Praise for
Christians & Jews—Faith to Faith:
Tragic History, Promising Present, Fragile Future

"Absolutely the most convenient panoramic analysis of the Jewish-Christian retrospect and prospect I've seen.... A masterpiece by the Jewish dean and most seasoned veteran of Jewish-Christian deliberations ... penetratingly clear and accessible for all readers.... A clarion call lest gains of recent decades lapse or even dissipate."
> —**Rabbi Michael J. Cook, PhD**, Bronstein Professor of Judeo-Christian Studies, Hebrew Union College, Cincinnati; author, *Modern Jews Engage the New Testament: Enhancing Jewish Well-Being in a Christian Environment*

"A comprehensive overview of a half century of Christian-Jewish relations. Rudin brings his long central involvement in the Christian-Jewish dialogue to bear in insightful ways on the major theological and political issues central to that conversation."
> —**John T. Pawlikowski, OSM, PhD,** director, Catholic-Jewish Studies Program, Catholic Theological Union (Chicago)

"Rabbi Rudin has brought his wealth of experience and uncommon wisdom to shed light on the complex world of interreligious relations. Important and useful."
> —**Rabbi Gary Greenebaum**, director of Interreligious and Intergroup Relations, American Jewish Committee

"Does not dodge any of the painful issues.... [A] rewarding, always stimulating book."
> —**Peter Steinfels**, co-director, Fordham University Center on Religion and Culture; former *New York Times* religion correspondent and columnist

"A vibrant, timely study by one of America's distinguished leaders and shrewd analysts of the Jewish-Christian encounter. Rudin succeeds brilliantly in laying bare the past and illuminating the present so Jews and Christians may wisely and respectfully press forward to model a more authentic relationship for the good of the other and the future of all humanity."
> —**Marvin R. Wilson, PhD**, Ockenga Professor of Biblical Studies, Gordon College

"Offers us all a Jewish 'take' on our times, allowing us to see and hear the news with the eyes and ears of Jews. Here also is a clear-eyed understanding for both Christians and Jews of the evils of establishment, religion and state coupled together, predicated upon replacing suspicion with respect and apathy with empathy. Urgently needed!"

   —The Rev. Dr. James M. Dunn, professor of Christianity
and public policy, Divinity School at Wake Forest University

"This thorough, engaging and accessible [resource] on Jewish-Christian relations examines the complex history of two formidable faith communities and makes concrete suggestions for action. Rudin's rich experience in Jewish-Christian dialogue is apparent from beginning to end."

   —Rabbi David A. Teutsch, PhD, Wiener Professor
of Contemporary Jewish Civilization and former president,
Reconstructionist Rabbinical College

"This is a must-have for anyone interested in the vital story of Christian-Jewish relations. Rabbi Rudin's polished prose and sharp observations guide the reader on a stimulating journey through time, and provide invaluable insights into the future of one of the world's most complicated religious relationships. Indispensable for academics, interfaith activists and general readers interested in religion and its impact on world history."

   —Rabbi Eric J. Greenberg, director, Department
of Interfaith Affairs, Anti-Defamation League

"Rabbi Rudin has written the best guide to Jewish-Christian dialogue that I have ever seen. Popular but sophisticated, sobering but hopeful, it provides a searching analysis of the vocabulary and history of Christian-Jewish relations, reminding us why these relations are so difficult and why they are so important."

   —Rabbi Eric H. Yoffie, president, Union for Reform Judaism

Christians
&Jews
Faith to Faith

Christians & Jews
Faith to Faith

Tragic History, Promising Present, Fragile Future

Rabbi James Rudin

For People of All Faiths, All Backgrounds
JEWISH LIGHTS Publishing
Woodstock, Vermont

Christians & Jews—Faith to Faith:
Tragic History, Promising Present, Fragile Future

2011 Hardcover Edition, First Printing
© 2011 by James Rudin

Grateful acknowledgment is given for permission to use material from the following sources: Excerpt from *Modern Jews Engage the New Testament: Enhancing Jewish Well-Being in a Christian Environment* © 2008 Michael J. Cook. Permission granted by Jewish Lights Publishing, P.O. Box 237, Woodstock, VT 05091, www.jewishlights.com. Scriptural quotations from the *New American Standard Bible*, copyright © 1960, 1962, 1963, 1968, 1971, 1972, 1973, 1975, 1977, 1995 by the Lockman Foundation are used by permission. www.lockman.org.

Library of Congress Cataloging-in-Publication Data
Rudin, A. James (Arnold James), 1934–
   Christians & Jews—faith to faith : tragic history, promising present, fragile future / James Rudin. — 2011 hardcover ed.
       p. cm.
   Includes bibliographical references and index.
   ISBN 978-1-58023-432-0 (hardcover)
   1. Judaism—Relations—Christianity. 2. Christianity and other religions—Judaism. 3. Christianity and antisemitism. I. Title.
   BM535.R75 2010
   296.3'96—dc22

                                                                2010033375

10 9 8 7 6 5 4 3 2 1
Manufactured in the United States of America
Jacket design: Tim Holtz
Jacket art: © iStockphoto.com/aperture8, modified by Tim Holtz
Interior design: Kristi Menter

For People of All Faiths, All Backgrounds
Published by Jewish Lights Publishing
A Division of Longhill Partners, Inc.
Sunset Farm Offices, Route 4, P.O. Box 237
Woodstock, VT 05091
Tel: (802) 457-4000   Fax: (802) 457-4004
www.jewishlights.com

In memory of six giants of Christian-Jewish relations—
The Rev. Edward Flannery
The Rev. Linda Blagg Harter
Rabbi Leon Klenicki
Cardinal John O'Connor
Rabbi Murray Saltzman
Rabbi Michael Signer

Contents

Acknowledgments

I could not have written this book without the guidance, support, cooperation, and inspiration of many people and institutions.

I am especially appreciative of the wonderful staffs of the Sanibel Island Public Library and the New York Society Library in New York City. Both libraries provided superb writing areas and extraordinary research facilities.

Two gifted people put this book together: Stuart M. Matlins, the publisher of Jewish Lights, and Richard Curtis, my literary agent. Emily Wichland and Lauren Hill were excellent editors. Gerald and Deborah Strober, talented authors and lifelong friends, provided constant encouragement and advice.

While this book is the work of a single author, my many Jewish and Christian colleagues taught me more than they will ever know, and I am grateful to all of them. I appreciate the suggestions and comments of Dr. Amy-Jill Levine of the Vanderbilt Divinity School and Dr. Marvin R. Wilson of Gordon College. The American Jewish Committee (AJC) has been my professional home for more than forty years, a precious gift I never take for granted. Since 1991 the Religion News Service (RNS) has distributed my newspaper columns, and I thank the RNS staff and management for that unique opportunity. It is an honor to be part of the Center for Catholic-Jewish Studies (CCJS) that the AJC cosponsors with Saint Leo University (SLU).

The views and opinions expressed in this book are my own, however, and do not necessarily reflect those of the AJC, RNS, SLU, or CCJS.

Finally, the best for last. Four remarkable Jewish women have taught me humility and given me enormous joy: my daughters, Rabbi Eve and Jennifer; my granddaughter, Emma Mollie; and my wife, Marcia, who every day provides meaning in my life and has shared our journey together for more than forty years. Unlike my biblical ancestors who were compelled to wander in the wilderness for four decades, thanks to Marcia, I long ago entered the Promised Land of love and companionship.

What's in a Name?

Hebrews, Israelites, or Jews?

In the beginning were the names.

Three names for the people of the Bible—Hebrews, Israelites, and Jews. And the people were with God, and God was with the people. And it was good.

And although the trio of scriptural names had diverse linguistic roots and were used during distinct periods of ancient history, each name, while different from one another, identified the same people.

But a bitter and long-lasting quarrel began two thousand years ago when a new faith, Christianity, emerged from within the community of Hebrews/Israelites/Jews.

Jesus of Nazareth, a Jew living in the Land of Israel two millennia ago, was believed by a nascent group of Jewish followers to be the theological fulfillment and replacement of Judaism, the religion that had spiritually nurtured Jesus during his brief lifetime of about thirty-three years.

In an effort to buttress their claim, the followers of Jesus took one of the three biblical names for themselves and declared it now belonged to them. They boldly called themselves the "New Israel" as a visible sign that they had separated from the "Old Israel" (Hebrews 9:11, 9:15), and they believed the Jewish vocation as a people of God ended with the coming of Jesus.

However, Jews refused to cede their revered name to the new faith community. They asked the rabbis, their spiritual leaders, several probing and painful questions: "Why was 'Israel' taken from us? Must we share our traditional name with members of another faith who teach that our own religion is incomplete, even null and void?"

The people of Israel also asked, "We entered into an eternal covenant with God at Mount Sinai following the Exodus from Egypt; do we not earn, do we not merit sole rights to 'Israel'? Why did the Christians expropriate our venerated name and deny our spiritual legitimacy?"

For two thousand years, Jews, the original "Children of Israel," have posed these and similar questions, and during the same two millennia, Christians have claimed that they are the authentic bearers of the title "Israel." Battling over the same name was not an auspicious start to Christian-Jewish relations, and the debate continues to this day. The question, Which people is the true, indisputable Israel? remains a source of controversy.

As proof the debate is not settled, here is an exercise I use to spark serious discussion whenever Christians and Jews encounter one another in a dialogue setting.

I provide each person with a standard three-inch by five-inch index card and ask the group to print the word "Israel" on one side of the card, and then I ask them to write the definition of that word on the reverse side. The participants' names do not appear on the cards, and after collecting them, I read aloud each definition.

The Many Meanings of "Israel"

It is easy to tell whether a Jew or a Christian has filled out a card because the results always reflect two different responses based upon the participants' specific religious identities.

Jews overwhelmingly define "Israel" as the traditional name for the Jewish people as well as their biblical homeland. In addition, Israel is the name of the Jewish state that achieved political independence in 1948. The Jewish responses are consistently linked to people, land, and state.

However, Christians invariably perceive themselves as the New Israel, another name for the church. Sometimes, Christian respondents define Israel as the "people of God," a broad term lacking any reference to a particular land or community. A minority of Christian respondents list the modern Jewish state as their first choice of identification, but most focus on Israel as a theological term devoid of ethnic, geographical, or political meaning.

My index-card drill reveals the wide interreligious breach and sharp differences that exist between Christians and Jews. Why, after two thousand years, do the synagogue and the church each still claim the name "Israel" for itself? Can the gap be closed? Should we even try to bridge the differences?

Before exploring those questions, it is necessary to look at the biblical names. The Hebrew word *ivri* (pl., *ivrim*) has three letters as its root—*ayin, vet, reish*—and is translated as "Hebrew." But the same combination of letters also means "across from the other side," as well as being the name of Eber, an ancestor of Abraham mentioned in the book of Genesis (10:21). In Genesis 40:15 is the phrase *eretz ha-ivrim*, the "land of the Hebrews," and in the book of Exodus *ivrim* is used to describe the slaves in Egypt who were freed from Pharaoh's "house of bondage."[1] In the New Testament, Saul of Tarsus/the apostle Paul describes himself as a "Hebrew born of the Hebrews" (Philippians 3:5).

Ivrit is the Hebrew language. A calendar written in Hebrew that included various holidays was used in the Israelite city of Gezer in the tenth century BCE.[2] What is called the Hebrew Bible was written in that language except for several Aramaic sections in the books of Jeremiah, Ezra, and Daniel. Aramaic is a Semitic language with many similarities to ancient Hebrew.

Avoiding the "J" Word

The word "Jew" stems from the Hebrew *Yehudah* or *Judah*, the fourth son of the Hebrew patriarch Jacob, and Judah was one of Israel's twelve tribes. Because King David was from that tribe, in time the name was applied to an entire people. Over the centuries, the word "Jew" took on a more pejorative meaning than either "Hebrew" or "Israelite," two names that appear more frequently in the Bible than "Jew." Another reason for the negative meaning may be that "Jew," and its various forms in other languages, is often a one-syllable word that easily becomes an epithet. While "Hebrew" describes a particular language, it has often been employed to avoid using the more familiar "Jew" or "Jewish." "Hebrew" is not the name of a religion, unlike "Christian," with which it is sometimes linked.

The word "Jew" had a negative connotation in some English literary works, especially Geoffrey Chaucer's *The Prioress' Tale* (1390), Christopher Marlowe's *The Jew of Malta* (1590), and William Shakespeare's *The Merchant of Venice* (1596). Chaucer made reference to nine-year-old Hugh of Lincoln, who died in 1255. Jews in England were falsely accused of killing him and using the youngster's blood in the baking of matzah, the Passover unleavened bread—an early example of the infamous blood libel, a ghoulish anti-Semitic canard. Marlowe and Shakespeare featured negative Jewish characters in their plays, notably Shylock in *The Merchant of Venice*.[3]

The derogatory tradition about "Jew" or "Jewish" is one reason the Reform Jewish movement in the nineteenth century called its rabbinical school the Hebrew Union College (HUC) and its synagogue body the Union of American Hebrew Congregations (UAHC). It was not until 2003 that the UAHC officially changed its name to the Union for Reform Judaism.[4]

The Hebrew University, established in Jerusalem in 1925, was a significant sign of the revival of the ancient language among Jews living in British Mandate Palestine. There are other institutions with Hebrew in their titles: Hebrew Immigrant Aid Society, Hebrew College, Young Men's/Women's Hebrew Association (YMHA/YWHA), and even Hebrew National hot dogs.

Jacob, the third Jewish patriarch, whose Hebrew name *Yaakov* means "supplanter," became a changed personality following his nocturnal wrestling with a mysterious messenger from God (Genesis 35:10). As a result of that struggle, Jacob became "Israel," or *Yisrael*, meaning "he who struggled with God." That proud designation became the name of the Jewish people and its biblical homeland. Israel is a combination of two Hebrew word roots that can mean "God is upright/straight" or "you have striven with God." The name is applied later to the twelve tribes, the children of Jacob. Israel was also the name of the combined kingdom ruled by David and Solomon, and in later centuries the name Israel was given to the northern kingdom and the name Judah to the southern kingdom.

Unlike the terms "Hebrew" and "Jew," "Israel" has a potent theological meaning, and that is why early Christians wanted to be the "New Israel" and not "New Hebrews" or "New Jews." Unlike "Hebrew," a linguistic term, or "Jew," a word that stems from a name, "Israel" is prescriptive and descriptive in its origins.

As part of its anti-Semitic campaign, the Nazi regime forced every Jew in Germany to take the name "Israel" or "Sarah."[5] The Nazis perceived "Israel" as a pejorative, an insulting name, but only three years after the collapse of Hitler's Germany, the independent Jewish state proudly called itself "Israel."

Of the three ancient names, "Jew" has been the one most used in hostile ways over the centuries, and even today, many Jews prefer "Jewish" instead. The word was first a tribal description; only later did it encompass an entire people. While most of the Bible uses either "Hebrew" or "Israel," the book of Esther represents an early biblical reference to "Jew" and "Jews." Martin Luther (1483–1546), the Christian Reformer, disliked the book, especially its usage of those two terms; he much preferred "Hebrews" or "Israelites."[6] Would Luther have still detested the book if it had described Haman's potential victims as "Israelites" or "Hebrews" instead of "Jews"?

The word "Jew" entered into many languages, and in some of them, especially German, Polish, and Russian, the word is despoiled because it has been used as an epithet. The linguistic variations include *Yehudi* (Hebrew), *Judaeus* (Latin), *Ioudaios* (Greek), *Juif* (French), *Yahud* (Arabic), *Jude* (German), *Zyd* (Polish), *Jood* (Dutch), *Yid* (Yiddish), and *Zhid* (Russian).

A Misleading Hyphen

Some people, including American politicians who want to sound "inclusive" and do not want to offend Jews, have taken the Latin term *Judaeus* and melded it with "Christian" to describe a so-called "Judeo-Christian" tradition or heritage. While there are many Christians in the world, there are no "Judeos." The accurate phrase should be "Jewish and Christian" traditions or heritages, without a hyphen. Each faith community has many religious streams; there is no one single "Jewish tradition" or "Christian tradition," and there is certainly not a "Judeo-Christian" one.[7]

In attempting to be constructive, those who use the latter term speak of something that has never existed. Often, such efforts are well intentioned and seek to develop positive interreligious relations, but the result is a watering down of both faiths.

But Christian-Jewish relations are more complicated than ownership of the contested name "Israel." Both communities claim the towering biblical figure of Abraham as their own, and both feel inextricably bound to the "first Hebrew." Jews call him *Avraham avinu,* "Abraham our father," and feel physically linked to him, the first Jewish patriarch. However, Christians revere him as the first person of faith in the one God. As we shall see, it was Paul, the Apostle to the Gentiles, who rejected any need for a flesh-and-blood connection to Abraham; faith alone was sufficient (Romans 2:28–29).

Paul argued that God's spiritual pledges and guarantees that began with Abraham are not the possession of Jews. Abraham's seed is predestined not for an entire people, the Jews, but rather for only one Jewish individual in the future, Jesus of Nazareth. This Christian belief stems from the New Testament verse "Now the promises were spoken to Abraham and to his seed. He does not say, 'And to seeds,' as referring to many, but rather to one, 'And to your seed,' that is, Christ" (Galatians 3:16, *New American Standard Bible* [NASB]).

For Jews and Christians, the "seeds" of their long-running debate were sown long ago; it is a debate that has, for good or ill, shaped our world.

2 The Ancient Big Three

Jews, Greeks, and Romans

This is a tale of three cities—Jerusalem, Athens, and Rome—and three languages—Hebrew, Greek, and Latin. Both Judaism and Christianity arose in the lands of the Mediterranean basin, and many of our religious and philosophical foundational documents were originally written in Hebrew, Greek, or Latin.

Because they are distinctive in history and demography, people sometimes forget that the three capital cities are geographically near one another when contrasted with the vast travel distances we take for granted today. It is 1,434 miles from Jerusalem to Rome, similar to the mileage between Houston and Baltimore. Jerusalem and Athens are 778 miles apart, about the distance between Columbus and Minneapolis–St. Paul, and a trip from Athens to Rome is only 656 miles, the approximate distance between Charlotte and New York City.

Soul Cities

We do not need a world atlas to locate Jerusalem, Athens, and Rome, nor do we require a jet plane to transport us to these locations to recognize their importance. Each one, in its unique way, occupies an indelible place in our personal and collective memory banks even if we have never physically visited the famous capitals.

Jerusalem, Athens, and Rome are embedded in our thoughts, beliefs, governance, cultures, and languages. Even now, thousands of years after they first gained world prominence, the cities' remarkable influences remain, as do their ancient languages.

Jerusalem, Athens, and Rome allow us to time travel in our heads, in our hearts, and most of all, in our souls. We are forever part of each city because of religion, philosophy, literature, architecture, law, and history. In a mystical way, we have never left them. We will always remain emotionally and historically linked to these three cities.

Every schoolchild knows the basic drill:

- Jerusalem brought monotheistic religion, the Bible, and a system of ethics and morality anchored to an omnipresent and invisible God.
- Athens was the source of democracy (itself a Greek word), timeless theatrical dramas, noteworthy philosophy, and magnificent sculpture and architecture.
- Rome provided a complex system of laws combined with classical literature and the legacy of a vast empire based upon military and economic power.

The three cities, while different from one another in many ways, do share one common geographical similarity: none is a harbor or a port despite the fact that water traffic was a major form of transportation and commerce in ancient times.[1]

Jaffa, on Israel's coastline, was Jerusalem's gateway to the Mediterranean Sea, and one of the capital's oldest roadways is Rehov Yafo, or Jaffa Road. It begins at the Jaffa Gate, an entry point into the walled Old City, and heads westward. Piraeus served as Athens's nearby port, and Rome, although located on the Tiber River, required the neighboring city of Ostia for its maritime enterprises, both military and commercial. But whatever the commercial and strategic importance of Jaffa, Piraeus, and Ostia, they are far less remembered today than Jerusalem, Athens, and Rome.

The ports remind us that the ancient peoples were not sedentary, living inside hermetically sealed religio-cultural "bubbles," as we sometimes believe. The residents of Jerusalem, Athens, and Rome were not isolated from the powerful influences and pressures of the various competing cultures, religions, and political movements that were integral parts of the ancient Middle East and the Mediterranean basin.

Throughout history, emperors frequently conquered the three cities, and political rulers proclaimed themselves divine figures and demanded submissive worship from their subject peoples (1 and 2 Maccabees). Sacrifices, including child sacrifice, were offered up to appease capricious gods; and philosophers, prophets, and other "troublemakers" were forced to commit suicide or were jailed or executed because of their beliefs.

Yet, against this backdrop of blood, conflict, and idolatry, there were also moments where the human spirit soared, leaving us extraordinary gifts of religion, philosophy, ethics, prophecy, law, and language. Throughout history, the populations of the three cities were in constant flux, but Jerusalem, Athens, and Rome remained permanent centers of civilization.

It is impossible to understand Judaism and Christianity today without an awareness of the three cities and their dynamic civilizations and cultures, which permeated the ancient Mediterranean basin and influenced the followers of both faiths.

The "City of Peace"?

Although the Hebrew name *Yerushalayim* is translated as "City of Peace," and Muslims call it *al-Quds*, "the Holy," Jerusalem has experienced more warfare, conquest, hatred, and strife than perhaps any other city in the world. Geography helps explain Jerusalem's turbulent history, which continues into the twenty-first century.

The city is located atop a group of small but strategically important hills, and control of Jerusalem was and continues to be the key to the entire Land of Israel. While the city's precise date of founding is shrouded in the mists of history, archaeologists believe Jerusalem was inhabited at least four thousand years ago.

David, the second king of Israel, made Jerusalem his capital sometime between 1000 and 980 BCE, and ever since it has remained the spiritual focus of Jews and the political center of Jewish national independence and sovereignty. Forty years later, David's son, Solomon, a name meaning "peace," was given the task of building Judaism's First Holy Temple (1 Kings 5:1–5), which became the focal point of the Israelite religion.

The Bible recounts that David, with his bloody history as a warrior, albeit a successful one, was denied that role. Solomon's Temple stood until the Babylonians destroyed it in 586 BCE. It was the first of two Temples erected in Jerusalem. The Second Temple was also destroyed by an invader, the Romans, in 70 CE. Because of its key role in ancient Jewish history, "Jerusalem" appears in the Hebrew Bible 750 times and Zion, a small hill within the city, is mentioned in 150 places.

Jerusalem is also a central focus of Christianity. It was the scene of Jesus's death at the hands of the Romans and the site of his resurrection. While Jerusalem is not specifically mentioned in the Qur'an, it still ranks as the third holiest city for Muslims, after Mecca and Medina.

The fabled walled Old City of Jerusalem occupies about a third of a square mile, but it is supersaturated with spiritual meaning for Judaism, Christianity, and Islam. Within that tiny area are the Temple Mount, the Western Wall (a remnant of the Holy Temple), and the Jewish Quarter—sacred spaces for Jews. The Old City also contains the Church of the Holy Sepulchre, believed to be the crucifixion site, and the Via Dolorosa (the Way of Sorrow), the route Jesus took carrying a cross on the walk to his death. The Christian and Armenian quarters are also in the Old City.

Muslims revere the city because of the Islamic belief that Muhammad the Prophet (570?–632) miraculously traveled from his home in the Arabian Peninsula to Jerusalem on his steed, al-Barak (Lightning), and once there the founder of Islam ascended to the seventh heaven.[2] The Arab conquerors of the city built the Dome of the Rock in 691 atop the site of the two Jewish Holy Temples. Though not a mosque, the Dome of the Rock is the oldest existing Islamic structure in the world.

Eric H. Cline, an American historian, has studied Jerusalem's complex history and determined that its residents have witnessed two destructions of the city, twenty-three sieges, and fifty-two armed attacks and that Jerusalem, always a coveted prize, has been captured and recaptured forty-four times.[3] With that grim background, Jerusalem represents both the dashed hopes of interreligious amity as well as the perpetual dream for harmony among Jews, Christians, and Muslims.

The Golden Age of Athens

Athens is one of the oldest inhabited cities in the world; its history goes back at least seven thousand years. It was named for Athena, the Greek goddess of wisdom and justice. During the fifth century BCE, Athens was a powerful city-state and a rival of Sparta, its more militant neighbor. Their conflict, the Peloponnesian War, lasted nearly thirty years of that century, and a defeated Athens was permanently weakened. The wars are recounted in the writings of Thucydides, Plutarch, and Aristophanes.[4]

Prior to the Spartan military victory, Athens was the cradle of democracy and the home of both Aristotle and Plato. That era, the Age of Pericles, is celebrated today for its literature, philosophy, and magnificent architecture. But the glory of Athens, and indeed of Greece itself, ended in 146 BCE when the Romans overran the city and converted it into a protectorate, a vassal state.

By then, Athens had already lost much of its political dominance because of the success of Philip of Macedonia (a region about 190 miles north of Athens) and his more famous son, Alexander the Great (356–323 BCE). Alexander's huge empire, which stretched to India, established new centers of power outside of Greece. That robbed Athens of its former prominence.

Although it can be argued that Athens was the main creator of Hellenistic culture, a dazzling civilization that challenged and even threatened the existence of Judaism, the city itself never again achieved its past glory. That was left to other cities in the Alexandrian Empire, including Antioch in Asia Minor (a city that played an important role in the rise of Christianity) and Alexandria, named for the young Macedonian empire builder.

Yet Athens's philosophers, especially Aristotle, directly impacted Jewish and Christian religious thinkers fifteen hundred years later and shaped the theology of both faiths. Moses Maimonides (1135–1204), Judaism's renowned philosopher, was influenced by Aristotelian thought, as was the Christian theologian Thomas Aquinas (1225–74).[5]

The books of the New Testament were written in Greek, even though they focused on Jesus, a Jew who lived in Israel, spoke Aramaic, and knew the Hebrew Bible. An important Jewish biblical translation was the Septuagint, a Greek-language version of the Hebrew Scriptures, which was completed in 132 BCE. This classic translation reflected the need of Greek-speaking Jews to read the Bible in their vernacular, because Greek was more accessible to them than the Bible's original languages. In fact, the term "synagogue" is a Greek word meaning a "place of assembly." The Septuagint is quoted in the New Testament and in the writings of the church fathers.[6]

The Jewish philosopher Philo of Alexandria (20 BCE–50 CE) wrote in Greek and was also influenced by the thinkers who had lived centuries earlier in Athens. It is likely Philo knew little or no Hebrew.

Athens went into a long decline following the Roman conquest and only emerged as an important center with Greek national independence in 1830, an event that marked the end of Ottoman Turkish control.[7] Athens never achieved the imperial power of Rome or the spiritual influence of Jerusalem, but the city has made lasting contributions to Western civilization.

The dominant religious community today in both Greece and its capital city is Eastern Orthodox Christianity. Its spiritual leader, the ecumenical patriarch, is traditionally a Greek cleric who resides in Istanbul, Turkey, a city Orthodox Christians refer to as Constantinople in honor of Emperor Constantine (272–337 CE), who converted to Christianity in the fourth century and linked his Byzantine Empire to the Christian Church.

Rome's Positive and Negative Legacies

The legendary story of the twins Romulus and Remus dates the founding of Rome to 753 BCE, about the same time the Hebrew prophets were in full flower in ancient Israel. According to this account, Romulus killed his brother and then named the city on the Tiber in honor of himself.[8]

Beginning in the eighth century BCE, Rome was the center of a kingdom that became a republic in 510 BCE, and the city decisively entered the world stage as the capital of the Roman Empire in 27 BCE under the first emperor Octavian (63 BCE–14 CE), whose imperial name was Augustus. He established a *Pax Romana*, a "Roman peace," in the first and second centuries CE. From Rome's perspective, it was a period of relative calm and few military battles. Of course, the Jews living under imperial occupation in the Land of Israel had a different view: brutality, bloodshed, mass executions, and unsuccessful rebellions against Roman authority.

The Roman Empire controlled much of the Mediterranean basin, including the Land of Israel. During those centuries of power, Rome also dominated major areas of Europe, the Middle East, and North Africa by employing a brutal combination of military and economic power. Rome reached its apex of influence in 117 CE under Emperor Trajan.[9]

The decline and fall of the Roman Empire (Edward Gibbon's famous book title) occurred in stages as its power waned, until Rome itself was sacked in 410 by Alaric, the king of the Visigoths, and the year 476 marked the empire's official demise.[10] It is often overlooked that Arab Muslims invaded Rome in 846 and looted the original St. Peter's Basilica, which was replaced in the seventeenth century by the current basilica of the same name.[11]

In 756 the Papal States, a religio-political power, emerged and remained a major diplomatic and military player in Europe until 1870, when the Italian Republic was established and the Vatican, by treaty, became a mini city-state devoid of territorial holdings or military power. The official name for the Vatican is the Holy See; the latter word stems from the Latin for "seat." The Holy See is the center of authority of the Roman Catholic Church.

Rome also plays an important role in Jewish history. Judah Maccabee, the hero of the Hanukkah holiday story, sent two diplomatic representatives to the city during the second century BCE to form an alliance with the then extant republic (1 Maccabees 7:23–29). There may have been Jewish residents in the city earlier in time, but scholars record that Jews came to Rome within the same period as Judah's ambassadors, and the city represents one of the oldest continuous Jewish communities in the Diaspora.

The Roman Jewish population, though never large in number, significantly increased following the Jerusalem Temple's destruction in 70 CE, when Jewish prisoners were brought as slaves in chains to the imperial capital along with the fabled Temple menorah, gold, and other looted spoils following the Roman military victory in Israel. It is estimated that perhaps ten thousand Jews resided in Rome during the late stages of the empire; two thousand years later, the number of Jews in the city is about twenty thousand.

Despite the community's small size throughout its long history, Roman Jews have remained faithful to their religion and are proud of their survival despite the oppression and persecution they faced, first from church authorities and later from the Nazis during the Holocaust.

The community's Grand Synagogue, built in the 1890s, has in recent years been the scene of two important events in Christian-Jewish relations. In April 1986, Pope John Paul II became the first pontiff since Peter, nearly two millennia earlier, to visit a synagogue. The pope's address broke new ground when, speaking as the leader of one billion Catholics, he affirmed the "irrevocable"

Jewish covenant with God and called Jews "our elder brothers in faith." John Paul II also denounced the sin of anti-Semitism. His historic visit to the synagogue, located only a few miles from the Vatican, was a combination of rich pageantry and theological substance.[12]

Nearly a quarter century later, in January 2010, Pope Benedict XVI retraced his predecessor's steps and also made a major speech at the Rome synagogue. The pope reaffirmed the validity of the Jewish covenant and urged even greater cooperation between Christians and Jews. Benedict, himself a German who was drafted into the Nazi German army at the end of World War II, recounted the tragedy of the Holocaust, especially the deportation of many Roman Jews to Nazi death camps in October 1943, after the collapse of the Fascist government of Benito Mussolini; of 1,259 Jews rounded up, only 15 survived the war.[13]

The German deportation of Rome's Jews was the focus of historian Susan Zuccotti's book *Under His* [Pope Pius XII's] *Very Windows: The Vatican and the Holocaust in Italy*. The role of the wartime pope during the Shoah and his possible sainthood remain serious issues between Catholics and Jews.

3 The World's Longest Running Religious Debate Begins

Christianity and Judaism have an asymmetrical relationship with one another based upon the life of a Jew born during the Roman Empire, which occupied Jerusalem and other areas of ancient Israel. Christian faith requires a belief, among other things, in Jesus as God made flesh, the second part of the Trinity, the personal Savior, and the divine Son of God. Simply put: no Jesus, no Christianity. But no such spiritual beliefs are necessary for Jews or Judaism. Judaism stands alone without requiring Christianity's existence, but Christianity cannot stand without affirming and understanding its Jewish roots.

A number of early Christian leaders, including some church fathers, did not affirm those roots. Instead, they spewed forth hostility and contempt toward Jews and Judaism in their efforts first to discredit and then to delegitimize the older faith. One church father, John Chrysostom (347–407) was especially vicious in his denunciations and hostile attacks.

Unsaintly Words

Chrysostom, an archbishop of Constantinople, who later became a Catholic and an Orthodox saint, lived for a period of time in Antioch, a city in today's Turkey. Ancient Antioch had an established Jewish community during Chrysostom's lifetime, and it was the victim of harsh church laws and edicts. Even so, in Antioch Christians attended synagogues, where they were welcomed by Jews.

Chrysostom gave eight sermons in Greek, covering one hundred pages that are an explosive volcano of venom and rage against the Jews, replete with vicious stereotypes and obscene caricatures. Whatever the reason for his pathological and theological hatred of all things Jewish, Chrysostom remains a prime example of religious anti-Judaism. Sixteen centuries after he first wrote his "Eight Homilies against the Jews," the Nazis used Chrysostom's sermons as anti-Semitic propaganda in their "war against the Jews."

Chrysostom's writings provided a theological justification for the deicide (Christ-killer) charge, and they still stun a modern reader:

> The Jewish people were driven by their drunkenness and plumpness to the ultimate evil; they kicked about, they failed to accept the yoke of Christ, nor did they pull the plow of his teaching. Another prophet hinted at this when he said: "Israel is as obstinate as a stubborn heifer."... Although such beasts are unfit for work, they are fit for killing. And this is what happened to the Jews: while they were making themselves unfit for work, they grew fit for slaughter.... Before they committed the crime of crimes, before they killed their Master, before the cross, before the slaying of Christ, [Jewish sacrifices were] an abomination.... Nothing is more miserable than those people who never failed to attack their own salvation. When there was need to observe the Law, they trampled it underfoot.... You [Jews] did slay Christ, you did lift violent hands against the Master, you did spill his precious blood. This is why you have no chance for atonement, excuse, or defense.... The Jews are enduring their present troubles because of Christ.[1]

For Chrysostom, synagogues are evil nests of idolatry and the devil, this despite the strict Jewish prohibition against the presence of any "graven images" or statues in a place of worship. The church father branded a Christian's visit to a synagogue an act of blasphemy, and a Christian attending a Passover Seder meal is a direct insult to Jesus. Worst of all in Chrysostom's eyes is a Christian being in the company of a Jew on Easter, the day the Jews "did slay" Jesus.

As a natural reaction to this fierce campaign of animus, Jews, led by their rabbis, became cautious, even defensive, in encounters with the new faith and its adherents. They avoided studying the tenets of Christianity and reading the New Testament, even though most of its twenty-seven books were written by Jews.

Jews, with rare exceptions, were wary of learning about the new religion that sprang from their midst. Christianity, especially following the bloody massacres carried out by the Crusaders in Europe and in the Land of Israel beginning in 1096, was perceived by Jews not as a religion of love, but rather as the faith of their tormentors, and in time, it became forbidden spiritual fruit. Little wonder that Jews, defamed and demeaned for nearly twenty centuries, remained suspicious of a threatening religious doctrine that proclaimed it had superseded Judaism.

How could the reaction to Christianity have been otherwise in the face of constant withering attacks, both verbal and physical? The anti-Jewish rhetoric and actions of Christian theologians and political leaders throughout history often produced a malevolent combination of church and state that blocked most meaningful contact between the two faith communities.

Church + State = Persecution

Whenever the Christian church—Roman Catholic, Eastern Orthodox, or Protestant—became the "established" religion in a nation or an empire, a vast array of harsh anti-Jewish legal measures generally followed that were sponsored by either the ecclesiastical or the temporal authorities or both. It was a litany of woe that included forced conversions, physical assaults on Jews (called pogroms in czarist Russia), the creation of ghettoes, and destruction of synagogues, religious objects, and texts. These actions were justified by repressive laws and decrees that denied Jews full citizenship and discriminated against them in areas of daily life, including education, housing, military service, ownership of land, travel, and employment.[2]

For centuries, Jews, the original people of Israel, endured intense psychological and physical pressure from Christians, when the New Israel demanded the Old Israel abandon Judaism and convert to Christianity. If the calls for baptism were not heeded, the "stubborn" Jews were often exiled from the nations, regions, and cities where they had resided, sometimes for hundreds of years. They suffered death at the hands of fervent Christians who believed it was necessary to destroy Jewish life and the Jewish religion in order to theologically "save" them and "prove" Christianity's supremacy. The horrific actions of Christians against Jews were carried out in the name of Jesus, the Jew from Nazareth.

It was a brutal history, which at first impeded and finally prevented constructive encounters between the two religious groups. However, in our own day, the development of positive interreligious relations, especially in North America and in parts of Europe, has provided Jews with the necessary intellectual and historical knowledge of Christianity as well as the political freedom and the emotional sure-footedness to explore the meaning of Jesus's teachings and life as part of the Jewish cavalcade of history. Conversely, Christians engaged in interreligious relations can gain an authentic understanding of the Jewish people and their religion, an understanding built upon mutual respect and knowledge.

Jews today are emotionally and religiously secure enough to ask who Jesus was. They are able to view the rise of the new religion without anxiety or anger and, hopefully, without the physical and psychological hostility many Christians exerted in the past.

Cleaning Out the Stables of Bigotry

At the same time, Christians, both clergy and laypeople, have begun cleaning out their own stables of bigotry and anti-Jewish prejudice. This involves a critical self-examination of Christian religious traditions and history vis-à-vis Jews and Judaism. The intent is to eradicate anti-Jewish bigotry and prejudice from their faith.[3]

But even as these efforts are under way, the questions still remain: How much do the world's Christians know about Jews and Judaism? And how much do Jews know about Christians and their religion, whose origins reside within Judaism?

As mentioned above, for centuries many Jews were wary of asking questions about Christianity, a religion that professed love, grace, and charity. But those qualities were generally lacking in the real world when Jews lived under Christian domination. Because of this negative existential reality, Jews often perceived the religion of Jesus as one of hatred, contempt, and dread.

Today Jews and Christians can figuratively stand atop the debris of the past and, viewing one another with mutual respect and understanding, can turn their attention to exploring together the events that took place during the first Christian century.

Jesus (ca. 3 BCE–30 CE) was a Jew born in the Land of Israel toward the end of the Second Jewish Commonwealth. It was a turbulent period because the Jewish community chafed under the brutal occupation of the Roman Empire. Whatever knowledge we have about Jesus comes solely from the writings about him in the New Testament. His life and teachings are not mentioned in any other existing literature of that era, nor do we have any text actually written by him.[4]

Gospel Truth?

Within the New Testament, the three books attributed to Matthew, Mark, and Luke are called the "Synoptic"—from the Greek for "looking"—Gospels because they can be analyzed side by side and because they represent somewhat similar, but not identical, accounts of the life and death of Jesus at the hands of the Romans. The three Gospels differ in significant ways from one another; "gospel" is a variation of an old Middle English term meaning "good story" or "good news."

Scholars have never agreed and probably never will about the precise dating of the Synoptics. However, the consensus is that they were composed after the death of Jesus, probably in the decades of the 50s and 60s of the Common Era.[5] That is why the three books make no mention of the catastrophic event in the year 70 CE—the Romans' destruction of the Jewish Holy Temple in Jerusalem.[6]

There is general agreement that the fourth Gospel, the book of John, was composed decades after the completion of Matthew, Mark, and Luke, but it, too, contains no mention of the Temple's destruction, even though it was likely written around 90–100 CE, at least sixty years after Jesus's death and perhaps twenty years after the Roman conquest of Jerusalem.

The author of John introduces more problematic themes and negative descriptions about Jews and Judaism than do the three Synoptics. John's Gospel, particularly its pejorative images concerning the two words "the Jews," presents enormous difficulties and challenges in overcoming and erasing the toxic anti-Judaism within much of Christianity.

But none of the Gospels, and certainly not John, can be considered books of history as we define the term. Instead, they represent a series of narratives, episodes, events, and beliefs about Jesus that were collated after his death and used to further the cause of the men and women who were faithful to him. The Gospels became key foundational documents of Christianity.

Some contemporary scholars have attempted to mitigate or soften John's negative descriptions of "the Jews." One explanation is that the Greek word *Ioudaioi*, which appears seventy-one times in the fourth Gospel, really refers to the Jewish leaders who collaborated with the Romans and not the entire people. Another approach is to translate the word as "Judeans," the residents of Judea (the Roman name for the region), rather than the better-known "Jews." But for many people these are differences without any real meaning or significance.

An Ancient Family Feud

A more plausible explanation is that the Gospels, especially John, represent a bitter intra-Jewish family feud. It was an internal clash between the followers of Jesus and members of the older faith. The former asserted their spiritual leader, Jesus, was the Jewish Messiah and had fulfilled the promises of the Hebrew Bible, while the latter group maintained its traditional faith commitment. Those vigorous angry debates took place within the *mishpacha*, the Hebrew word for "family." Those holding this view argue that people often utter or write more derogatory words and phrases in family disputes than they would ever use with strangers, those outside the family circle.[7]

It may have been a family fight, but it was more bitter in tone and substance than the other intra-Jewish polemics among Pharisees, Essenes, Zealots, and Sadducees, some of the Jewish groups that existed during the lifetime of Jesus and the rise of the new faith community. John's hostile rhetoric reflects the intense struggle for religious legitimacy that was taking place about sixty years after Jesus's death. The fierce struggle centered on a critical question: which religious group merited the religiously important title of "Israel"?

The first thirty years of Jesus's life are quite vague in the Gospels; the New Testament's focus is on the last years of his life between the ages of thirty and thirty-three. But much is known about the dynamic Jewish life of the period. It was a time of military occupation, years filled with religious ferment and political turbulence that took place against the backdrop of the barbaric punishment meted out by the Romans upon the Jews living in ancient Israel. The restive Jewish population had no judicial, political, or military power—a classic definition of subjugated and occupied populations.

Capital Punishment, Roman Style

The Romans were well practiced at executing anyone suspected of preaching rebellion, sedition, or insurrection, particularly Jews who challenged the existing religious and political order. They executed people in a number of ways: beheading, burning, and wild beasts.

But crucifixion was widely used, and it was considered the cruelest method by both the Romans and their victims. It was akin to today's electric chair, firing squad, or lethal injection. Indeed, thousands of Jews suffered this extreme form of capital punishment.[8]

The Jewish historian and military leader Josephus (37–100 CE) has written that when the Romans were besieging Jerusalem in the year 70, Titus, the Roman commander, crucified five hundred or more Jews a day,

> a number so great that there was not enough room for the crosses and not enough crosses for the bodies.... The air was redolent with the stench of rotting flesh and rent by the cries and agony of the crucified. But the Jews held out for still another year, the fourth year of the war.[9]

Many contemporary Jewish and Christian scholars are devoting increased attention to that important period. Their research reveals a spiritually restless Jewish community, one filled with apocalyptic hopes, fears, and anticipations. Basic religious terms like "Messiah" (the Greek term is *Christos*), meaning "anointed," and "Son of Man," mentioned in the book of Daniel and in seventy-nine other places in the Hebrew Bible, developed within a complex society rife with expectations that its painful travails under the oppressive Romans would soon end.

While there were many Jewish groups, factions, and divisions during the Roman occupation, four major groups stand out: Sadducees, Pharisees, Zealots, and Essenes. Each one represented a response to the political and religious situation of the time, and each group has impacted both Christians and Jews.

Bitter Rivals: The Sadducces and the Pharisees

The Sadducees were an aristocratic, upper-class religio-political movement that began in the second century BCE. They derived their name from Zadok, the priest appointed by King Solomon to administer the rites of the First Holy Temple in Jerusalem.

The Sadducees were bitter foes of the Pharisees ("Separatists"), a religio-political party credited with shaping Rabbinic Judaism. The Sadducees insisted on a literal reading of the Hebrew Bible, akin in some ways to those today who believe the Bible is not subject to interpretation. The Pharisees had a different view, one that prevailed and influenced Judaism and in some ways Christianity as well. That is true even though the Pharisees have for two thousand years received "bad press" from Christianity.

The Pharisees believed that not one but two Torahs, or sets of religious teachings, were revealed at Mount Sinai. The Written Torah was given to Moses, but it was not complete and needed enrichment, fresh insights, and constant interpretation. The Oral Torah was also divine in origin, but that set of religious teachings was memorized and transmitted orally from one generation of Jewish teachers to the next until it, too, was finally written down and became the Talmud.[10]

Central to such a concept, familiar to both Jews and Christians, is the belief in continuous revelation; that is, revelation did not end with the Mount Sinai experience for Jews or with Jesus for Christians. Instead, spiritual enlightenment and God's teachings are continuous, and all religious revelations, whether ancient or contemporary, are equal in holiness.

The belief that spiritual revelations and teachings are constantly evolving constitutes a radical breakthrough in religious thought and represents a major Pharisaic principle. In addition, the Pharisees honored the Rabbis and sages who participated in the necessary process of making religion relevant in a changing society. Indeed, without such efforts, Judaism might have stagnated and disappeared from history.

When the Temple was destroyed, the Sadducees, without their tangible physical base, disappeared from history, but the Pharisees and their adaptable approach to religion guaranteed the survival of Judaism. They taught that the Written and Oral Torahs do not require a central shrine, a Temple; instead, a schoolhouse or synagogue is the institution that defines Judaism and allows it to develop and survive.

One key example illustrates the major differences between the Sadducees and their Pharisaic rivals—the biblical law of retribution, or *lex talionis* in Latin:

> If anyone maims his fellow, as he has done so shall it be done to him: fracture for fracture, eye for eye, tooth for tooth. The injury he inflicted on another shall be inflicted on him.
>
> —Leviticus 24:19–20, Jewish Publication Society *Tanakh* (JPS)

These verses and similar ones in two other places in the Torah have been a constant source of anti-Judaism and anti-Semitism. Jews are allegedly bloodthirsty in their demand for a literal retribution for any wrongs committed. If a person destroys or removes another person's eye, the perpetrator's eye must be removed as punishment. That was, in fact, the position of the Sadducees, who opposed any Rabbinic interpretation of the Torah.

But the Pharisees advocated a different form of punishment or retribution for a crime: the *value* of an eye, or what we today call "compensatory damages." They offered an interpretation of these verses and many others that mitigated the actual words of the ancient biblical text. Their view prevailed, and the Sadducees' insistence on a literal interpretation did not.

Anyone who believes Jews desire or require an actual eye as compensation for a lost eye is totally wrong. Yet traces of that discredited point of view can still be seen in those who demand a literal reading of the Bible and those who either minimize or reject any method of biblical interpretation. Such people are modern Sadducees.

Freedom Fighters: The Zealots

The Zealots, a third group that existed during the last years of the Second Temple, had a far different response to Roman rule. They urged their fellow Jews to kill and maim the hated occupiers of Judea, and the Zealots came into their own as a distinct group around 28 CE. Their violent acts brought severe counteractions by the Romans, but the Zealots continued their strong opposition and were the leaders of the unsuccessful Jewish rebellion in 66 CE against Roman power.

As often happens with such groups in history, the Zealots targeted not only the despised Romans but also Jews suspected of cooperating or collaborating with the occupation authorities. When the Temple was destroyed, the Sadducees faded away, the Pharisees turned to prayer and study in synagogues, but some Zealots regrouped on the top of Masada, a small mountain in the forbidding Dead Sea area, and conducted a "last stand" against the Roman Tenth Legion. It took the Legion three years and ten thousand men to reach the top of Masada, and when the Roman soldiers overran the Jewish stronghold, they discovered the Zealots had killed themselves and their families to escape capture. The number of Jewish dead was 967; it required a Roman Legion force ten times larger than the number of Jewish Zealots to capture the fortress at Masada.

In modern Israel, elements of the Israel Defense Forces take a collective oath that "Masada shall not fall again!"[11] But despite its iconic status in Jewish history, many question both the Zealots' strategy of fighting the vaunted Romans from an isolated fortress in the Dead Sea wilderness and, more importantly, the ethics of mass suicide even in the face of a cruel enemy. Critics point to the Pharisaic response instead: disperse, establish synagogues, and teach Torah, both the written and the oral varieties, and in so doing, ensure the survival of Judaism.

The Essenes, People of the Dead Sea Scrolls

The severity of the Roman occupation compelled one group of Jews, the Essenes, to live a secluded, hermitlike existence far away from both urban centers and rural villages. Seeking spiritual "purity" and political freedom, Essenes chose to reside as religious communities in the caves of the bleak Judean wilderness east of Jerusalem or in isolated, remote communes near the Dead Sea.

There are several explanations about the origin of the word "Essene." Some believe it is a variation of *hesed*, the Hebrew word for "pious." Other scholars see Essene roots in the Hebrew word *hashim*, or "silent ones," not because the Essenes were forbidden to speak to one another but perhaps because they "silently" provided anonymous sustenance and gifts to the poor. Some students of the period believe Christian monasticism is a direct outgrowth of the ancient Jewish Essene experience. Interestingly, the Essenes are not mentioned in either the New Testament or in postbiblical Jewish literature, including the Talmud.

What is clear, however, is that Essenes strongly rejected the priestly class and life in Jerusalem a century before the Roman occupiers arrived. They chose to live an intensely religious and ascetic life. As part of their commitment, Essenes neither took wives nor handled money. It is widely believed that the famous Dead Sea Scrolls, discovered in 1947 in a cave in Qumran near Jerusalem, were written by Essenes.[12]

Jesus the Preacher

Essene newcomers spiritually and physically cleansed themselves by water immersion in a *mikveh*, Hebrew for a ritual pool. Other immersions sometimes took place in the Jordan River. Thus, Yeshu (the name "Jesus" is the Greek form of the original Hebrew), the son of Joseph and Miriam (Mary), was immersed in the river by an important Jewish religious personality of the day, Yohanan (John the Baptist). It is believed Jesus was about thirty years old when he was baptized.

For the next year or two, Jesus preached messages of otherworldly hope to his oppressed Jewish brothers and sisters. He delivered his teachings on various mountains and hills, in fields, and in synagogues along the shores of Lake Kinneret (the Sea of Galilee), including Kfar Nahum (the village of Nahum), or Capernaum. It is no surprise that Jesus and other charismatic Jewish religious teachers of the period, especially those offering a message of deliverance and relief from the hated Roman occupation, attracted enthusiastic followings.

Sometimes the supporters of such preachers were numerous, and sometimes they were small groups of ardent believers, but they all shared a reverence for their particular spiritual leader. The followers of Jesus believed he performed miracles, including the healing of the sick and infirm, powers attributed to many other charismatic individuals throughout history.

Jesus's Commandments from the Torah

The early Jewish followers of Jesus were convinced their leader possessed a special relationship with the God of Israel. In the usual rabbinic preaching style and manner of his era, Jesus peppered his religious teachings with anecdotes, parables, and stories, some of them rooted in the Jewish Bible, the only Scriptures Jesus knew. It is often forgotten or overlooked that the two "Great Commandments" attributed to Jesus in the books of Matthew (22:34–40) and Mark (12:28–34), "Love your neighbor as yourself" (Leviticus 19:18) and "Love the Lord your God with all your heart, soul, and might" (Deuteronomy 6:5), come directly from the Torah.

It seems likely that Jesus had some knowledge of Hellenistic civilization, which was to play an important role in the development of Christianity. His knowledge perhaps came from visiting Jerusalem, seeing Jewish religious pilgrims who came to the city from many countries, and having an awareness of the trade and other economic factors prevalent in ancient Israel.[13]

Jesus's followers were known as *Notzrim*—Hebrew for "Nazarenes," a name that remains in modern usage. The name indicates that Jesus's hometown in the Galilee was an important factor in identifying the new sect.

It is a pattern that has occurred many times in history: preachers, teachers, or healers emerge from small towns or villages and ultimately bring their "dangerous" ministry to larger, more populated areas, where they challenge the established religious or political authorities. In this case, Jesus, coming from rural Nazareth, carried out his final religious mission in the capital city of Jerusalem.

Following Jesus's death, the *Notzrim* were confident the Roman crucifixion was not the end of either their teacher or his ministry. Some followers proclaimed Jesus had, in fact, been resurrected. The concept of physical resurrection was neither radical nor new among Jews of that period; it was a tenet of Pharisaic Judaism. While it was rejected by the Sadducees, resurrection remains a traditional Jewish belief to this day. Jesus's followers also believed he would quickly return to earth, a "Second Coming."

His followers and disciples were convinced their rabbi was the longed-for *Mashiach*, or Messiah, who would return in universal glory to a world where there would be "neither Jew nor Greek," a world where all peoples would acknowledge Jesus as Lord. Even when the *Notzrim* realized their leader was not about to return soon, their faith was not undermined or weakened (Matthew 28:7–9).

Who and What Killed Jesus?

The most painful flashpoint about Jesus and Christian-Jewish relations centers on who and what forces brought about his crucifixion. For centuries, many Christians offered an inaccurate and malevolent explanation that has had devastating consequences: "The Jews killed Christ." The technical term for this belief is "deicide," the murder of God. This canard has been a theological cudgel used to attack the "guilty" Jews, who are forever blameworthy for "killing our Lord."

But the historical reality was very different. The Jewish appointees within the established Temple priesthood who owed their leadership positions to the Roman occupiers were naturally opposed to anyone who attracted a religious or political following among the people. Typical of such collaboration was Herod Antipas (ca. 20 BCE–39 CE), the son of the famous King Herod

(73–4 BCE). Antipas ruled a large area of ancient Israel and served at the pleasure of his Roman masters.

The obsequious Antipas built a city on the shore of the Sea of Galilee and called it Tiberias in honor of his patron, the Roman emperor. Ironically, centuries later the city, named for a pagan ruler, became an important center of rabbinic learning and is today venerated as one of Judaism's four "holy cities," along with Jerusalem, Hebron, and Safed. The medieval philosopher Moses Maimonides is buried in Tiberias, as is Akiba (50–135 CE), a rabbinic martyr executed by the Romans.

Antipas, fearful of any real or perceived political incitement, saw Jesus as a dangerous troublemaker. The puppet ruler, needing to maintain law and order and, of course, his own position of power, sought the Jewish preacher's death—standard operating procedure for insecure rulers against any person who excites the masses, attracts a following, and threatens the entrenched society. The agitator from Nazareth had to be curbed or silenced (Luke 13:31–33).

Like other observant Jews, Jesus made the yearly springtime Passover pilgrimage to worship within the precincts of the Holy Temple in Jerusalem. He was accompanied by his twelve disciples, and it was in the capital city where he shocked the authorities by predicting the Temple's destruction. Jesus also denounced the entrenched priesthood, many of whose members, especially the *Kohein Gadol,* or "High Priest," owed their positions to the Roman authorities. Because of these actions, Jesus was suspected of sedition.

Another canard hurled at the Jews throughout history focuses on Jesus chasing "the money changers" from the outer courts of the Holy Temple. The images conveyed in Matthew (21:12–17, 21:23–27), Mark (11:15–19, 11:27–33), Luke (19:45–48, 20:1–8), and John (2:12–25) are of grasping materialistic Jews who are obsessed with money at a sacred time—Passover—and in a sacred place—the Holy Temple—when they should, instead, be focusing on holiday prayers and religious worship.

What emerged from those New Testament passages is a harsh caricature of money-loving Jews and the stereotype of avarice and greed as permanent ugly traits of an entire people. But the historical reality about the so-called Temple money changers is far different.

Ancient ATMs

Because Jews came to Jerusalem as religious pilgrims from "every nation under heaven" (Acts 2:5), they brought with them different currencies, especially many different coins. The holiday visitors deposited with Temple officials the money necessary to cover pilgrimage expenses while they were in Jerusalem. In effect, the vilified money changers acted as bankers and currency traders who provided the required financial services that allowed the pilgrims to change their various types of money into usable funds.

The money changers of old were an indigenous part of ancient Near Eastern cultures, including Egypt. They were akin to modern banks and currency converters (like those at today's airports) that provide the means for international travelers to exchange dollars, rubles, euros, pesos, pounds, yen, and other currencies.

Absent such services, fiscal chaos would ensue, and the resulting crazy quilt pattern of different and confusing currencies would negatively impact travel and commerce. In the case of ancient Israel, without a coherent system of currency exchange, the number of Passover visitors to Jerusalem would have been drastically reduced. It would have prevented Jews from fulfilling their religious obligations to worship God within the Temple compound.

Travelers today, faced with similar situations, routinely use ATM machines, traveler's checks, and credit cards. Only the technology has changed from two thousand years ago; the need for fiscal liquidity remains the same.

It is inaccurate to believe that Jesus "cleansed" the Temple sanctuary or worship areas. That large shrine occupied many buildings and courts, and the Holy of Holies, the Temple's most sacred space, required no cleansing because it was open only to members of the priestly class and could never have been the scene of the "tables of money changers." But the venomous stereotype of

Jewish greed has been transmitted for nearly twenty centuries, with ugly consequences.[14]

A Blame Game with Lethal Results

The complex, tense interplay between Joseph Caiaphas, the Temple's High Priest, and Pontius Pilate, the Roman governor, is a central feature of the New Testament account of Jesus's crucifixion and is always the critical dramatic relationship in Christian Passion plays. In such productions, the High Priest, eager for Jesus's death, is frequently portrayed as manipulating, even badgering the weak, milquetoast-like Roman overlord of Judea.

Because of the deicide charge and the widespread Christian belief that Jews as a people are responsible for—even guilty of—Jesus's death, it is important to dig deeper and explore the High Priest–Roman governor connection.

In 18 CE Caiaphas succeeded his father-in-law, Annas, and began eighteen tumultuous years as the High Priest. From the start of his tenure, he was under the control of and dominated by the Roman authorities who had appointed him to his exalted leadership position. In return, the occupation authorities demanded that the high Jewish religious officials maintain peace in the troublesome province whatever the cost.

Throughout history the High Priest and his entourage have always been considered Jewish leaders. This assumption led to the charge that "the Jews" collectively killed Jesus. But were Caiaphas and the other Temple officials actual leaders? Or were they pawns of the Roman occupiers? Dr. Eugene Fisher is an American Catholic scholar who questions the "leadership" claim:

> Cut off from the people and living by collaboration with Rome, the Temple priesthood must have developed a quite natural "siege mentality." Eager to please their Roman superiors, they would zealously seek to bring to the attention of Pilate even the slightest hint of rebellion.... They were not the truly religious leaders of the day, [unlike] the Pharisees.

Rather the individuals involved were only the "chief priests and the scribes," the Sadducean party of the aristocracy who had sold out to Rome in the view of the people and represented no more than their own selfish interests.[15]

The last ten years of Caiaphas's term as High Priest in the Temple hierarchy coincided with the rule of Pilate, Rome's fifth governor of the rebellious Jewish region. The occupiers called the area Judea, a Latin variant on the Hebrew name for the southern biblical kingdom of Yehudah, or Judah.

The two men, one the dominant military ruler and the other the subservient religious functionary of a subject people, collaborated to rule ancient Israel with oppression and repression. Dealing with the problems created by Jesus and his perceived acts of sedition was not the only time the two men were thrown together to maintain stability in the Roman-occupied province. Interestingly, the dates of the births and deaths of these two men, so important in the New Testament, are shrouded in mystery. Historians have no definitive time lines for either man.

In 36 CE, Pilate's cruelty as governor forced his superior in Syria, Vitellius, to remove him from office and order his humiliating and disgraceful return to Rome. In the same year, as part of a sweeping leadership change in the Judean province, Vitellius also removed Caiaphas, the Jewish collaborator, from his religious position.[16]

It is believed that after his removal as governor, Pilate lived out the remainder of his life in exile far from the imperial capital because of his violent and corrupt (even for Rome!) actions. Caiaphas, after being stripped of his authority and lofty post, resided in Jerusalem until his death.

While no one is quite certain where Pilate's grave is—Lucerne, Switzerland, is one supposition—in 1990 an ossuary bearing the remains of the Caiaphas family was discovered in Abu Tor, a small town two miles from Jerusalem, an exciting find that rocked the world of archaeology. It was a first-century ossuary, or "bone box," with the inscribed words "Yehosef bar Kayafa," translated as "Joseph, son of Caiaphas." Excavator Zvi Greenhut of the Israeli Antiquities Authority recovered the artifact, which is now on display at the Israel Museum in Jerusalem.[17]

Pilate was the cruelest of all the oppressive Roman rulers of ancient Israel. However, in the New Testament, he is portrayed as an indecisive governor who is easily swayed by a hostile Jewish crowd intent on killing Jesus. The lasting image of Pilate, one that has endured for two millennia, is that of a weak ruler who washes his hands, symbolically removing himself from judging and sentencing Jesus to his death by crucifixion.[18]

Whitewashing Pontius Pilate

Was the New Testament whitewash of Pilate part of the effort to shift the blame for Jesus's death away from the ruling Roman authorities and onto the Jewish Temple establishment and, by implication, upon the entire Jewish people? Whatever the motivation of the Gospel writers, it has only been in recent years that scholars and theologians have begun to peel away the layers of alleged Jewish "guilt" and analyze the historical realities of Roman rule, especially the career of Pilate.

Pilate's utter contempt for his subject people is documented in the writings of two prominent Jews of the period: Josephus and Philo.[19] Because Josephus was a highly complex and conflicted personality, scholars question the accuracy of some of his writings. However, his grim account of Pilate's blatant disregard for Jews and their sensibilities confirms other descriptions of the well-known Roman overlord of Israel. Josephus's specificity is worth quoting at length for its portrayal of Pilate. In the work *The Great Roman-Jewish War*, Josephus wrote:

> After this he [Pilate] raised another disturbance, by expending that sacred treasure, which is called "Corban" upon aqueducts, whereby he brought water from the distance of four hundred furlongs. At this time the multitude had indignation; and when Pilate was come to Jerusalem,

they came about his tribunal, and made a clamour at it. Now when he was apprised aforehand of this disturbance, he mixed his own soldiers in their armour with the multitude, but ordered them to conceal themselves under the habits of private men, and not indeed to use their swords, but with their staves to beat those that made the clamour. He then gave the signal from his tribunal [to do as he had bidden them]. Now the Jews were so sadly beaten, that many of them perished by the stripes they received, and many of them perished as trodden to death by each other; by which means the multitude was astonished at the calamity of those that were slain, and held their peace.[20]

Josephus describes another of Pilate's anti-Jewish actions:

Pilate ... under cover of night brought into Jerusalem the images of Caesar known as standards.... This act ... engendered a fearful tumult among the Jews; [they] were seized with dismay, their laws ... being trampled underfoot, for those laws allowed no image to be placed in the city.... [T]hey implored him to remove the standards from Jerusalem and to preserve their ancestral laws. When Pilate rejected their pleas, they fell prostrate on the ground and stayed so for five days and nights.

On the following day Pilate ascended his tribunal ... and summoned the people, as if to give them the answer they craved; then he gave a prearranged signal to a body of armed troops to surround the Jews.... [T]he Jews were dumbfounded at the unexpected sight. Pilate, declaring that he would cut them down if they refused to admit the standards of Caesar, signaled to his soldiers to draw their swords. As if by preconcerted agreement, the Jews fell prostrate in a mass, and offering their necks, cried they would rather die than transgress the law. Amazed at the force of their devotion to their religion, Pilate ordered the immediate removal of the standards from Jerusalem.[21]

Philo described Pilate as "venal, violent, abusive, savage, ferocious" and a governor who carried out "frequent executions of untried prisoners and ... endless savage ferocity."[22]

Pilate is specifically mentioned in the Christian Nicene Creed written in 325: "[Jesus] was crucified also for us under Pontius Pilate...." However, the ruthless Roman governor is portrayed, especially in traditional Passion plays, as a weak and indecisive ruler torn by inner doubt and is even bullied by a bloodthirsty Caiaphas, who is intent on killing Jesus.

The attempt to whitewash Pilate resulted in transferring the blame for Jesus's death from Pilate and the Romans, where it rightly belongs, first to Caiaphas and the corrupt, bloodthirsty priesthood, and then ultimately to the entire Jewish people past, present, and future, eternally cursed "Christ killers" who are shunned by God for their alleged crime.

Naturally, the priests of the Temple were angered by Jesus, who appeared to them as a threatening activist from the Galilee, an area held in disdain by the more sophisticated Jerusalem religious leadership. The priests, serving at the pleasure of and dominated by the tyrannical Pilate, sought ways to weaken, silence, or curtail the activities of the upstart from Nazareth. Any disruption of the established order could be used by Pilate to terminate their own positions of religious authority.

In their need to protect their privileged status, they found precisely who they were looking for in the person of a deeply troubled apostle of Jesus: Judas Ish-Kariot (Judah the man of Kariot, a town in ancient Israel). Some Christian and Jewish scholars point out that Judas was a tortured personality who exhibited a psychological love-hate relationship toward his religious leader. They also speculate that perhaps Judas became jealous of Jesus's miraculous powers and his spiritual gifts.

Other scholars believe that Judas grew resentful of Jesus's growing fame and that the once faithful apostle was fearful the Romans would accuse Jesus and his immediate circle of followers, including himself, of the alleged crimes of sedition and rebellion, thus endangering the entire Jewish community. Whatever the reason, Judas took a bribe from the Temple priests and in return revealed Jesus's identity to them. The preacher from Nazareth was arrested following a festive last supper that included wine and unleavened bread. Both wine and bread later became parts of the Christian Eucharist.[23]

It is puzzling that the Jewish establishment required the services of an informer to accurately identify Jesus. This perhaps indicates that the preacher from Nazareth had not achieved a high profile in Jerusalem. If he had gained such recognition, no informant would have been needed. Was Jesus an unknown face in the crowd among the Jewish pilgrims who had arrived in Jerusalem for the Passover festival?

One of the world's foremost New Testament scholars, David Flusser of Israel's Hebrew University, has written:

> The Gospels in their present form contain descriptions of the so-called "trial" of Jesus rewritten in a way making them improbable from the historical point of view.... All Gospel writers to some degree exaggerated Jewish "guilt" and minimize Pilate's [the Roman governor] involvement.[24]

The brief life and early death of Jesus attracted great attention and fear from his devout followers—attention because their beloved teacher was dead, and fear lest his execution threaten the group's physical security. Would the Roman authorities condemn all of Jesus's followers as well? However, his death was little noted by the overwhelming majority of the Jewish community of the time or by the Roman authorities, because in those turbulent years, there were other Jewish troublemakers who were also executed in the Roman fashion: by crucifixion.

Was Jesus a Pharisee?

Jesus traveled throughout the Land of Israel and taught within a specific time frame and religious milieu—all within human history. His crucifixion took place at a distinct time, within a particular political setting and physical location. Jesus, as a Jew, acted within his people's religious tradition; indeed, his moral and ethical teachings are frequently similar to the Pharisaic precepts of the sage Hillel, who lived a generation earlier (ca. 60 BCE–10 CE). Both stressed love of God and of one's neighbor.

Jesus is similar to Essene and Pharisaic teachers of his era who stressed special concern for the humble, the poor, the oppressed, and the downtrodden. He probably saw himself as a rabbi or a prophet, but in the New Testament writings he never mentioned the word *Mashiach.*

He did refer to himself as "Son of Man," a term that appears seventy-nine times in the prophetic books of Ezekiel, Daniel, and Ezra and in numerous psalms. In its original usage, the phrase does not possess any unique or special theological meaning, nor are "sons of men" set apart from other individuals except perhaps for their leadership qualities.

However, in chapter 7 of Daniel, the phrase denotes a particular figure with supernatural power who will judge the world. Daniel's "Son of Man" became associated with a messianic figure who rewards the righteous and punishes the sinner. During the period of the Second Temple, the term acquired a mystical meaning, and Flusser believes Jesus, at the end of his life, "finally identified himself with this sublime figure."[25]

Christianity, the faith that grew up after the death of Jesus, began almost unnoticed in the last chaotic days of the Second Temple. Eventually, metaphysical interpretations and extraordinary cosmic claims about Jesus, some made centuries later, created a permanent theological separation, a rupture between Judaism and Christianity that has existed to our own day. But that clear division came only after Jesus's life and death.

It is important to distinguish between the human Jewish Jesus and the cosmic Christian Christ, as articulated by later Christian leaders, especially Saul, a Jew from Tarsus (ca. 5 BCE–ca. 65 CE). In the Greco-Roman world he lived in, he was called by the Latin name Paul.

Paul, sometimes called the founder of Gentile Christianity, never met or saw Jesus in person. It was Paul, the Apostle to the Gentiles, however, who through his extensive writings, which compose much of the New Testament, added new and controversial elements to the faith of Christianity. Those elements included the insistence that flesh is evil and should be suppressed and the conception of Jesus not as a man, but as God made into a human form. Jesus, in Pauline teaching, is the personal Savior for the entire human family, and the Messiah for all of history.

While Jews have never accepted Paul's basic teachings about Jesus or the apostle's radical negative interpretation of the Torah, they have never "rejected" Jesus, as has often been charged. For example, the theologian and philosopher Martin Buber considered Jesus a "Jewish brother."[26] Nor have Jews rejected Christianity's basic message of compassion and love, which are essential components of Judaism.

Jews have always remained convinced that the covenant established between themselves and God at Mount Sinai is eternal and irrevocable. They are to serve and worship the God of Israel, who in turn has promised to sustain and protect them forever. According to the covenant, God hears the prayers of the Jewish people, forgives their sins, and pardons their transgressions, while they in turn pledge to perform God's *mitzvot*, the Hebrew term for divine commandments.

The covenant requires no intermediary or vicarious savior. Judaism, for its adherents, is not an unfulfilled faith, nor is it incomplete. For Jews, there is no religious void that Jesus or any other figure could or needs to fill. In theological language, Judaism is a "perfected" religion.

However, the gap between Jews and Christians is more than a series of religious affirmations or deeply held beliefs. Sometimes it is hard for Christians to understand that even after Jews have heard the Christian claims and explanations about Jesus and his ministry for two thousand years, the two communities do not perceive Jesus the same way. In addition, the Jewish and Christian views of sin, repentance, atonement, and salvation are different from one another.

Repentance and atonement are central concepts for both religions. In Judaism it is within the power of each person to turn from sin (*teshuvah* in Hebrew) and purposefully change one's behavior. Because there is no original sin in Judaism, each person is responsible for individual actions and sins.

One of the twenty Hebrew terms for sin is the word *chet*, and it appears in the Hebrew Bible nearly five hundred times. Its root meaning is "to miss the mark," as an archer fails to hit the target. In that sense, sin is missing the mark in attaining ethical and moral behavior. But even as archers fail to reach their targets and try again, so humans often "miss the mark," but they, too, are able to try again.

Messianic Claims

Nor can Jews accept the messianic claims about Jesus. He was, sadly, neither the first nor the last to be proclaimed as the longed-for Jewish Messiah. Indeed, the nature of the Messiah or the messianic age has always been a shifting, emerging, and changing concept in postbiblical Jewish life. It has reflected the hopes of the people for deliverance in the various lands and societies in which they lived at various moments in history.

For Jews, Jesus was not the Messiah because the expectations for such a personage were not fulfilled. Rome's power was not broken in ancient Israel; in fact, it became more savage and led to armed Jewish uprisings against the occupiers of the biblical homeland, all unsuccessful. The royal line of King David was not restored; the dispersion of the Jews from the Land of Israel intensified; and hatred, war, famine, and injustice all continued as before. And Jews maintained a belief in the absolute unity and singularity of God, a belief also held by Muslims.

But many Jews, when freed of Christian religious coercion and physical persecution, are able to see Jesus as part of a long line of religious figures that extends to our day—figures who taught the Jewish people ways to enhance and strengthen their relationship with the God of Israel.

It is not whether the Jewish way is better than the Christian way; rather, the two paths to God are different. Many Jews and Christians, recognizing these differences, are content to let God resolve these differences "at the end of days."

4 Saul, Call Me Paul

The Controversial Apostle to the Gentiles

The life and career of Saul of Tarsus, a city of nearly three million people in today's Turkey, has attracted attention for nearly two thousand years. In addition to numerous religious studies of the Jewish "Apostle to the Gentiles," there are many literary, historical, philosophical, and psychological explorations of the man who became Paul, a Christian saint.

He was a bundle of emotional contradictions, wild swings of religious belief, spiritual ambivalences, and perpetual controversies. Saul's father was a Jewish Roman citizen who traced his family's roots to the biblical tribe of Benjamin and the Galilean village of Gush Halav in Israel. After Saul's conversion on the road between Jerusalem and Damascus around 36 CE, Saul changed his Hebrew name to the Latin "Paul." His own Roman citizenship status permitted him to travel freely throughout the Mediterranean basin as Christianity's most successful traveling spokesperson, with visits to synagogues in addition to the meeting places of the new faith in Asia Minor, Israel, Greece, Cyprus, and ultimately Rome.

Although he called himself a "Hebrew of the Hebrews," Paul was the major factor in transforming Christianity from a sect within ancient Judaism into a separate faith community overwhelmingly composed of Gentiles that in time became the older religion's theological rival and adversary. Christian tradition teaches he was beheaded in Rome on Emperor Nero's orders around 65 CE.

Paul was frequently loathed by both Jews and Gentiles; he was an early equal-opportunity target of distrust. But because of his teaching, writing, preaching, and peripatetic travel, Paul decisively impacted and shaped future relations between Jews and Christians.

But that happened only after young Saul received a traditional Jewish education and even studied with one of the great teachers of the time, Gamaliel the Elder (d. 50 CE). He was the grandson of Hillel, one of the most important Jewish religious figures in history. Saul's religious training was influenced by Pharisaic Judaism. As mentioned in an earlier chapter, the term "Pharisee" is frequently used as a pejorative in the New Testament and in later Christian writings, yet that important stream of Judaism was the foundational source of normative Judaism.

The Road to Damascus

Saul was a good student, and around 36 CE Temple officials sent him on a special mission to Damascus. He was directed to arrest some followers of Jesus, and Saul wrote that during this period of his life, he "persecuted" Christians. It was on the journey to Damascus that Saul underwent a sudden conversion when he was overcome by a blinding light from the sky and a heavenly voice that spoke to him.

The voice, Saul later wrote, belonged to Jesus of Nazareth, who questioned the Damascus-bound traveler: "Saul, Saul, why are you persecuting me?... I am Jesus whom you are persecuting, but get up and enter the city, and it will be told you what you must do" (Acts 9:4–6, NASB). The same event is described twice more in Acts chapters 22 and 26.

Saul pressed on to Damascus, where he was baptized, but surprisingly he did not return to Jerusalem, the center of the Jesus movement, for three years. The conversion experience changed Saul/Paul on a personal level, and it ultimately transformed Western civilization. Paul's sudden conversion, his ministry, and his writings have been revered by Christians for almost two millennia. While he may or may not have been the true founder of Christianity, Paul was a major factor in shaping the new faith's teachings and perceptions of Jews and Judaism, many of them negative.

Paul on the Couch

Because of his importance, religious scholars, historians, and others have probed deeply into Paul, the man and his personality. Indeed, modern-day psychoanalysts have figuratively put the "Christian Rabbi" on their therapeutic couches in an attempt to plumb the emotional and spiritual depths of this highly conflicted man. They point out that Paul's sudden and blinding conversion may have been the result of depression caused by a profound guilt complex.

Saul "persecuted" Christians, but those harsh actions may have triggered a sense of self-loathing, and one way to overcome such a painful emotion was to rid himself of the cause of the psychic pain and identify with those whom he persecuted, that is, to fully accept Jesus. For Saul, the conversion on the road to Damascus must have been an emotionally cleansing experience.

Or was Saul, despite being a faithful and observant Jew, secretly attracted to the forbidden fruit of the alien Hellenistic civilization of his day that featured gods who died and were reborn, and other forms of what we call mystery religions? Or perhaps Saul was influenced by Rabbi Gamaliel's sympathetic view of Jesus and the early Christians that is mentioned in the New Testament. In the book of Acts the rabbi intervenes on behalf of Peter and the other apostles who may be executed:

> But a Pharisee named Gamaliel, a teacher of the Law, respected by all the people, stood up in the Council and gave orders to put the men outside for a short time. And he said to them, "Men of Israel, take care what you propose to do with these men."
>
> —Acts 5:34–35, NASB

Christian tradition posits that Gamaliel became a Christian but withheld that fact from his Jewish colleagues.[1] The argument goes on to assert the famous rabbi did not reveal his religious decision because he wanted to secretly assist his fellow Christians. That description of a supposed conversion to Christianity is perhaps why the parents of the twenty-ninth president of the United States named their son Warren Gamaliel Harding. However, Jews have never accepted the conversion account, and Gamaliel is honored as one of the great teachers of Judaism.

Another theory is that Saul was a highly ambitious man who sensed he could not gain sufficient influence or fame within the well-established parameters of the Judaism of his day, a dynamic religious community that featured many brilliant teachers, rabbis, and preachers. One way to achieve a significant place in the world was to shatter his link with his Jewish colleagues and their Torah-centered Judaism and to avoid the embryonic Jerusalem church led by Peter and other followers who knew and had personal contact with Jesus, an experience that was not Paul's.

In such a psychologically difficult situation, either a breakdown or a breakthrough was inevitable. Would Saul remain "trapped" in the Jewish community in which he grew up? Must an ambitious man become merely another member of a new faith community whose leaders had actual flesh-and-blood personal experiences with the charismatic Jesus?

However, a prominent Lutheran scholar, Krister Stendahl, the former bishop of Stockholm and dean of the Harvard Divinity School, rejects such psychological speculation about the apostle. In his 1976 book *Paul among Jews and Gentiles*, Stendahl asserts Paul had no psychological depression or guilt-ridden conscience. Instead, the spiritual conversion was a momentous religious experience devoid of spiritual or emotional angst, and in fact Paul spent most of his energy not on himself, but on delineating the differences between Judaism and Christianity, between Jews and Christians. Stendahl's interpretation differs from Augustine's traditional view that Paul's conversion on the road to Damascus was the result of a troubled personality and inner religious turmoil. In the past fifty years,

Stendahl's interpretation has been both defended and opposed by various scholars.[2]

One can revere Paul as a Christian saint or scorn him as Saul, a formidable foe of traditional Judaism, but neither Jew nor Christian can ignore him or his lasting influence on both faith communities. The highly personal writings attributed to Paul, many of them "epistles" or letters sent to various early Christian communities, constitute more than half of the New Testament text. The twentieth-century Christian scholar Sydney Ahlstrom has written that "Christian theology is a series of footnotes to St. Paul."[3]

Paul offered a complex explanation of the theological attributes of Jesus that came to be called Christology. Paul taught that before his birth, Jesus was "with God" and then led a brief earthly life. After his death, Jesus was resurrected and returned to God, and the world awaits his Second Coming. Jesus is the longed-for Messiah, the Christ, who appeared in human form in ancient Israel and whom the divine figure Saul encountered in his conversion experience.

Paul Wins a Momentous Debate

One question the early *Notzrim* led by Peter had to answer was whether to preach the message of Jesus to non-Jews, the Gentiles. Would the followers of Jesus remain a "Jewish church," or would their message of Jesus as the Messiah be extended to and accepted by people who were not Jews?

The *Notzrim* also debated whether their religious message about the Jew from Nazareth would be welcomed by or acceptable to those Gentiles who were perhaps familiar with traditional Judaism. If the new faith community remained inside *Beit Yisrael*, "the House of Israel," it would be rooted in the traditions, beliefs, liturgy, rituals, and obligations of Judaism. But did the ministry of Jesus represent continuity or discontinuity with Judaism? Was that ministry meaningful beyond the Jewish community?

Thanks to Paul and his influence on Gentiles, the answers to such questions were not long in coming. It is estimated that by the year 130 CE, only a century after Jesus's death and shortly before the final climactic Jewish war against the Roman occupiers, the majority of Christians came from Gentile, not Jewish, backgrounds. That demographic fact has not changed since then, and the Gentile majority within Christianity has had a lasting impact upon its tortured relationship to Jews and Judaism.[4]

Despite the books and articles about Saul/Paul, and even after two thousand years of intensive study of both the man and his writings, the Greek-speaking Jew from Tarsus remains an enigmatic figure. While proudly maintaining his Jewish identity, Paul still rejected both the Torah as a path to spiritual fulfillment and many Jewish religious observances, especially the kosher dietary laws and ritual circumcision. He claimed that a belief in Jesus as the Messiah, the Christ, no longer required observing many of the Jewish religious laws and commandments.

Some followers of Jesus from within the Jewish community objected to Paul's sweeping abandonment of Jewish religious practices, and a conflict arose between the "Jerusalem church" that was Jewish in its membership and the Gentiles who became Christian as a result of Paul's teachings.

This dispute is described by Barrie Wilson, professor of humanities and religious studies at York University in Toronto:

> We automatically link Paul's teachings with those of the Jesus Movement [based in Jerusalem], although in fact, they were drastically different. The Jesus Movement was part of Judaism; Paul's enterprise was not. The Jesus Movement was Torah-observant; Paul's wasn't. The Jesus Movement was led by people who knew the historical Jesus; Paul's movement wasn't. Jesus and his early followers were anti-Roman and anti-Hellenistic; Paul's movement wasn't.
>
> Joining the two movements together was not something that happened at the time of Paul. In his letters, Paul was extremely insistent that he had only minimal contact with the leaders of the Jesus Movement. He was very clear

that his movement was separate and different.... It was a brand-new religion entirely. The Christ and the Jesus Movements are, in fact, different religions, not rival interpretations of the same religion.[5]

But Paul's point of view became the dominant element of the new faith. Paul, an indefatigable traveler and preacher, rejected traditional Jewish religious practices, calling the Law a "dispensation of death." He offered instead belief in the "Risen Christ" as the sole means of gaining spiritual salvation. At the same time, Paul also taught that God's earlier election of Israel was not abrogated. The apostle's seemingly contradictory stance regarding Christians and Jews reflected his inner, perhaps irreconcilable, positions.

Has God Abandoned the Jews? "By No Means!"

Paul expresses those views in chapters 9–11 in the book of Romans, considered to be his most authoritative religious statements. Many Christians and Jews have focused on these chapters to show that Paul believed that God's promises to Jews remain valid. Although he is mystified that his fellow Jews have not followed him into the new faith, he wonders whether God has forsaken the covenant and promises made to Jews. Paul answers, "God forbid!" that such a divine negation could take place. He also compares Judaism to a "good olive tree" and believes Gentiles can only be "grafted" onto that tree.

Because of the importance these three chapters play in Christian-Jewish relations, it is necessary to quote some of the key verses:

I am telling the truth in Christ, I am not lying.... For I could wish that I myself were accursed, separated from Christ for the sake of my brethren, my kinsmen ... who are Israelites, to whom belongs the adoption as sons, and the glory and the covenants and the giving of the Law and the temple

service and the promises, whose are the fathers, and from whom is the Christ.... But it is not as though the word of God has failed. For they are not all Israel who are descended from Israel.... That is, it is not the children of the flesh who are children of God, but the children of the promise are regarded as descendants.... I say then, God has not rejected His people, has He? May it never be! For I too am an Israelite, a descendant of Abraham, of the tribe of Benjamin.... But if some of the branches were broken off, and you, being a wild olive, were grafted in among them and became partaker with them of the rich root of the olive tree,... Do not be arrogant toward the branches; but if you are arrogant, remember that it is not you who supports the root, but the root supports you.... And so all Israel will be saved ... for the gifts and the calling of God are irrevocable.
 —Romans 9:1, 9:3–8, 11:1, 11:17–18, 11:26, 11:29, NASB

Romans 9–11 was a major element in the adoption of the *Nostra Aetate* Declaration at the Vatican Council in 1965. During the Evangelical conversion campaign "Key '73" in the United States, Billy Graham cited these same chapters to support his belief that Jews must not be singled out as specific targets for conversion.

Two Cardinals Disagree

Christian scholars have weighed in with their own interpretations of Romans 9–11, and two Catholic cardinals, Walter Kasper, a German theologian who formerly directed Catholic-Jewish relations at the Vatican, and Avery Dulles, an American theologian, presented opposing views of Paul's most famous writings.

In a 2002 address at Boston College, Kasper declared:

What we have in common is above all what Jews call the Hebrew Bible and we the Old Testament. We have in common our common father in faith, Abraham, and Moses and the Ten Commandments, the Patriarchs and Prophets, the covenant and the promises of the one and unique God, and the messianic hope. Because we have all this in common and because as Christians we know that God's covenant with Israel by God's faithfulness is not broken [Romans 11:29], mission as understood as a call to conversion from idolatry to the living and true God [1 Thessalonians 1:9] does not apply and cannot be applied to Jews. They confess the living true God, who gave and gives them support, hope, confidence and strength in many difficult situations of their history. There cannot be the same kind of behavior towards Jews as there exists towards Gentiles. This is not a merely abstract theological affirmation, but an affirmation that has concrete and tangible consequences, such as the fact that there is no organized Catholic missionary activity towards Jews as there is for all other non-Christian religions.[6]

But Dulles, the son of John Foster Dulles, the U.S. secretary of state in the Eisenhower administration, opposed Kasper's interpretation of Paul:

The most formal statement on the status of the Sinai covenant under Christianity appears in the Letter to the Hebrews, which points out that in view of the new covenant promised by God through the prophet Jeremiah, the first covenant is "obsolete" and "ready to vanish away" (Hebrews 8:13). The priesthood and the law have changed (Hebrews 7:12). Christ, we are told, "abolishes the first [covenant] in order to establish the second" (Hebrews 10:9).

These passages from Hebrews do not overturn Paul's insistence in Romans that the promises of God to Israel remain valid. The Hebrew Scriptures, containing God's promises, have enduring value, but are to be interpreted in the light of Christ to whom they point forward. The elect have obtained what was promised, though the rest were hardened (Romans 11:7). "And even the others, if they do not persist in their unbelief, will be grafted in" (11:23). Paul in fact looks forward to a day when all Israel will recognize Christ and be saved (11:26). He does not mean that Israel is already saved by adherence to the Sinai covenant.

Some Christians, in their eagerness to reject a crude supersessionism, give independent validity to the Old Covenant. They depict the Old and New Covenants as two "separate but equal" parallel paths to salvation, the one intended for Jews, the other for gentiles.... Joseph Fitzmyer, in his scholarly commentary on Romans, likewise opposes the theory of two separate ways of salvation: "It is difficult to see how Paul would envisage two different kinds of salvation, one brought about by God apart from Christ for Jews, and one by Christ for Gentiles and believing Jews. That would seem to militate against his whole thesis of justification and salvation by grace for all who believe in the gospel of Christ Jesus (1:16). For Paul the only basis for membership in the new people of God is faith in Christ Jesus."[7]

The Rev. Dr. John T. Pawlikowski, professor of ethics at Chicago's Catholic Theological Union and a pioneer in Christian-Jewish relations, supports Kasper's position. Pawlikowski has written that the early church's anti-Jewish writings and teachings were more than a bitter tirade. Rather, they represent a basic component of Christian teaching: the church has replaced the Holy Temple and the synagogue, and the Gospels have supplanted the Torah.

Yet, the overwhelming majority of Jews in Paul's day as well as today have remained loyal to Judaism; they have not become Christians, members of the church. Jews remain, in Paul's words, "beloved for the sake of the fathers; for the gifts and the calling of God are irrevocable" (Romans 11:28–29, NASB). Romans 9–11, with all of its ambiguities, remains a constant rebuke to Christian triumphalism, even though Paul longed for Jewish acceptance of Jesus as the Savior and Messiah and he believed the new covenant,

Christianity, was God's ultimate answer to the contradictions he described in Romans.

As this exploration of only three chapters of Paul's writings shows, there are divergent views of what they mean for Christians and Jewish-Christian relations. However, it is Paul's complex, ambivalent teachings, and not those of Jesus, that helped create the major theological differences between Judaism and Christianity, differences that continue to plague relations between these two "peoples of God."

Rome Kills Paul

Following the great fire in Rome around 64 CE, the emperor Nero blamed the Christians for the disaster, and in an act of imperial scapegoating, Paul, perhaps the most visible and articulate Christian in the entire empire, was beheaded. Persecution of the new Christian faith went on for several centuries after Paul's death, and the martyrs of that period are revered by Christians. After Paul's death, the crisis regarding the new faith's relationship to Judaism continued. Once the majority of Christian converts were Gentiles, the Jewish origins, milieu, and roots of the new religion were often minimized and even repudiated.

The early Christian missionaries after Paul had a serious problem as they preached his message of Jesus as Messiah. Most Gentiles, including Greeks and Romans, were unfamiliar with the various Jewish religious categories, practices, rituals, and liturgy that were important and familiar to the early *Notzrim*. The Gentiles could not or would not identify with Jewish traditions and the specific *mitzvot*, especially ritual circumcision, the dietary laws, and the observance of Saturday as the weekly Sabbath day.

In addition, the new Gentile adherents of Christianity did not share the same connection with the Land of Israel (*Eretz Yisrael*) as Jews did. For the former group, that region was given the name "Holy Land" not because of any personal link of their own, but because it was their description of the place where their Savior was born, lived, died, and was resurrected. It was also the land and the city—Jerusalem—where the anticipated Second Coming would take place.

As a result, Gentile Christians did not pray for and were not committed to the rebirth of Jewish national sovereignty in the Holy Land; instead, it became over the centuries a place of pilgrimage for Christians intent on "walking in the steps" of Jesus. The "theology of the land," an indigenous part of Judaism, is notably absent from Christian religious teachings. The dichotomy between Christian reverence for the Holy Land and the Jewish passion for *Eretz Yisrael*, the biblical homeland and the place for a reborn Jewish Commonwealth, remains a source of major difference and tension between the two communities.

Marcion's Heresy

An extreme example of anti-Jewish teachings occurred as early as the second century when a Christian theologian, Marcion (85–160 CE), called for the total elimination of the Hebrew Bible from Christianity. He believed Jesus as the Christ was completely separate and distinct from any historical or religious connection with Judaism and the God of Israel. Marcion saw a total disconnect, an abyss between what he believed was the wrathful tribal God of the Hebrew Bible and the loving God of Jesus. For him, the God of the Hebrews was a vicious deity to be cast aside and replaced by the universal God of Christianity. In addition, he wanted a major revision of the New Testament, with certain books deleted from the Christian canon.

Because of his radical views, Marcion was deemed a threat to the unity of Christianity, and he was declared a heretic and eventually excommunicated from the church. But today, nearly two thousand years later, whiffs of Marcionism still exist within Christianity. His ideas, especially the total rejection of Judaism and the Hebrew Bible and his abandonment of any Christian roots in Judaism, opened the doors for religious anti-Semitism and even provided proof, albeit from a heretic, that Christianity represents a total fulfillment of the older faith; that the "New Israel" completely displaces the "Old Israel" and severs all connections with the religion of Jesus.[8]

Pope John Paul II denounced Marcionism in this way:

> [God] is faithful to his covenant. To ignore this most basic principle is to adopt a Marcionism against which the church immediately and vigorously reacted, conscious of a vital link with the Old Testament, without which the New Testament itself is emptied of meaning.[9]

Even without Marcionism, Christianity early on began a systematic campaign to diminish the spiritual value of Jews and Judaism. That denigration, called the "teaching of contempt," has poisoned relations between the two faith communities. To use modern technological jargon: when the church's centuries-old anti-Jewish historical and theological tradition, the "teaching of contempt" toward Jews and Judaism, continues to be programmed into the Christian teaching and preaching "computer" of today's church, that same toxic, negative teaching will come out, and until and unless permanent systemic changes are made, the "teaching of contempt" is likely to continue.

5 The Partings of the Way

Jews and Christians Take Separate Paths to God

Yogi Berra has taught, "When you come to the fork in the road, take it." And that is what most people believe happened when Christianity supposedly "broke" with Judaism and emerged as a fully formed separate faith.

For centuries, it was believed the early Christians abruptly took that fork in the road around the year 85 CE, about five decades after the Romans executed Jesus and fifteen years after the Romans destroyed the Temple in Jerusalem.

For members of the new Christian faith community, that momentous event was evidence that Jews had lost God's favor because they "rejected" Jesus as their Messiah and Savior. But, of course, since the early followers of Jesus were Jews, there was no mass Jewish "rejection." No vote was taken, no referendum was held in ancient Israel regarding the claims made about Jesus. The majority of the Jews of that era, whether living in Israel or in the Diaspora, the Jewish communities outside the biblical homeland, probably never heard of Jesus, his teachings, or his death.

As described in a previous chapter, by the time Jesus was born, there was already in existence a rich and diverse Jewish religious tradition based upon the Jewish Scriptures and a strong collective memory of the Exodus, the prophetic teachings, the Maccabean rebellion (the Hanukkah story), and other defining events.

As the church grew in adherents and influence, Christians believed they had won their rightful place as the religious successor to Judaism. Judaism had lost. Except it wasn't true.

Winning the Battle, but Losing the War

As the centuries unfolded, Jews living under Christian domination, but secure in their own religious beliefs, felt a sense of disdain bordering on condescension toward the younger faith. One of my rabbinical school professors, a 1930s refugee from Nazi Germany, summed it up in a few pithy words: "We Jews won the theological battle with Christianity, but we lost the war numerically."

The harsh Roman occupation and the destruction of the Temple in Jerusalem, which ended centralized worship in that majestic building, forced some of the surviving Jews to flee the Land of Israel for hopefully safer homes in the Diaspora, most notably Babylonia, today's Iraq. However, there were also Jewish communities in North Africa, including Egypt, as well as in Greece, Italy, and other lands.

Once in the Diaspora, Jews developed new ways and methods of being faithful to their religion that did not require the existence of the Temple and its cultic worship. What emerged has been called Rabbinic Judaism. Synagogues existed before 70 CE, but following the Temple's destruction they became central to Jewish life. At the same time, rabbis became the main teachers of Judaism, and the existing Jewish Diaspora became even larger in size.

In the years that followed, Jews established hundreds and later thousands of houses of assembly, worship, and study—*beit knesset* in Hebrew—decentralized spaces where Judaism was kept alive and where it ultimately survived. The Temple's destruction was a cataclysmic event, but it did not mean the end of Jewish life or an abrogation of the Sinai covenant. The growth of the synagogue was a remarkable example of religious adaptation.

However, the early Christians saw something different in the Temple's destruction: the catastrophe was God's eternal punishment of an unfaithful people, and the physical ruins marked the

name of the Jews' chief enemies, the Philistines, whose most notable leader in biblical times was Goliath, David's foe.[5] In time, the area became known simply as Palestine, although Jews continued to call it *Eretz Yisrael*, the Land of Israel.

In one final act of anti-Jewish egotism, the Roman emperor renamed Jerusalem as Aelia Capitolina, in honor of himself and the pagan god Jupiter Capitoline. No Jews or *Notzrim* were allowed to enter the newly constructed pagan city except on the ninth day of the Hebrew month of Av, the traditional fast day of mourning when the Holy Temple was destroyed.

Jewish Independence Ends until 1948

The results of the devastating Roman victory over Bar Kochba and his forces, though less known than the siege of Jerusalem and the Temple's destruction in 70 CE, were far more lasting. In this war, the majority of Jews living in the Land of Israel were killed, exiled, or sold into slavery. The entire city of Jerusalem, not just the Holy Temple, was completely destroyed, and all vestiges of Jewish national independence were wiped off the face of the earth and did not reappear until May 14, 1948, with the birth of modern Israel, a wait of 1,813 years.

But despite Hadrian's obscene intentions, he did not end Jewish life in the land of the Bible. The Jerusalem Talmud was compiled in the Galilee between the second and fourth centuries. Historians remind us that in the sixth century, four hundred years after Bar Kochba's defeat, there were still forty-three extant Jewish communities: a dozen communities were on the Mediterranean coast, in the Negev wilderness of the south, or east of the Jordan River; the remaining thirty-one were in the Jordan Valley or the Galilee.

James Parkes, the British historian, has written of this underreported and little recognized period in Jewish history, years when most people believe there were no Jews living in the Land of Israel:

> It was, perhaps, inevitable that Zionists should look back to
> the heroic period of the Maccabees and Bar Kochba [the

last name of Israel's first prime minister, David Ben-Gurion, is in honor of one of Bar Kochba's generals] but their real title deeds were written by the less dramatic but equally heroic endurance of those who had maintained the Jewish presence in The Land all through the centuries, and in spite of every discouragement. This [little-known] page of Jewish history ... allowed the anti-Zionists, whether Jewish, Arab, or European, to paint an entirely false picture of the wickedness of Jewry trying to re-establish a two-thousand-year-old claim to the country, indifferent to everything that had happened in the intervening period. It allowed a picture of The Land as a territory which had once been "Jewish," but which for many centuries had been "Arab." In point of fact any picture of a total change of population is false ... from Roman up to modern times. If the number of Jewish inhabitants has constantly varied, it has been because of circumstances outside Jewish control, and not because Jews had themselves lost interest in living in the "promised land." On the whole it may be said that it was always as large as possible in view of conditions existing at any one time.[6]

Cautious Rabbis and a Portable Homeland

Following Bar Kochba's defeat, and for centuries after, the Rabbis grew cautious in making messianic claims and urged Jewish withdrawal from political insurrections. Some rabbis, chastened by the catastrophic losses of the past, even dampened hopes for a restoration of Jewish national independence.

The Rabbis attempted to minimize the valor and military prowess of Judah Maccabee's triumph in 165 BCE. A Talmudic reference (*Shabbat* 21b) asks a strange rhetorical question: "What is Hanukkah?" The Rabbis surely knew the story, but they emphasized the "miracle" of the cruse of oil in the newly rededicated Jerusalem Temple that lasted eight days instead of one. The Rabbis of the Talmud engaged in self-censorship by focusing more on spiritual matters and less on how a small insurgent group was successful against a large imperial army, clearly not a message the Roman overlords wanted to hear from a subjugated people.

The synagogue, the schoolhouse of a people, became the center of Jewish life, and the Torah scroll housed in its Holy Ark became a "portable homeland" replacing the lost glory of the Temple, national sovereignty, and military strength. Jews were weighed down by harsh imperial rule and the emergence of a Gentile Christianity hostile in many ways to Judaism. After Constantine's conversion, religion and state became coupled together. These twin pressures forced Jews to turn inward, and the biblical and Talmudic scholar, not the soldier-warrior, became the model of Jewish identity until the rise of the modern Zionist movement in the late nineteenth and early twentieth centuries.

This view of a slow emergence of Christianity from Judaism is in accord with human behavior. New movements, whether religious, political, social, or cultural, take time to mature, grow, and become distinct from their roots. That is why the current efforts toward reconciliation and mutual respect between Jews and Christians cannot be completed in a sudden burst or by suddenly taking a new fork in the road. Significant changes in human development do not occur in a single moment in history.

Instead, today's relationships, filled with promise and perplexity, certainty and ambiguity, will take time, patience, and commitment by all parties over many years, perhaps decades, to reach full maturity.

6 Why "Old Testament" Is Not a Term of Endearment

I remember an interreligious conference on the Bible that nearly resulted in a fistfight among some of the academic participants. The meeting opened with a panel that included me and five otherwise coolheaded Christian professors of Scriptures. The quintet argued with one another because they could not agree among themselves on an appropriate or mutually acceptable name for the Jewish Holy Scriptures.

The first panel member offered the well-known term "Old Testament" to describe the ancient collection of books that Jews and Christians both consider holy. The prominent professor used the traditional terminology—"Old Testament" and "New Testament"—which Christians have employed for centuries to express their belief in the sacredness of both scriptural collections. Indeed, he pointed out that 75 percent of the Christian Scriptures consists of the Old Testament. However, it is a term I reject for many reasons.

I have attended and spoken at many church services where selections from both "Testaments" were read, with one critical and striking difference. During the Old Testament reading, usually selections from the Hebrew prophets or psalms, the congregation—Roman Catholic or Protestant— remained seated. When the Gospel (Matthew, Mark, Luke, or John) verses were spoken, the worshippers stood as a clear sign of reverence. Was the custom of standing for only New Testament readings a lack of respect for the only Scriptures Jesus knew? Probably not, but the implication of the "New," especially the four Gospels, being somehow spiritually more important than the "Old" was clear.

I have also visited Eastern Orthodox churches where members of the congregation stand during the entire worship service. But even in such settings, it seemed the readings from the New Testament were accorded greater honor than those from the Old Testament.

An infuriated colleague followed the first conference speaker, her ire perhaps reflecting this widespread disparity in liturgy and ritual. She charged that the term "Old Testament" is highly pejorative when used in conjunction with or in contrast to the "New Testament." The professor of Bible added that something "New" frequently trumps something "Old," and the angry scholar insisted instead on using the terms "First Testament" and "Second Testament" to describe the writings.

Of course, she was historically and chronologically correct. No one questions that the Second Testament, with its central focus on Jesus, was written centuries after the First Testament had become the scriptural canon of the Jewish people. For me, the professor's two titles sounded less like a theological or literary definition and more like the legal language frequently used by attorneys who specialize in wills and estates.

The well-meaning Bible scholar, striving to be nuanced and fair to both faith communities, could just as easily have labeled the two collections "the first and second codicils" to God's contracts or covenants with Jews and Christians.

Another professor on the panel chose "Early Testament" and "Later Testament." The interreligious audience had trouble accepting this tortured attempt to avoid offending anyone. It was a nimble effort to describe an obvious historical reality. I found this particular formula worse than using "First" and "Second," since "Early" is, in general parlance, almost always perceived as inferior to the new and improved "Later" model of a product, whether it be a car, a computer, or religious texts.

Lacing his words with a wry smile, another distinguished professor of biblical studies rejected the earlier descriptions and opted for "Jewish Bible." But even before he could offer his preferred term for the New Testament, he was interrupted by a fellow academic in the audience who correctly noted that Christians as well as Jews consider the books in question as "biblical." Following this not-so-polite put-down, the scholar lamely concluded by using "Christian Bible" alongside "Jewish Bible."

Still another panel member dismissed "linguistic confusion" and chose the phrases "Hebrew Scriptures" and "Christian Scriptures." But even those terms were criticized, because certain parts of the "Hebrew" Bible were actually written in Aramaic, especially sections of the book of Daniel. Aramaic is a kindred but distinct tongue from the Hebrew language.

In addition, there is an obvious imbalance in the two terms, since Hebrew is, among other things, not a specific religious term, while "Christian," a word that appears only three times in the New Testament books of Acts and First Peter, denotes a distinctly religious or theological identity.

Quarreling Christian Scholars Require a Jewish Referee

By now, the restless audience was bemused when, as the final speaker and the only Jewish member of the divided conference panel, I rose to speak. I attempted to act as both referee and peacemaker with my sly suggestion that "for the purposes of this meeting we should only employ the traditional Jewish term *Tanach*, the Hebrew acronym for *Torah* (Teaching), *Nevi'im* (Prophets), and *K'tuvim* (Writings), the three components of the Jewish Holy Scriptures." However, the *Tanach* does not contain the books of the Maccabees, Tobit, and Judith that are part of the Catholic, Eastern Orthodox, and Anglican canon. I added that people were free to use any title they wished for the second collection of books even as I expressed my own aversion to the use of "Old Testament," a term I find unacceptable and depreciatory.

I affirmed the earlier assertions that something "new" is frequently considered better than the "old." But the issue is more complex. Much of Christian teaching affirms the "New" Testament reflects a universal God of "Grace" and theologically fulfills the "Old" Testament, which expresses a parochial God of "Law." It is an inaccurate and mischievous comparison because it sets up a false dichotomy between the two faiths.

Dr. Walter Kaiser Jr., the former president of Gordon-Conwell Seminary in South Hamilton, Massachusetts, has written:

> Evangelical Christians can and ought to use the Mosaic law, for as Paul affirmed, "The law is good if we use it rightly" (1 Timothy 1:8). The ... "law is holy, just, spiritual and good" (Romans 7:13–14); that is not where the problem ever existed, for Israel or the church: the problem always was with people, not the law.[1]

Dr. David Blumenthal, professor of Judaic studies at Emory University, makes clear that grace is a basic component of Judaism:

> The Jewish concept of grace is bound up with the Hebrew word "hesed."... Creation is God's first act of grace.... The motif of creation of grace recurs in the daily liturgy of rabbinic Judaism.... The motif occurs again in medieval Jewish philosophy [Moses Maimonides].... Finally, the motif of creation as grace occurs in the Jewish mystical tradition [Levi Yitzhak of Berditchev].[2]

There was applause from the audience following my remarks about using the term *Tanach*. The collective conference temperature immediately dropped, allowing a positive tone to return to the previously tense and testy proceedings. But the truce on biblical nomenclature I had brokered ended when the conference concluded. The arguments over the various names given to the two sets of Scripture had taken almost forty minutes, and the deep fissures among the Christian biblical scholars on the panel were evident for all to see.

The names given to the ancient religious texts reveal more about the person who provides the labels than the actual content of the books themselves. The spectacle of well-respected biblical scholars confronting one another over the "right" scriptural titles illustrated some significant facts that require exploration and analysis.

First, *Tanach*, the Hebrew-language acronym, requires no supplemental elaboration or multiple names to define it. While Jews may sometimes call their Scripture by several other terms, the use of *Tanach* is accurate and comprehensive.

Because Jews anchored their religious beliefs to a specific "holy text," the new Christian faith community followed suit and designated a collection of twenty-seven books written in Greek as its primary religious focus: the "New Testament." It is also likely that Islam, which developed nearly six hundred years after the death of Jesus, was influenced by the centrality of both the *Tanach* and the New Testament, and it, too, chose a text, the Qur'an, as its sacred book.

Even though Paul rejected much of Jewish religious "Law," the Christian church regards the Hebrew Bible as Scripture. As a result, while both Jews and Christians may revere the same text, they perceive and study it in fundamentally dissimilar ways. This is especially true in the diverse definitions each faith community has given to a series of shared theological terms, including "Messiah," "salvation," "sin," and "redemption."

For Jews, the *Tanach* is the bedrock of their faith, the ancient story of their people and the source of eternal instruction, inspiration, and teaching. Christians early on saw the same biblical books differently: a necessary but insufficient component of their own belief system. For them, the "Old" Covenant or Testament was fulfilled in the person of Jesus, through his death and resurrection, and that fulfillment is reflected in the Christian usage of "New" Covenant or Testament.

It is little wonder that in such a competition, the "harsh Old Testament" often became spiritually inadequate, even inferior, when compared to the "loving New Testament." In that false dichotomy, the people of the Old Testament were denigrated and viewed as a religiously surplus population, while the people of the New Testament were celebrated as members of the new true religion. The comparison conveniently overlooks harsh verses contained in the New Testament and omits references to loving texts in the *Tanach*.

Christians have used various verses, themes, institutions, and events in the *Tanach* as vital "proof texts" that, it is believed, predicted or pointed the way for the coming of Jesus. This was a key teaching of early church leaders, one that has continued to this day and represents a major difference and theological flash point between the two faith communities.

The Only Sacred Text Jesus Knew

The *Tanach*, as mentioned above, was the only Scripture that Jesus knew, and his reverence for and knowledge of those books was evident when he spoke. Paul's constant references to the sacred text, probably the Septuagint, are a major feature of his writings. I have met many Christians who feel themselves closer to the rabbinic "Jewish Jesus" who was part of the Jewish community of his time than the more distant and imperial "Christian Christ" who represents the later infusion of Hellenistic themes and beliefs.

Because Jesus was spiritually "at home" in the *Tanach* and Paul in the Septuagint, it became imperative for Christians to validate themselves religiously by using various selections from those texts as biblical confirmations of their faith. They achieved this goal by incorporating into the New Testament some of the same verses from the *Tanach* that Jesus used in his preaching.

When asked which were the great commandments of God (Matthew 22:37–40), Jesus responded by citing, "You shall love the Lord your God with all your heart, with all your soul and with all your might," directly from Deuteronomy 6:5. He followed with "Love your neighbor as yourself," a commandment in Leviticus 19:18. Jesus recited the opening words of Psalm 22, "My God, my

God, why have You forsaken me?" as he faced death on the Roman cross (Matthew 27:46).

But the use of the *Tanach* within Christianity involved more than simple familiarity with the verses known and used by Jesus and his early followers. The *Tanach* had first to be redefined and reformulated as a predictive set of books and then presented as a foretelling of both Jesus and the emergence of the new Christian faith. It was essential to see that the New Testament, especially the coming of Jesus, was forecast within the Old Testament as a way of bolstering the faith of the Christian community.

Christianity could not stand alone without strong references to its taproots within Judaism, the religion of Jesus. But at the same time, it was also necessary to transfer the divine promises and the spiritual legitimacy of the older faith to the new one. It was, and still remains, a delicate balance: to link Christianity to the Jewish Scriptures while at the same time declaring that the earlier faith is religiously fulfilled, or, as I have often heard from some Christian leaders, "Judaism became null and void" with the arrival of Jesus.

The technical name for using the *Tanach* to validate Christianity's truth is "typology," a term derived from the Greek linguistic root "to strike" or "to make an imprint." In modern English, it means to leave an impression of the letter or letters typed by either a typewriter or a computer. In biblical typology many of the Old Testament events, institutions, rituals, and personalities become holy leading indicators, "impressions" or predictions of what was to come following the birth of Jesus.

Typology is also described as biblical prefiguration and is a form of eisegesis, that is, reading an event or a person's life back into a text long after it was written. The opposite of eisegesis is exegesis, the delving into and the exploration of a text in an attempt to discover its original meaning.

There are many examples of Christian typology, but a few illustrations will indicate how this biblical system operates and why it has separated Jews and Christians. The Hebrew word *navi* is translated as "prophet." The English term has come to mean a person who can predict events of the future, but the Hebrew word root means something different. A *navi* is one who is a truth teller, not a fortune-teller.

Even though Isaiah, Jeremiah, Ezekiel, and the other Hebrew prophets in the *Tanach* often spoke in allegorical or poetic terms, they always remained rooted to their own time and place in ancient Israel's history. Jeremiah speaks about the desperate situation of his beloved city of Jerusalem. He declares that the sinful people of Israel will face the devastating Babylonian invasion led by Nebuchadnezzar.

Jeremiah's soulful expressions of grief about the destruction and desolation of Jerusalem constitute the separate biblical book of Lamentations, which is read in synagogues on the gloomiest day in the Jewish liturgical calendar: the ninth day of Av.

Yet, despite these links with the events of sixth-century-BCE Jerusalem and Jeremiah's specific references to Israelite king Josiah, Christian typology has identified Jeremiah as a prophet of the Passion of Jesus, an event that took place about six hundred years after the end of Jeremiah's life. Sculptures of the Hebrew prophet appear in the thirteenth-century French cathedrals in Chartres and Amiens. In the former edifice, a Christian cross is even part of the Jeremiah sculpture, a blatant form of religious expropriation.

Jews do not accept the Christian use of the Hebrew Bible as a source of predictions for the coming of Jesus as Messiah. Despite the fact that the prophets lived hundreds of years before Jesus, early Christian leaders retroactively read Jesus back into the Hebrew Bible as proof of their own claims.

The Catholic historian Friedrich Heer describes Christian typology as "[the] greatest robbery in the history of the world from the Jewish viewpoint (and a true Christian who takes himself seriously must take account of it), reduc[ing] the Old Testament to the service of the Christian Church. What was created in the course of more than a thousand years by Jewish prophets ... now becomes the booty of the 'New Israel,' the Church, as the inalienable inheritance of the Church."[3]

While the entire biblical book of Isaiah is 66 chapters in length, there is general agreement that the first 39 chapters were composed by the prophet during the years 740–700 BCE and the remaining chapters, 40–66, were written much later, probably around 540 BCE during the Babylonian exile. The unknown author of the last 27 chapters is called Deutero-Isaiah or Second Isaiah.

"The Suffering Servant of Israel"

Beginning with Isaiah 40, the anonymous prophet offers hope and consolation following the Temple's destruction in 586 BCE, and it seems clear he was writing while living among the exiled Jews in Babylonia. Beginning at the end of chapter 52 and running through the first dozen verses in the next chapter, the unknown prophet describes what Christians call the "Suffering Servant of Israel":

> *"Indeed, My servant shall prosper,*
> *Be exalted and raised to great heights.*
> *Just as the many were appalled at him—*
> *So marred was his appearance, unlike that of man,*
> *His form, beyond human semblance—*
> *Just so he shall startle many nations.*
> *Kings shall be silenced because of him,*
> *For they shall see what has not been told them,*
> *Shall behold what they never heard."*

> *"Who can believe what we have heard?*
> *Upon whom has the arm of the Lord been revealed?*
> *For he has grown, by His favor, like a tree crown,*
> *Like a tree trunk out of arid ground.*
> *He had no form or beauty, that we should look at him:*
> *No charm, that we should find him pleasing.*
> *He was despised, shunned by men,*
> *A man of suffering, familiar with disease.*
> *As one who hid his face from us,*
> *He was despised, we held him of no account.*

Yet it was our sickness that he was bearing,
Our suffering that he endured.
We accounted him plagued,
Smitten and afflicted by God;
But he was wounded because of our sins,
Crushed because of our iniquities.
He bore the chastisement that made us whole,
And by his bruises we were healed.
We all went astray like sheep,
Each going his own way;
And the Lord visited upon him
The guilt of all of us. "

He was maltreated, yet he was submissive,
He did not open his mouth;
Like a sheep being led to slaughter,
Like a ewe, dumb before those who shear her,
He did not open his mouth.
By oppressive judgment he was taken away,
Who could describe his abode?
For he was cut off from the land of the living
Through the sin of my people, who deserved the punishment.
And his grave was set among the wicked,
And with the rich, in his death,
Though he had done no injustice,
And had spoken no falsehood.
But the Lord chose to crush him by disease,
That, if he made himself an offering for guilt,
He might see offspring and have long life,
And that through him the Lord's purpose might prosper.
Out of his anguish he shall see it;
He shall enjoy it to the full through his devotion.

"My righteous servant makes the many righteous,
It is their punishment that he bears;

Assuredly, I will give him the many as his portion,
He shall receive the multitude as his spoil.
For he exposed himself to death
And was numbered among the sinners,
Whereas he bore the guilt of the many
And made intercession for sinners."

—Isaiah 52:13–53:12, JPS

These verses are among the most analyzed and controversial in the entire *Tanach*. They represent the best-known and most widely used example of how Christianity used the Hebrew Bible to predict the coming of Jesus. The prophet, living in the exiled Diaspora community in Babylonia, offers an idealized description of a servant of God, and many Christians believe that while this chapter was written six centuries before Jesus's birth, it is a proof text predicting and describing his life and death. Indeed, these verses represent the high-water mark of Christian typology or prefiguration.

However, Jews and many contemporary Christian scholars have a completely different view of the prophet's description of the so-called Suffering Servant. For Jews, Isaiah 52–53 is extraordinary prophetic poetry intended to exalt and inspire an exiled people following the destruction of the First Temple. Most believe the words apply either to the people of Israel or to the prophet himself. The *Tanach* writing style often refers to peoples and nations in the singular form, and in this case the Servant of God may not be a single personage, but rather the entire people who suffered the traumatic loss of the Jerusalem Temple, an event followed by a painful exile that only ended when Cyrus, the Persian king, defeated the Babylonians and allowed the exiles, led by Nehemiah and Ezra, to return to the Land of Israel and its capital city.

During the twentieth century these Isaiah verses were sometimes used to describe the millions of Jews who were led to their slaughter "like sheep," even though the historical record of the Holocaust indicates there were many instances of Jews, with extremely limited military capability, fighting the Nazi Germans and their collaborators both in and out of the death camps.[4]

Who or what did the prophet have in mind? Jews believe Second Isaiah is describing in painful and poetic terms the people of Israel. The sense is that the so-called Suffering Servant who will redeem an exiled people is the future faithful people of Israel, not the current population trapped in exile. It will be a people who are truly the collective Servant of God, men and women who have undergone severe testing and trauma and who will emerge from the crucible of suffering as a perfected community bound in faith to the God of Israel.

For Christians, however, the Servant of God who has suffered is Jesus, and the prophet is predicting the travails Jesus will endure nearly six hundred years after Second Isaiah's words were written. In typology, the Old Testament's veracity is not dependent on historical time periods, specific locations, or time-sensitive events. Rather, the New Testament is prefigured, folded into the Old Testament, and all that is required is to employ various Old Testament stories and personalities to definitively "prove" the truth of Christianity.

Isaiah 53 is used by Christian proselytizers who cite these verses as predictive evidence of Jesus's messiahship. The various Hebrew Christian groups, including the Jews for Jesus, base much of their efforts on this chapter. Christian missionaries cite the Isaiah passages when they attempt to convert Jews, a tactic especially used on college and university campuses: "You see, your own Bible predicts the coming of Jesus!"

There are Christian and Jewish biblical scholars who reject the idea that the Hebrew prophet predicted Jesus and his ministry, including Harry M. Orlinsky, the only Jewish member on the translation team of the Revised Standard Version (RSV) of the Bible (1952). He was also among the translators of the New Jewish Publication Society version (NJPS, 1985) and the New Revised Standard Version (NRSV, 1989), and Orlinsky taught at the Hebrew Union College–Jewish Institute of Religion in New York City. He wrote:

Why would any scholar have thought of treating chapter 53 differently from any other chapter in our Book [Isaiah] had it not been for the theological aura created for it in early Christianity?... The personage in Isaiah 53 is not Israel (personified or ideal or otherwise) but an individual person, a spokesman of God, and that person is Second Isaiah himself. The element of vicariousness was completely unknown [among Jews] ... until long after his [Second Isaiah] career had come to an end, indeed, until after the death of Jesus.... It was long after Isaiah 53 was composed, and only ... in conjunction with the death of Jesus, that the servant came to be dubbed ... "the Suffering Servant" ... an appellation unknown in the Hebrew Bible and unsupported by it. It was then that our prophet came to be pushed out of the picture, as that person, in favor of Jesus or Israel, or the Messiah; in short, eisegesis has pushed out exegesis.[5]

Pretext without Context

Rabbi Leon Klenicki, the Anti-Defamation League's former interfaith director, called typology a "pretext without understanding the context" in which the words of the *Tanach* were written or spoken.

Another example of typology is the story of the Israelites who spent forty years in the Sinai wilderness following the Exodus from Egypt. It required four decades to develop a new generation of free Israelites who were capable of entering the Promised Land and becoming a "people of God." According to the typology formula employed by many Christians, Jesus spent forty days living in the Judean wilderness near Jerusalem as spiritual preparation for his life's work.

Elijah, a central figure in the book of Kings, raised the dead, retrieved fire from the sky, and at the end of his life, ascended into heaven. Elijah, according to Jewish tradition, will return to earth in the future, settle all disputes, and turn the hearts of children to their parents and parents to their children. Elijah's return to earth will happen on "the awesome, fearful day of the Lord" (Malachi 3:23, JPS). Finally, Elijah will be the herald who announces the coming of the Messiah (Malachi 3:1). In sum, Elijah is the "Great Deliverer" of the Jewish people.

Church typology linked Elijah, who lived in the ninth century BCE, with both Jesus and John the Baptist. For Christians, the three are miracle workers and leading figures in religious history. Jesus and John the Baptist are in some ways the physical and spiritual continuation of the ancient Hebrew prophet Elijah (Matthew 11:7–14).

Jewish baby boys are ritually circumcised on the eighth day of their lives as a tangible symbol of the covenant God made with Abraham, the first patriarch of the Jewish people. This ritual, called in Hebrew *brit milah* (the covenant of circumcision), is why the Christian liturgical calendar observes January 1 as the Feast of the Circumcision, the day when Jesus entered into the Jewish covenant with God. Paul, however, negated the religious requirement for the circumcision of the flesh and proclaimed instead that circumcision "of the heart, by the Spirit, not by the letter" (Romans 2:29, NASB) was all that was required for a follower of Jesus.

Another example of Christian typology is the biblical story of Jonah, the description of a reluctant person who attempts to flee God's plan for him to become a prophet in the large Assyrian city of Nineveh, today's Kirkuk in Iraq. Jonah flees his responsibility by sailing from the port of Jaffa on a ship headed for Spain at the opposite end of the Mediterranean.

An intense storm arises, and the frightened sailors, believing their Hebrew passenger is the cause of the storm, toss Jonah overboard, where he is consumed by a great fish. Jonah spends three days trapped inside the fish's stomach before he is spat up on a dry shoreline. Only then does Jonah begin his divine mission of preaching to the residents of Nineveh.

Christian typology teaches that Jesus, like Jonah, spent three days alone—not in the belly of a "great fish," but in the tomb following his execution by the Romans. Like Jonah, he too is freed from his imprisonment, and in Jesus's case he is resurrected.

The sexually graphic biblical book *Shir HaShirim,* the Song of Songs, is a collection of poems celebrating physical love between human beings. It earned a place in the *Tanach* because the erotic book was symbolically interpreted as the love between the God of Israel and the covenanted Jewish people. But Christians placed a different meaning on the lush Song of Songs; for them, the book represents the love between Jesus and his church.

Passover is an eight-day holiday that annually commemorates the Israelites' Exodus from Egyptian bondage. To mark the festival, a paschal lamb was offered in ancient times as a sacrifice to God expressing a people's gratitude for the divine deliverance from slavery to freedom.

Christian typology makes Jesus the paschal lamb of God who was sacrificed to achieve human liberation and spiritual salvation. Because Jesus, an observant Jew, came to Jerusalem as a pilgrim during Passover, his death and the Christian observance of Easter closely coincide with the dates of the Jewish holiday.

To save his Israelite people, Samson gives up his life by destroying a pagan temple in Gaza. Jesus surrenders his life, similar to Samson's act of selflessness, in order to bring his followers freedom even as the Holy Temple faces destruction by the Roman Empire.

Typology also involves the use of numbers from the *Tanach.* Four major Hebrew prophets—Isaiah, Jeremiah, Ezekiel, and Daniel—are prefigurations of the four Gospel writers. The twelve tribes of Israel are invoked as predictors of the twelve apostles of Jesus.

The use (and some would say abuse) of typology remains a major difference between Judaism and Christianity. Jews reject efforts to use the *Tanach* as "proof" Jesus fulfilled Judaism, while Christians believe biblical prefiguration is a major component of their faith.

Christian typology provided justification for Christian "triumphalism" and "supercessionism," two terms signifying that Christianity emerged victorious in its contest with Judaism and replaced the older faith community to become the authentic "people of God," the universal perfected religion for humanity. It is, of course, a claim that has never been accepted by Jews and was later rejected by Muslims, Hindus, Buddhists, and members of other religions.

A refrain running through Christian typology is the belief that the people of Israel, the Jews, have been unfaithful to God, and the covenant made with God at Mount Sinai has been replaced by the new covenant made at Calvary through the death and resurrection of Jesus (Jeremiah 31:31–34; Hebrews 8:6–13, 10:16).

"Law" versus "Love": A False Dichotomy

In their efforts to discredit Judaism, Christian teachers and theologians stressed the alleged limited religious value of ancient Israel's complex sacrificial system, the people's desecration of the Sabbath, the rite of ritual circumcision devoid of religious meaning, the heavy-handed Temple priesthood in Jerusalem that pressed the Roman authorities to ensure Jesus's death, and the contrast between the synagogue's suffocating "law" and the Church's liberating "love."

Jews have a different self-understanding and view of themselves, their covenant with God, and their religious vocation. After two thousand years, much has changed in the world of science, technology, travel, communication, and medicine. During the past two millennia humans have fully explored our planet and begun the exciting exploration of space, but Christian typology and its negative views of Jews and Judaism have remained almost intact, even unchanging, despite the efforts of many Jews and Christians to build a new and constructive relationship between their two ancient faith communities.

For some Christians, neither the horrific events of the Holocaust that took place in what Pope John Paul II called "Christian Europe"[6] nor the rebirth of an independent Jewish state in the biblical homeland has caused a widespread Christian reexamination of the long-held system of biblical prefiguration. The centuries-old typological understanding of Jews, Judaism, and the *Tanach* remains embedded within Christianity, but some Christians are beginning to reevaluate that system of belief.

Typology has been attacked by scholars and religious leaders who employ the historical-critical method of biblical interpretation, a system that began in Europe with the Age of Enlightenment in the nineteenth century.[7] Scholars seek to place biblical texts in their original historical settings of specific times and places, and the historical-critical approach usually minimizes typology or discards it entirely. A major critique is that typology does not perceive or understand the *Tanach* in situ as the story of early Jewish history, but only as a lengthy prefiguration of both Jesus and the Christian church.

Historical-critical scholars use the German phrase *Sitz im Leben*, or "sit in life," as a basic component of biblical interpretation. The phrase describes the religious, cultural, and political settings and time frames of biblical texts. *Sitz im Leben* allows readers of the Bible to recognize the context of the various texts—many of which differ widely from one another in linguistic style, vocabulary, and intended audiences. Central to the method is the view that the *Tanach* was collected into the Jewish canon perhaps two hundred years before the birth of Jesus; as a result, it must stand alone. For that reason, the New Testament must also stand alone as a separate canon that focuses on the life, death, resurrection, and ministry of a single Jew who lived during the Roman occupation of Israel.

Typology was a key factor in justifying the church's anti-Jewish teaching, preaching, and actions directed against the Jewish people. That bitter history includes the Crusades of the medieval period, forced exiles, expulsions, and lethal physical attacks upon defenseless Jewish communities in many parts of Europe.

It is beyond the scope of this book to document in detail the lengthy series of catastrophes that fell upon Jews. But scholars agree this hostile campaign against the kinsfolk of Jesus could never have achieved its baleful results without the use of typology and prefiguration as driving forces in creating and sustaining the "teaching of contempt" of Jews and Judaism.

7 Anti-Judaism and Anti-Semitism

The Poisoned Branches of Paul's "Good Olive Tree"

It may surprise readers to learn there is a difference between "anti-Judaism" and the better-known "anti-Semitism." The former term describes traditional Christian and Islamic religious bias against Jews and Judaism, while the latter expression is a modern creation that goes beyond religious bigotry as the source for fomenting hatred of the Jewish people and their religion.

The term "anti-Semitism" was invented in 1879 by Wilhelm Marr, a little-known German Lutheran left-wing political activist, who participated in the unsuccessful 1848 revolution in Hamburg. Perhaps disillusioned by the dashed liberal hopes of the revolution, Marr in later life became a reactionary figure who endorsed human slavery, especially as it applied to blacks. He opposed the growing political power of the proletariat in Germany, and most of all, he assailed Jews. One of Marr's central canards was that throughout history Jews had systematically attacked Gentiles to achieve world domination.

In 1879 he wrote *Der Sieg des Judenthums über das Germanenthum von nicht confessionellen Standpunkt*,[1] "The Victory of Jewry over Germandom, Considered from a Nonreligious Point of View." Marr's book went through a dozen printings in a single year—a remarkable feat in that era—and in the book he coined the term "anti-Semitism," which quickly became a code word for hatred of Jews and Judaism. Marr created the euphemism "anti-Semitism" for a specific purpose: he desired a sophisticated "scientific" term instead of the traditional religious "anti-Jewish" language. "Anti-Semitism" with its academic-sounding veneer provided a convenient and respectable cover to express bigotry and prejudice.

Pseudo-Scientific Mumbo Jumbo

British historian James Parkes scoffed at "anti-Semitism." He called it "pseudo-scientific mumbo jumbo." Others joined Parkes in rejecting the concept or existence of "Semitism," and they chose "antisemitism" instead. They believed Marr's nonscientific term is not entitled to either a hyphen or a capital letter.[2]

The phrase implied that Jews were a dangerous foreign element, a Middle Eastern/Asiatic "Semitic" people who could never be part of authentic European Germany. The origin of the term is the biblical Shem, one of Noah's three sons, whose name became associated with Jews and later with Arabs, who are also considered "Semites." But for Marr and other anti-Semites throughout modern history, there was never any doubt about the intended meaning or the true target of his cunning term.

Following publication of his book, Marr attempted to organize an anti-Semitic political movement in Germany. His efforts failed, but tragically, in the years that followed, other more effective and dangerous German and Austrian political leaders took up Marr's cause. His pioneering efforts in fostering hatred earned him the title "patriarch of anti-Semitism."

In addition to Marr, there were two other prominent anti-Semitic leaders of the pre–World War I period: Adolf Stoecker, a Lutheran pastor in Germany, and Kurt Lueger, a Catholic politician in Austria. Both were more successful in their political efforts than Marr was.

Anti-Semitism as a Political Movement

In 1874 Adolf Stoecker became Kaiser Wilhelm I's *hofprediger*, or court chaplain, in Berlin. Stoecker's high-profile position enabled him to write and speak widely about the perceived danger of

Jewish "control" of Germany, and he urged the establishment of a restrictive quota system that limited the number of Jews permitted in many professions and universities.

In time, Stoecker left the Kaiser's court to enter political life, and he organized an anti-Semitic party, the Christian Socialists. He attempted to link Christianity, especially the German Lutheran church, to an anti-Semitic platform. The former court chaplain was elected to the Reichstag in 1881, where he served, except for a five-year hiatus, until 1908, a year before his death.

Lueger was the mayor of Vienna between 1897 and 1910. Following Stoecker's example in Germany, Lueger organized the Christian Social Party in Austria, which made anti-Semitism one of its major public policies. Adolf Hitler, who was a baptized Austrian Catholic, acknowledged that Lueger had influenced him when the future Nazi führer lived in Vienna during the early years of the twentieth century (1908–13).[3]

Lueger's anti-Semitism was mild compared to Hitler's horrific and violent program of physical annihilation of the Jews. However, having an outspoken anti-Semite as the mayor of Vienna in the years prior to World War I poisoned the political, cultural, social, and religious environment of the faltering and soon-to-be-dissolved Austro-Hungarian Empire led by the aged emperor Franz Joseph, who had assumed the royal throne when he was only eighteen years old.

The World's Oldest Pathology

Although the expression "anti-Semitism" is a product of nineteenth-century Germany, hatred of Jews and Judaism is one of the world's oldest pathologies. It predates the rise of Christianity.

The American Catholic priest Edward H. Flannery was a pioneer in the effort to expose and document the anti-Judaism within Christianity. Flannery's book *The Anguish of the Jews: Twenty-three Centuries of Anti-Semitism*, first published in 1965, was an interreligious milestone, a breakthrough in the development of new and positive relations between Christians and Jews.[4]

The Providence, Rhode Island, native was the first director of Catholic-Jewish relations for the U.S. Bishops' Committee on Ecumenical and Interreligious Affairs, a position that was created following the conclusion of the Second Vatican Council in 1965 and its historic call for "mutual respect and knowledge" between Catholics and Jews. Flannery served in that position between 1967 and 1976, when he was succeeded by Eugene Fisher, who retired in 2007.

A theologian and historian, Flannery constantly challenged his fellow Christians to confront and root out the pernicious anti-Semitism within their religious tradition:

> The anti-Semite, not the Jew, is the real Christ killer. He thinks he's religious, but that's a self-delusion. Actually he finds religion so heavy a burden, he develops "Christophobia." He's hostile to the faith and has an unconscious hatred of Christ, who is for him, Christ the Repressor. He uses anti-Semitism as a safety valve for this hostility and is really trying to strike out at Christ.[5]

Flannery listed four basic types of anti-Judaism or anti-Semitism: political/economic, religious, nationalist, and racist.

Political and economic anti-Semitism existed before the emergence of Christianity. A prime example of this pre-Christian bigotry is Cicero, a Roman statesman and philosopher (106–43 BCE). A member of Rome's elite class, he became a consul in 63 BCE and was a superb orator and philosopher. Cicero's prejudicial attitude toward Jews is revealed in this brief quotation:

> Justice demands that the barbaric superstition [Judaism] should be opposed; and it is to the interest of the state not to regard that Jewish mob which at times breaks out in open riots.... At one time the Jewish people took up arms against the Romans; but the gods showed how little they cared for this people, suffering it to be conquered and made a tributary [of the Roman Empire].[6]

Of course, during Cicero's lifetime there were few successful armed uprisings by any subjugated people against the vaunted and dreaded military power of Rome. Yet this early hater of Jews believed the pagan "gods" had turned against the "superstitious" followers of the God of Israel.

American Anti-Semites

Cicero had modern twentieth-century counterparts in the United States—religious and political leaders with oratorical skills. In the 1930s, Father Charles E. Coughlin of Royal Oak, Michigan, was America's most vocal and best-known anti-Semite. His weekly radio program reached an estimated thirty million listeners. The centerpiece of each broadcast was an anti-Semitic diatribe, and several of Coughlin's quotations from that era capture the "Radio Priest's" vitriol and poisonous rhetoric.

During the night of November 8–9, 1938, the Nazi regime carried out a coordinated series of physical attacks on the Jews of Germany and Austria that included the destruction of many synagogues and Jewish-owned businesses. During the attacks, many glass windows of homes, stores, and shops were shattered, and the assault quickly became known as *Kristallnacht* (night of the broken glass). It marked a violent turning point in the Nazi anti-Semitic campaign, a shift from political prejudice and legal discrimination against Jews to lethal physical violence and increased concentration-camp internments.

In late 1938, less than three weeks after the *Kristallnacht* pogrom, Coughlin told his large national radio audience:

> If Jews persist in supporting communism directly or indirectly, that will be regrettable. By their failure to use the press, the radio and the banking house, where they stand so prominently, to fight communism as vigorously as they fight Nazism, the Jews invite the charge of being supporters of communism.[7]

During the same year, speaking at a rally in the Bronx in New York City, Coughlin gave the stiff-armed Nazi salute and declared, "When we get through with the Jews in America, they'll think the treatment they received in Germany was nothing."[8]

Coughlin was finally silenced by several powerful forces and events. In 1942, Detroit archbishop Edward Mooney ordered him to cease his political activities (something Mooney's predecessor refused to do) or Coughlin would be defrocked. Earlier, the Roosevelt administration took legal steps to remove the anti-Semitic priest from the airwaves, and the Japanese attack on Pearl Harbor on December 7, 1941, combined with Hitler's declaration of war against the United States four days later, silenced the isolationist, pro-Nazi movement in America.

Because of his demagoguery, Coughlin has been called "the father of modern hate radio" in the United States. One of the highlights of my professional interreligious career with the American Jewish Committee occurred in Michigan during the 1980s when I spoke from the pulpit of the National Shrine of the Little Flower, Coughlin's home parish in Royal Oak.

Coughlin's anti-Semitic attacks ended during World War II when America was leading the global effort to destroy the anti-Semitic regime of Nazi Germany. However, even as that titanic struggle was taking place, two members of the United States Congress, American "statesmen" of that era, Senator Theodore G. Bilbo and Representative John E. Rankin, both from Mississippi, were outspoken in their raw anti-Semitism.

Rankin called the popular newspaper columnist Walter Winchell "the little kike" on the floor of the House of Representatives, while Bilbo wrote to Leonard E. Golditch of New York, secretary of the National Committee to Combat Anti-Semitism:

> If Jews of your type don't quit sponsoring and fraternizing with the negro [sic] race you are going to arouse so much opposition to all of you that they will get a very strong invitation to pack up and resettle in Palestine.... There are just

a few of you New York Jew "kikes" ... socializing with the
negroes [*sic*] for selfish and political reasons.... You had better stop and think.[9]

A more "polite" anti-Semite of the time was the celebrated aviator
Charles Lindbergh, who saw Jews as a political threat to America.
Lindbergh wrote in his diary:

> We must limit to a reasonable amount the Jewish influ-
> ence.... Whenever the Jewish percentage of total popula-
> tion becomes too high, a reaction seems to invariably occur.
> It is too bad because a few Jews of the right type are, I
> believe, an asset to any country.[10]

Religious Anti-Semitism

Although there are many kinds of anti-Semitism, Flannery's second category—the religious variety—remains a pervasive force
within many people around the world, and it is the primary source
and theological justification for other forms of anti-Semitism.

As mentioned in an earlier chapter, with the founding of
Christianity, "Old Israel" was considered no longer part of the
divine economy; it had forfeited its spiritual vitality. In such a
worldview, Judaism had completed its historic mission—that is, the
spiritual preparation for Christianity. By all measures of reason and
faith, Jews and Judaism should have disappeared from history. One
contemporary Christian missionary has described Judaism as a
"booster rocket" that was jettisoned once the "main rocket,"
Christianity, was launched into orbit.

Dr. Eugene Fisher believes religious anti-Judaism did not
become violent until the Crusade period beginning in 1096, which
was when Christian malice—physical and psychological—toward
Jews and Judaism intensified. Fisher sees the Crusades as a turning
point in the church's relationship with Jews and Judaism.[11]

Rabbi Michael J. Cook, author of *Modern Jews Engage the New
Testament: Enhancing Jewish Well-Being in a Christian Environment*

(Jewish Lights), believes there are ten New Testament themes that have created great tension and have been a source of Christian anti-Judaism and anti-Semitism:

1. The Jews are culpable for crucifying Jesus—as such, they are guilty of deicide.
2. The tribulations of the Jewish people throughout history constitute God's punishment of them for killing Jesus.
3. Jesus originally came to preach only to the Jews, but when they rejected him, he abandoned them for Gentiles instead.
4. The Children of Israel were God's original chosen people by virtue of an ancient covenant, but by rejecting Jesus they forfeited their chosenness—and now, by virtue of a new covenant (or "testament"), Christians have replaced the Jews as God's chosen people, the Church having become the "People of God."
5. The Jewish Bible ("Old" Testament) repeatedly portrays the opaqueness and stubbornness of the Jewish people and their disloyalty to God.
6. The Jewish Bible ("Old" Testament) contains many predictions of the coming of Jesus as the Messiah (or "Christ"), yet the Jews are blind to the meaning of their own Bible.
7. By the time of Jesus' ministry, Judaism had ceased to be a living faith.
8. Judaism's essence is a restrictive and burdensome legalism.
9. Christianity emphasizes love, while Judaism stands for justice and a God of wrath.
10. Judaism's oppressiveness reflects the disposition of Jesus' opponents called "Pharisees" (predecessors of the "rabbis"), who in their teachings and behavior were hypocrites.[12]

The "Teaching of Contempt"

But whenever and wherever it began, religiously inspired anti-Judaism has spanned centuries of time and covered many geographical locales. Jules Isaac, a French historian and the inspector-general of that nation's public educational system in the 1930s, termed the church's long history of anti-Judaism the "teaching of contempt." Isaac's phrase has entered into the permanent lexicon of interreligious relations.[13]

Isaac's wife and daughter were killed at Auschwitz, and as a Holocaust survivor, he devoted the rest of his life to documenting the Christian roots of anti-Semitism. His work as a historian and an educator was essential in creating a foundation for the development of constructive and positive relations between Jews and Christians. Isaac's research into the sources of Christian anti-Judaism, some of it conducted while he was in hiding or on the run during the German wartime occupation of France, showed that anti-Judaism emphasizes three false accusations, all fostering hatred:

- The dispersion of Israel, the Jewish people, was God's just punishment for rejecting Jesus as the Messiah.
- Jews had committed deicide.
- Judaism was highly corrupt and spiritually unfaithful during Jesus's time.

Following the war, Isaac had two papal meetings—the first with Pius XII in 1949, and the second ten years later with John XXIII. On both occasions Isaac documented the roots of religious anti-Semitism and urged that concrete steps be taken to eradicate the "teaching of contempt" within the Catholic Church.

Isaac's meeting with Pius XII yielded few positive results, but his conversation with John XXIII motivated the pope to seek a change in the church's teachings about Jews, Judaism, and anti-Semitism. His efforts paved the way for historic changes in the Catholic Church's Good Friday prayers vis-à-vis Jews as well as the reforms of the Second Vatican Council, achievements that Isaac did not live to see.

He had a difficult task because the writings of many church fathers, especially Chrysostom, constitute a significant body of

Christian teaching and preaching that demonize Jews as deniers of Jesus, at best, or as Christ killers, at worst. For centuries, Judaism was dismissed as a necessary prerequisite for the triumphant entrance of Christianity into the world as the universal religion for humanity. A central theme of the church fathers' writings was the Jews' alleged "rejection" of Jesus, which resulted in God's eternal punishment of the "stiff-necked, stubborn" people.

Aquinas Reads Maimonides

Thomas Aquinas (1225–74), an Italian Dominican priest, was the most important Christian philosopher of the medieval period. His writings were influenced by the Jewish philosophers Solomon ibn Gabirol (1021–58) and Moses Maimonides. Aquinas has been portrayed as sympathetic to Jews because of his familiarity with Jewish religious thought and because he opposed forced conversions and physical violence against the kinfolk of Jesus.

Jeremy Cohen, a scholar of medieval religious history who teaches at Israel's Tel Aviv University, presents a more critical picture of the famous Christian theologian. In his book *The Friars and the Jews*, Cohen emphasizes that, beginning in the thirteenth century, the Christian friars commenced a strong campaign to convert all nonbelievers, including Jews, pagans, and Muslims, to Christianity. Aggressive measures, including physical force, could be used against those who refused to convert.[14]

Cohen notes that while Aquinas eschewed harsh conversionary measures and did not call for physical assaults on Jews, nonetheless the Catholic theologian regarded Jews as "sinful" because of their continuing refusal to accept Jesus as their Savior. Expropriation of Jewish property was seen by Aquinas as a legitimate activity of the state. He had negative views of pagans, but Aquinas was harsher toward Jews, who (he claimed) knew they had killed Jesus and who, as a people, remained unfaithful to the laws found in the Hebrew Bible.

Perhaps because he was influenced by the philosophical and theological writings of Maimonides and other Jewish scholars,

Aquinas opposed drastic methods to gain converts to Christianity. However, much of his writing reflects a strong antipathy toward both Jews ("greedy usurers") and Judaism itself. Aquinas perceived Jews as "infidels" and legitimate targets for conversion, despite their adherence to the Hebrew Bible:

> Among unbelievers there are some who have never received the faith, such as the heathens and the Jews. [These] arc by no means to be compelled to the faith ... because to believe depends on the will. [N]evertheless they should be compelled by the faithful ... so that they do not hinder the faith by their blasphemies or ... by their open persecutions. It is for this reason that Christ's faithful often wage war with unbelievers, not indeed for the purpose of forcing them to believe ... but in order to prevent them from hindering the faith of Christ.[15]

Aquinas, in effect, provided the Christian conversion campaign with two theological rationales. First, the infidels, including Jews, are simply blind in not accepting Jesus, and second, their very existence "obstructs" the church and its faithful.

While modern anti-Semitism drew heavily upon traditional anti-Judaism as expressed by Chrysostom, Aquinas, and other church leaders throughout history, Pope John Paul II was careful to differentiate between "anti-Judaism," a tragic legacy of Christianity, and "anti-Semitism," a contemporary term employed to express "Jew-hatred."

Luther's Horrific Plan for Jews

In his early writings, Martin Luther was hopeful that Jews would convert to Christianity. When that did not happen, the Great Reformer mounted an attack on Jews and Judaism that was one of the "justifications" used by the Nazis in their "final solution of the Jewish question." In 1543 Luther wrote *Von den Juden und ihren Lugen*, "On the Jews and Their Lies."

With that title, no one should be surprised by Luther's lengthy assault on a people he once had believed would become Christians. According to Luther,

> If I had power over the Jews, as our princes and cities have, I would deal severely with their lying mouths.... We are at fault in not avenging all this innocent blood of our Lord....
>
> I wish ... that our rulers who have Jewish subjects exercise a sharp mercy towards these wretched people.... They must act like a good physician who, when gangrene has set in, proceeds without mercy to cut, saw, and burn flesh, veins, bone, and marrow. Such a procedure must also be followed in this instance.

In an appalling prediction of what was to take place four hundred years later in Germany, Luther wanted Jewish schools and synagogues burned and rabbis blocked from preaching and teaching, and he described the synagogue as an "incorrigible whore and an evil slut." He said Jewish property should be expropriated, since Jews are "worms," and even though Luther was a revered religious leader, he warned fellow Christians they were "at fault for not slaying" their Jewish neighbors.[16]

Lutheran Church bodies in both the United States and Europe have in recent years publicly faced up to the Reformer's horrific words and officially distanced themselves from Luther. Franklin Sherman, who taught at the Lutheran Seminary in Chicago, was a pioneer in the successful campaign to recognize and repudiate Luther's reprehensible teachings.[17]

Anti-Judaism can only be overcome by positive teaching and a systematic campaign to eliminate it from church life that includes seminary training for clergy, biblical studies, sermons, hymns, liturgy, and other forms of Christian teaching and preaching. Anti-Semitism, on the other hand, is based on blood and birth, neither of which is reversible or subject to change.

Jewish Converts: No Escape from Nazis

It is often forgotten that Jews who converted to Christianity and were baptized were still considered Jews by the Nazis, who gave no credence to conversion. For them, the "curse of Jewish blood" could not be washed away by the waters of the Christian baptismal font.

Dietrich Bonhoeffer was a German Lutheran pastor and theologian who was executed by the Nazis in April 1945 just weeks before the end of the war in Europe. He was a foe of the Nazi regime and is revered today by many Christians as a spiritual hero, a modern martyr who courageously opposed the Nazis and was hanged as an "enemy of the Third Reich."

Bonhoeffer was a foe of the "Aryan paragraph," a key part of the Nazi anti-Jewish legislation enacted in the 1930s. The Nazi law and the paragraph in question nullified Jewish conversions and declared that even a baptized Jew remained a Jew, subject to legal discrimination, persecution, and death. Bonhoeffer opposed the "Aryan paragraph" because it undermined the efficacy of baptism. But few of his fellow Christian clergy joined him in that effort, and baptized Jews were among the six million Jewish victims of Nazism.[18]

Perhaps the most famous example of the Nazis' belief in Jewish "blood and birth" is the case of Edith Stein. She was a student of Edmund Husserl and Martin Heidegger, both prominent German philosophers. The former was a Jew, and the latter became a Nazi supporter.

Stein was born in Breslau when it was part of Germany (today it is the Polish city of Wroclaw), and she was raised in an observant Jewish family. In her youth Edith was an atheist, but at age thirty-one she converted to Catholicism and became a Carmelite nun, taking the name Teresa Benedicta of the Cross.

As a nun, she wrote an appeal to Pope Pius XI in 1933 begging the pontiff to intervene against the already evident Nazi persecution of the Jews. Her poignant words were written during the first days of the Nazi regime:

For years the leaders of National Socialism have been preaching hatred of the Jews. But the responsibility must fall, after all, on those who brought them to this point and it also falls on those who keep silent in the face of such happenings.

Everything that happened and continues to happen on a daily basis originates with a government that calls itself "Christian." For weeks not only Jews but also thousands of faithful Catholics in Germany, and, I believe, all over the world, have been waiting and hoping for the Church of Christ to raise its voice to put a stop to this abuse of Christ's name.[19]

She received no reply from the pope, and scholars speculate he never received the pleaful missive. In 1942 the Carmelite order placed the Jewish convert in a convent in Holland to provide a more secure residence. But it was to no avail.

In late July 1942, the Dutch Catholic bishops issued a public condemnation of the Nazis, and in response, the Gestapo arrested Edith Stein and her sister, Rosa, also a Jewish convert. Within two weeks of their arrest, Edith and Rosa were gassed at Auschwitz. Stein's conversion to Catholicism, becoming a nun, and living in a sequestered convent provided no defense against the Nazis, for whom her birth as a Jewish woman trumped all. Indeed, she was the only Carmelite nun taken from the supposedly safe Dutch convent where Stein lived.

In 1998 Edith Stein was canonized as a Catholic saint. Some Jews and Christians expressed the view that she was not a martyr because of her Catholicism, but rather she was deported to a death camp because the Nazis identified her as a Jew. Edith Stein died, the critics claimed, not as a Catholic heroine of the faith, but as one of the six million Jews murdered during the Shoah.[20]

Conflicting Images on the Strasbourg Cathedral

Anti-Jewish beliefs, attitudes, and myths infected much of Christian teaching, preaching, hymnology, and even church architecture.

The Strasbourg Cathedral in France, built between the eleventh and fifteenth centuries, has famous images on its facade where Judaism and Christianity are sharply contrasted.

Judaism is portrayed as a blindfolded woman clutching a broken Torah, while Christianity is represented as an effervescent young woman holding a book of the Gospel. No written commentary is required to understand the sculptures' message of defamation and denigration.

This traditional Christian understanding of Jews and Judaism as a spiritually empty, surplus people has provided theological justification for destructive images, negative teachings, and odious comparisons. Judaism was regularly described as a dry, static religion of strict law, while Christianity was portrayed as a merciful faith of compassionate love. And sometimes, depending upon the time and place, the Christian attitude toward Jews and Judaism went much further than mere theological contempt and hostility: enter the monstrous "deicide" charge.

Deicide, literally the killing of God, proclaimed that Jews collectively had willfully murdered Jesus of Nazareth. As punishment for this infamous act, the Jewish people then, now, and forever are guilty of the heinous crime of murdering divinity.

The Deicide Battle at the Second Vatican Council

For centuries, the deicide charge was used as divine license to harm Jews. But in October 1965, at the conclusion of the Second Vatican Council, and after three years of debate, the world's Roman Catholic bishops overwhelmingly repudiated the teaching of Jewish "guilt" for the death of Jesus and implicitly repudiated the deicide charge that Jews were "Christ killers." The historic *Nostra Aetate* ("In Our Time") Declaration was adopted by a vote of 2,221 to 88.[21]

But the achievements at the Vatican Council were no easy thing. They required the talent, energy, and commitment of many courageous Catholic leaders, including Popes John XXIII and Paul VI, to guarantee the adoption of *Nostra Aetate*. Indeed, in the early months of 1964, the entire Catholic-Jewish enterprise at the Vatican Council was floundering and in danger of collapsing.

A coalition composed of ultraconservative, mostly European bishops along with prelates from Arab countries opposed the papal-led efforts to improve Catholic-Jewish relations. The coalition, while small, raised serious objections to the adoption of any statement. Other critics urged the bishops to focus on the major issue of internal church reform; anything else, especially the energy and debate time spent on anti-Semitism and deicide, was peripheral to the Council's major tasks.

The conservative bishops clung to the traditional anti-Judaism of past centuries, while the cluster of Middle Eastern bishops believed any positive Vatican Council statement about Jews or their religion represented implicit church support for the State of Israel. However, Israel was never mentioned in the *Nostra Aetate* Declaration or in any other Vatican Council document. Full and formal diplomatic relations between the Vatican and Israel had to wait until 1994, nearly thirty years after the Vatican Council vote on *Nostra Aetate.*

But at the critical moment when the traditionalist Arab coalition threatened to block any statement on the Jewish people, two American cardinals, Richard Cushing of Boston and Francis Spellman of New York, personally intervened by delivering important public speeches, one in the United States and the other in Rome. They threw their influence, charisma, and leadership into the Vatican Council deliberations by urging their fellow bishops to adopt strong positive statements on the church's relationship to Jews. Their efforts proved to be a decisive factor in beating back the anti-Jewish coalition.

It was a daring move by Cushing and Spellman to intervene as they did, because they were publicly challenging their church's long history of anti-Jewish teaching and preaching, including the deicide charge and the widespread Catholic belief that Judaism as a religion was exhausted and fulfilled by Christianity.

Because Cushing and Spellman were both religiously and politically conservative, many people did not expect them to be champions of any constructive church change toward Jews and Judaism. But such expectations were wrong.

At the April 1964 American Jewish Committee (AJC) annual meeting in New York City, Spellman called for stronger ties and understanding between the Jewish and Christian communities. Repudiating the charge of deicide, the archbishop declared:

> It is simply absurd to maintain that there is some kind of continuing guilt which is transferred to any group and which rests upon them as a curse which they must suffer.... Anti-Semitism can never find a basis in the Catholic religion.[22]

By 1964, Cushing had become a global religious figure because of his close ties to the Kennedy family in Massachusetts. The Boston archbishop officiated at the wedding of Senator John F. Kennedy and Jacqueline Bouvier in 1953, and ten years later, Cushing led the funeral service for JFK following the president's assassination.

As the Vatican Council moved toward its conclusion, Cushing was fearful no action would be taken on the issues of deicide and anti-Semitism. He felt an urgent need to express his concerns in Rome, and Cushing first composed a speech in English and then requested an abbot to translate it into Latin, the language used at the Council. He delivered his address on September 28, 1964, and when he finished speaking, his fellow bishops from around the world applauded the Boston archbishop.

Cushing's powerful words resonate today, nearly a half century after they were first delivered:

> We must cast the Declaration on the Jews in a much more positive form, one not so timid, but much more loving.... For the sake of our common heritage we, the children of Abraham according to the spirit, must foster a special reverence and love for the children of Abraham according to the flesh. As children of Adam, they are our kin, as children of

Abraham they are Christ's blood relatives. So far as the guilt of Jews in the death of our Saviour is concerned, the rejection of the Messiah by His own, is according to Scripture, a mystery—a mystery given us for our instruction, not for our self-exaltation.... We cannot sit in judgement on the onetime leaders of Israel—God alone is their judge. Much less can we burden later generations of Jews with any burden of guilt for the crucifixion of the Lord Jesus, for the death of the Saviour of the world, except that universal guilt in which we all have a part.... In clear and unmistakable language, we must deny, therefore, that the Jews are guilty of our Saviour's death. We must condemn especially those who seek to justify, as Christian deeds, discrimination, hatred and even persecution of Jews.... I ask myself, Venerable Brothers, whether we should not humbly acknowledge before the whole world that, toward their Jewish brethren, Christians have all too often not shown themselves as true Christians, as faithful followers of Christ. How many [Jews] have suffered in our own time? How many died because Christians were indifferent and kept silent?... If in recent years, not many Christian voices were raised against those injustices, at least let ours now be heard in humility.[23]

The strong interventions of Spellman and Cushing helped ensure the overwhelming passage of *Nostra Aetate* in October 1965. The key provisions of the Declaration read:

What happened in his [Jesus's] passion cannot be charged against all the Jews, without distinction, then alive, nor against the Jews of today.... The Jews should not be represented as rejected by God or accursed, as if this followed from Holy Scripture. All should see to it, then, that in catechetical work, and in the preaching of the Word of God they teach nothing save what conforms to the truth of the Gospel and the spirit of Christ.[24]

The Second Vatican Council Declaration also stated:

> [I]n her rejection of every persecution against any man, the
> Church, mindful of the patrimony she shares with the Jews
> and moved not by political reasons but by the Gospel's spiri-
> tual love, decries hatred, persecutions, [and] displays of anti-
> Semitism directed against Jews at any time and by anyone.[25]

Protestants Condemn Anti-Semitism

Similar statements repudiating anti-Semitism have been issued by
other major Christian bodies, including two international groups:
the World Council of Churches and the Lutheran World
Federation. In the United States, the Southern Baptist Convention,
the United Church of Christ, the Presbyterian Church (USA), the
United Methodist Church, the Anglican Communion, and other
Protestant denominations have also adopted statements condemning anti-Semitism.

One American Protestant response to religious anti-Semitism
came from the 1987 General Synod of the United Church of Christ
(UCC), when it adopted a statement affirming that "Judaism has
not been superseded by Christianity" and that "God has not
rejected the Jewish people."

The UCC's highest policy body publicly acknowledged in a
confessional tone:

> The Christian Church has throughout much of its history
> denied God's continuing covenantal relationship with the
> Jewish people.... This denial has led to outright rejection of
> the Jewish people ... and intolerable violence.... Faced with
> this history which we as Christians cannot, and must not,
> disassociate ourselves, we ask for God's forgiveness.[26]

In 1972 the United Methodist General Conference, the denomina-
tion's top legislative authority, which meets every four years,
unequivocally denounced all forms of anti-Semitism and issued a

strong call for Methodists to affirm the spiritual vitality of the Jewish covenant with God. The Methodist statement has been a model for other Christian groups to emulate:

> Christians must also become aware of that history in which they have deeply alienated the Jews. They are obligated to examine their own implicit and explicit responsibility for the discrimination against and the organized extermination of Jews, as in the recent past [the Holocaust]. The persecution by Christians of Jews throughout centuries calls for clear repentance and resolve to repudiate past injustice and to seek its elimination in the present.... The Christian obligation to those who survived the Nazi Holocaust, the understanding of the relationship of land and peoplehood, suggest that a new dimension in dialogue with Jews is needed.... In such dialogues, an aim of religious or political conversion, or of proselytizing, cannot be condoned.... There is no tenable biblical or theological base for anti-Semitism.... A reduction of Jewish or Christian beliefs to a tepid lowest common denominator ... is not sought in this [dialogue] process.[27]

Nearly a quarter century later, in 1996, the United Methodist Church (UMC) in the United States passed another resolution at its General Conference affirming the dual religious covenants that both link and separate Jews and Christians. Although it is not a belief shared by all Christian bodies, the UMC spoke in unambiguous terms:

> While church tradition has taught that Judaism has been superseded by Christianity as the "new Israel," we do not believe that earlier covenantal relationships have been invalidated or that God has abandoned Jewish partners in covenant. We believe that just as God is steadfastly faithful to the biblical covenant in Jesus Christ, likewise God is

steadfastly faithful to the biblical covenant with the Jewish people. The covenant God established with the Jewish people through Abraham, Moses, and others continues because it is an eternal covenant. Paul proclaims that the gift and call of God to the Jews is irrevocable (Romans 11:29). Thus, we believe that the Jewish people continue in covenantal relationship with God.

Both Jews and Christians are bound to God in covenant, with no covenantal relationship invalidated by any other. Though Christians and Jews have different understandings of the covenant of faith, we are mysteriously bound to one another through our covenantal relationships with the one God and Creator of us all.

The 1996 United Methodist Statement also declared:

We believe that God has continued, and continues today, to work through Judaism and the Jewish people.... We deeply repent of the complicity of the Church and the participation of many Christians in the long history of the persecution of the Jewish people.[28]

During his twenty-seven-year reign between 1978 and 2005, Pope John Paul II declared:

Anti-Semitism ... has been repeatedly condemned by the Catholic teaching as incompatible with Christ's teaching.... Where there was ignorance and ... prejudice ... there is now growing mutual knowledge, appreciation, and respect.[29]

The pope on numerous occasions repeated the Second Vatican Council's statement that the church "deplores the hatred, persecutions, and displays of anti-Semitism directed against Jews at any time and by anyone."

The Jewish Response to *Nostra Aetate*

As we've seen here, in the three and a half decades since 1965, many church bodies and their leaders issued a series of constructive statements, proclamations, notes, guidelines, resolutions, and reports about the Christian religious imperative to oppose anti-Semitism, build positive relations with Jews, and develop a better and more accurate understanding of Judaism.

Some groups also published personal and collective admissions of guilt and responsibility regarding Christianity's negative actions and teachings toward Jews and their religious tradition. But, during the same years, only a few Jewish thinkers publicly grappled with the question of how their community should view and relate to Christianity in light of the significant interreligious advances that had been achieved.

It wasn't until 2000 that the Jewish community issued a response to these Christian efforts. Because the year 2000 marked the beginning of the third millennium of Christianity, the date was commemorated in many churches throughout the world. The new century was also a chronological reminder that two generations had grown into adulthood since the end of World War II and the Shoah. And finally, 2000 marked thirty-five years since the world's Catholic bishops at the Second Vatican Council adopted the *Nostra Aetate* Declaration on Jews and Judaism. It was perhaps with this background in mind that some prominent scholars of Judaism crafted a religious response to Christianity that received the endorsement of more than 220 Jews, mostly rabbis and scholars. The title of their carefully and tightly worded statement bore the Hebrew words *Dabru Emet* (Speaking Truth), a phrase found in the biblical book of Zechariah (8:16).

Dabru Emet's introduction recognized and welcomed the

> public statements of … remorse about Christian mistreatment of Jews and Judaism. These statements have declared that Christian teaching and preaching can and must be reformed so that they acknowledge God's enduring

covenant with the Jewish people and celebrate the contribution of Judaism to world civilization and to Christian faith itself.

The authors listed "eight brief statements" on how Jews and Christians may relate to one another:

1. Jews and Christians worship the same God.
2. Jews and Christians seek authority from the same book—the Bible (what Jews call "Tanakh" and Christians call the "Old Testament").
3. Christians can respect the claim of the Jewish people upon the Land of Israel.
4. Jews and Christians accept the moral principles of the Torah.
5. Nazism was not a Christian phenomenon.
6. The humanly irreconcilable difference between Jews and Christians will not be settled until God redeems the entire world as promised in Scripture.
7. A new relationship between Jews and Christians will not weaken Jewish practice.
8. Jews and Christians must work together for justice and peace.[30]

Dabru Emet was published as an ad in the *New York Times* and the *Baltimore Sun*; it also appeared in both the general and the religious media. Since its initial publication in English, the statement has been translated into French, German, Polish, Portuguese, Russian, and Spanish.

Christian groups in North America and Europe mostly praised *Dabru Emet*, but it was criticized by several prominent Jewish scholars, including David Berger of Yeshiva University and Jon Levenson of the Harvard Divinity School. Among the latter's criticisms was his belief that *Dabru Emet* could lead to a weakening of religious commitment among Jews, while Berger took issue with the document's contention that despite the worship of Jesus by Christians, the two faith communities still "worship the same God." Berger found the document's assertion that "Christian worship is not a viable choice for Jews" to be "thoroughly inadequate and a bland assertion."[31]

On a personal note, I did not sign *Dabru Emet* even though I respected the four scholars who were the primary authors: Tikva Frymer-Kensky, University of Chicago; Rabbi David Novak, University of Toronto; Peter Ochs, University of Virginia; and Rabbi Michael Signer, University of Notre Dame. Sadly, Frymer-Kensky and Rabbi Signer are now dead, and, indeed, Michael was one of my closest friends and colleagues, as this book's dedication attests.

My main objection to *Dabru Emet* focused on the fifth statement that asserted "Nazism itself was not an inevitable outcome of Christianity. If the Nazi extermination of the Jews had been fully successful, it would have turned its murderous rage more directly to Christians." Given the reputation and stature of *Dabru Emet*'s authors, I was disappointed by this superficial explanation of the complex, multifaceted relationship between the Jew-hating tradition that is part of Christianity and the lethal racial anti-Semitism of Nazism.

Also, I was not convinced that Nazism, once it was done murdering as many Jews as possible, would then have "turned its murderous rage" against Christians. Thank God, we will never know whether *Dabru Emet* or critics like me were correct. What is clear, however, is that the victorious Nazis would have intensified their previous aggressive attempts to make over the Christian churches into their own image, complete with swastika symbolism accompanied by a systematic attempt to turn Jesus into an "Aryan," an idolatrous worship of the führer, a new National Socialist liturgy, and many other programs to Nazify the churches.

But would there have been a "murderous rage" directed against Christians similar in fury and genocidal goals to the Nazis' "war against the Jews"? I think not.

Nationalist Hatred of the Jews

Turning to Flannery's third category, modern nationalist hatred of Jews and Judaism became more visible and virulent with the rise of European nation-states during the nineteenth century. Anti-Semites in many nations asserted Jews could never be trustworthy citizens of any country; they were parasitic "outsiders," a foreign and disloyal element within an otherwise racially homogeneous society.

History gives high marks to the famous French philosopher François-Marie Arouet, better known by his pen name of Voltaire (1694–1778). He was deeply committed to diverse opinions, freedom of speech, and civil liberties. Yet even Voltaire, whose famous character in *Candide*, Dr. Pangloss, believed he lived in the "best of all possible worlds," had a cold spot in his heart for Jews, who didn't fit into his Age of Enlightenment conception of humanity.

While Voltaire was critical of religion in general and of Christianity and Judaism in particular, his public attacks on Jews were especially vicious, seemingly out of character for a leading French *philosophe* of the Enlightenment. In his book *The French Enlightenment and the Jews*, Arthur Hertzberg wrote:

> His [Voltaire's] writings were the great arsenal of anti-Jewish arguments for those enemies of the Jews who wanted to sound contemporary.... Voltaire's own views cannot be explained, or rather explained away in such fashion as to defend a view of the Enlightenment as ultimately completely tolerant. An analysis of everything that Voltaire wrote about Jews throughout his life establishes the proposition that he is a major link in Western intellectual history between the anti-Semitism of classic paganism and the modern age. In his favorite pose of Cicero reborn he ruled the Jew to be outside society and to be hopelessly alien even to the future age of enlightened men.... In his own time Voltaire's work encouraged anti-Semitism.... For the next

century he provided the fundamentals of the rhetoric of secular anti-Semitism.[32]

Extreme xenophobia and jingoism, especially the chauvinistic (named for Nicolas Chauvin, a legendary figure who espoused a narrow French nationalism) variety, was a major element in the famous *l'affaire Dreyfus* (Dreyfus affair) in which Alfred Dreyfus (1859–1935), an innocent French Jewish artillery officer, was falsely convicted of passing military secrets to Germany. The rigged trials, beginning in 1894, Dreyfus's solitary imprisonment on Devil's Island in South America, and his ultimate vindication were saturated with anti-Semitism, particularly within the French military elite and the Roman Catholic hierarchy.

Herzl's Tragic Prediction

Theodor Herzl (1860–1904), the founder of modern Zionism, the Jewish national movement, was a Paris-based correspondent representing a Viennese newspaper when Dreyfus first went on trial for treason. The overt anti-Semitism Herzl witnessed in the French capital horrified him, and in 1896 he published his personal remedy to that social pathology. He wrote a slim volume entitled *Der Judenstaat*, "The State of the Jews."

One of Herzl's most famous and prescient sentences in *Der Judenstaat* was the following:

> We [Jews] might, perhaps, be able to merge ourselves entirely into surrounding races, if these [nations] were to leave us in peace for a space of two generations. But they will not leave us in peace. For a little period they manage to tolerate us, and then their hostility breaks out again and again.[33]

Just thirty-seven years after Herzl wrote those ominous words, Hitler became chancellor of Germany and the Jews were "not left in peace."

Flannery's fourth category—racial anti-Semitism—is based upon a mystical, sometimes occult belief in a racially "pure" nation, most notably, but not exclusively, in Germany, Spain, and Portugal. In the fifteenth century, anti-Jewish leaders on the Iberian Peninsula celebrated and acted violently upon their shared belief in *limpieza de sangre* in Spanish and *limpeza de sangue* in Portuguese, phrases meaning "purity of blood." Five hundred years later the Nazis glorified the "Aryan race" and the supremacy of the German *volk* while at the same time mounting a campaign of mass murder against the *untermenschen*, or subhuman, Jews.

Racial anti-Semitism added a modern "scientific" component to traditional Christian anti-Judaism. It was a poisonous brew that led to the murder of six million "racially impure" Jews.

Anti-Zionism: The New Anti-Semitism

In recent years a "new anti-Semitism" has intensified in many parts of the Islamic world as well as among some European political, religious, and educational elites. For them, the Jewish state of Israel is the world's chief villain among the family of nations, the major obstacle to world peace because its citizens and their "Nazilike" government allegedly commit war crimes, including "genocide" and a "holocaust" against the Palestinians.

In 1975 the "new anti-Semites" achieved a major, albeit temporary, victory when the United Nations General Assembly, led by Islamic countries and the then extant Communist bloc, adopted a resolution that defined Zionism, the national Jewish liberation movement, as a "form of racism and racial discrimination." The vote was 72 in favor, 35 against, including the United States and many Western nations, and 32 abstentions.

Shortly before the collapse of the Soviet Union and its European satellite states, the resolution was repealed by the UN in 1991 by a vote of 111 in favor, 25 against, and 13 abstentions. It was the only time a General Assembly resolution has ever been reversed since the world organization was founded in 1945.

Among the nations supporting the 1975 anti-Zionism resolution were Mexico, India, and China, while Japan abstained. Sixteen years later when the "Zionism is racism" resolution was repealed, India, Mexico, and Japan joined in the action, and the Soviet Union also supported negating the anti-Zionist resolution it had once championed. China, Egypt, Kuwait, Morocco, Oman, and Tunisia were notably absent for the 1991 vote.

Since 1945 and the end of the Shoah, two new generations of Europeans, many of them Christians, have entered adulthood and assumed leadership positions in their home countries. There are now tens of millions of people who have no personal remembrance of the mass murder of Jews that took place on their continent. Despite the large number of films, stage dramas, TV documentaries, monuments, and books dealing with the Holocaust, the tragic events of 1933–45 remain for many members of the postwar generations the stuff found in dreary history books and in rarely visited museums that document the Nazi campaign of slaughter.

As a result, there now exists among many people, in Europe and elsewhere, the potential to overlook, minimize, or tolerate the current anti-Semitic attacks that are still fueled by traditional religious ideology, political extremism, and historical amnesia.

One of the current tactics is to attack the State of Israel by using the slogan of "anti-Zionism." Those who employ such a tactic declare that it is possible to be against Zionism without being anti-Semitic. They believe that criticizing Zionism, and sometimes even questioning the legitimacy of modern Israel, is not anti-Jewish.

It is important to analyze the motives of the persons or groups who claim to be anti-Zionist and not anti-Semitic. The harshest critics of ancient Israel were the biblical prophets, and today some of Israel's toughest critics are Diaspora Jews or Israelis themselves. Self-criticism is a sign of a vigorous democracy.

But in both cases, ancient and contemporary, the criticisms were given in a spirit of support, even love, for the erring nation and people. But neither the prophets, even at their gloomiest, nor modern Israelis filled with self-criticism seek the end or destruction of the Jewish state.

The same cannot always be said about the self-proclaimed anti-Zionists. Underneath their alleged critique of various Israeli policies, it is apparent that their ultimate goal is not to reform Israel or Zionism, but to weaken and eventually destroy the state itself.

The Vatican recognized this deceptive tactic, and in 1989 the Pontifical Commission for Peace and Justice issued "The Church and Racism." In that official document, the commission defined anti-Semitism as "the most tragic form that racist ideology has assumed in this century." But the Vatican document went further by condemning anti-Zionism, which "questions the state of Israel and its policies," and it warned the use of anti-Zionism "serves at times as a screen for anti-Semitism." The Vatican commission declared, "Harboring racist thoughts and entertaining racist attitudes is a sin."[34]

Father Edward Flannery was correct: anti-Semitism remains the world's "oldest social pathology."

8 Mission, Witness, and Conversion

"Missionary" is a term that resonates positively among Christians for several reasons. Followers of Jesus serve in churches and other institutions far away from their homes and families in an effort to convert "the entire world" to their faith. They proselytize despite the fact that they frequently face spiritual and even physical resistance from the non-Christian populations they seek to convert.

There are, of course, Christian missionaries who remain in their native lands and bring their religious message to neighbors and fellow citizens. These missionaries also often face resentment and rejection.

"Rice Christians"

I witnessed resistance to American Christian missionary efforts in Japan while serving as a United States Air Force chaplain in Asia. The Japanese who did convert to Christianity were derisively called "rice Christians" by other Japanese. The derogatory nickname implied that missionaries provided material or financial benefit as inducements to converts.

However, Christian missionaries throughout the world have established hospitals, colleges and universities, medical clinics, technical training schools, hospices, orphanages, and other institutions. Indeed, for many Christians, "mission" today means less focus on converting individuals and more emphasis on providing assistance and education to people in need.

While fully recognizing the various humanitarian efforts of Christians, the term "missionary" triggers feelings of resentment and even rage among Jews. For nearly two thousand years zealous Christians in their quest for converts have assailed Jews with hostile proselytizing campaigns that have included forced conversions and humiliating public religious debates in medieval Europe. Such "disputations" sought to prove Christianity's spiritual superiority over Judaism and forced unwilling rabbis to "debate" priests, who were often Jewish converts. In some cases, the alleged debates were sponsored by the Christian ruling authorities, who acted as "judges."

Rigged Debates and Book Burnings

In 1240 there was a public disputation in Paris between four rabbis on one side and a Jewish convert to Christianity. Not surprisingly, the rabbis "lost" the theological contest. Two years after the collective rabbinical "defeat," twenty-four carriages containing twelve thousand precious handwritten copies of the voluminous Talmud were publicly burned in Paris as a sign of Christian supremacy over Judaism. Unfortunately, the Paris bonfire was not an aberration.[1]

Several popes instigated the destruction of Jewish manuscripts beginning with the reign of Pope Gregory IX (1227–41) and continuing for nearly four hundred years through the pontificate of Clement VIII (1592–1605). However, Johann Gutenberg's invention of movable type in 1439 guaranteed that books of all types could be printed in large numbers by a host of publishers with no possibility of permanent eradication or destruction. After Gutenberg, religious and political leaders continued to stage book burnings as public spectacles to express their contempt or hatred for a particular work.

One such book-burning spectacle took place in Berlin in May 1933. The Nazis set fire to nearly twenty-five thousand volumes, which included the writings of Jewish authors Albert Einstein, Sigmund Freud, Heinrich Heine, and others. But the Nazi flames of hatred also consumed books by Berthold Brecht, Helen Keller, Jack London, Thomas Mann, and H. G. Wells, none of whom were Jewish.[2]

In 1995 a memorial was dedicated on the site of the book burnings that included a plaque with the prescient 1821 quotation by Heine: "Where books are burned, in the end people will burn."

In 1263 in Barcelona the Jewish scholar Moses ben Nachman (1194–1270), or Nachmanides, was compelled to debate Pablo Christiani, a Jewish convert who, as a Dominican monk, had assumed this new name to reflect his religious fervor. The rabbi performed brilliantly in the faux debate against his opponent, but even extraordinary rabbis like Nachmanides were destined to "lose" the staged confrontations.

The rabbi, whose biblical and philosophical works are still studied, was so good that King James I of Aragon awarded the Jewish "loser" a monetary prize and remarked that never had "an unjust cause been so nobly defended." Even so, Nachmanides was exiled from the region, and his written report about the debate was burned by the "victorious" Christians.[3]

The predetermined results transmitted the message that particularistic Judaism was false and inferior when compared to the true and universal faith of Christianity. Because Jews were members of the losing religious "team," they were subject to persecution that included forced baptism, physical exile, and death.

Physical Expulsions

In addition to the so-called debates, there have been nearly seventy-five physical expulsions of Jews from various nations, regions, and cities during the past eighteen hundred years. Many of these acts were incited by Christian missionaries who were unsuccessful in their conversionary efforts. They considered the existence of faithful and viable Jewish communities within Christian regions of

Europe and North Africa an affront to God and Jesus and a living refutation of Christianity's claim that it had superseded Judaism.

One of the first recorded evictions of Jews took place in 250 in Carthage in what is today's Tunisia, but the most famous expulsions of Jews were in Spain in 1492 and in Portugal five years later. While both Iberian expulsions were ordered by Catholic monarchs, missionaries spurred on those ghastly events. One object of ridding a country of its Jewish population was to purify and strengthen the Christian presence in a particular locality. However, in many cases the expulsions provided welcome opportunities to expropriate Jewish property and wealth, a clear case of fiscal avarice cloaked in pious clothing.

Sometimes Jews were expelled from a country and then later asked to return in the expectation they would bring economic prosperity with them. Such a recall occurred in France in 1306 when Jews were forced to leave, but then permitted to return just sixteen years later. England expelled its Jews in 1290 and did not allow their official reentry until the seventeenth century, although Jews did live in Britain, sometimes with hidden identities, during that four-hundred-year interval.[4]

The pain and dislocation continued for nearly seventeen hundred years, culminating in the Holocaust and the expulsions of Jews from many Arab countries in the years following the establishment of the State of Israel.

The list of expelled Jewish communities reads like a travel brochure, but each expulsion, whether involving large or small numbers of people, resulted in lasting bitter memories. The upheavals created physically and emotionally wounded Jewish communities; each forced expulsion entered into the collective psyche of the Jewish people.

The lachrymose litany includes Alexandria, Italy, Switzerland, Hungary, Germany, Austria, Lithuania, Bohemia, Bavaria, Naples, Genoa, Prague, the Papal States, Holland, Frankfurt, Kiev, Russia, Warsaw, Ukraine, Vienna, Moravia, Bordeaux, and Bremen. In many cases, when Jews were not expelled from an area, they were persecuted and killed when angry missionaries failed—as they usually did—in their efforts to "bring Christ to the Jews."

Ghettoes and Forced Conversions

One example of unsuccessful Christian missionary efforts is the Catholic chapel in Rome, Santa Maria della Pietà, located near the former Jewish ghetto. After residing for more than seventeen hundred years in various areas of the city, Roman Jews were forced to live within a small, walled segregated area established by the papal *bullum* (the Latin word for "seal") *Cum nimis absurdum,* issued by Paul IV in 1555. The opening words capture the odium of the Vatican decree:

> Since it is completely senseless and inappropriate to be in a situation where Christian piety allows the Jews (whose guilt—all of their own doing—has condemned them to eternal slavery) access to our society and even to live among us ...[5]

In addition to creating the restrictive ghetto, the Vatican edict curtailed Jewish economic opportunities and activities and limited each city or town under papal control to only one synagogue, and finally, the *bullum* prohibited personal contact between Christians and Jews.

One result of the forced separation was the requirement that one hundred Jewish men and fifty Jewish women attend weekly religious services inside Santa Maria della Pietà, where they were compelled to listen to conversionary sermons, frequently delivered by converted Jews. As a final degrading obligation, the Roman Jews had to pay a fee for the "privilege" of hearing former members of their community attack Judaism.

As a constant reminder of alleged Jewish perfidy, the chastising words of Second Isaiah (65:2) uttered during the Babylonian exile in the sixth century BCE and in a completely different context are still inscribed above the chapel's entrance in both the prophet's original Hebrew and in Latin: "I have spread forth My hands all the day to an unbelieving people, who walk in a way that is not good, after their own thoughts; a people that continually provoke Me to anger before My face."

My professional responsibilities with the American Jewish Committee brought me to Rome and the Vatican many times. During each trip to the Eternal City, I visited the conversionist chapel facing the ghetto. It remains a vivid reminder of the great distance both faith communities have come since the bleak days of the past.

I shuddered upon entering the small worship area and tried to imagine the terror and dread Roman Jews must have experienced when they were forced to sit through a service that demanded they abandon their ancient faith and become Catholic. Each time I departed the church and reentered the modern world in physical safety and religious security, I offered a personal prayer praising the members of the Jewish community who had the spiritual strength not only to survive but also to triumph as Jews in Rome.

The ghetto was not legally ended until the establishment of the modern Italian Republic in 1870, and the physical walls of segregation were finally destroyed in 1888. It was the last European ghetto to remain until the Holocaust period, when the Nazis created new ones for their Jewish victims.

When Pope Benedict XVI visited Rome's Great Synagogue on January 17, 2010, he concluded his remarks with a reference to the historic Jewish community of that city. Although he did not mention the anti-Jewish persecutions of the past and the existence of the ghetto for more than 330 years, Benedict's words represent an extraordinary change from some of his anti-Jewish predecessors:

> I offer a particular reflection on this, our city of Rome, where, for nearly two millennia, as Pope John Paul II said, the Catholic Community with its Bishop and the Jewish Community with its Chief Rabbi have lived side by side. May this proximity be animated by a growing fraternal love,

expressed also in closer cooperation, so that we may offer a valid contribution to solving the problems and difficulties that we still face.[6]

Christian missionary efforts seeking to sever Jews from their faith, family, community, and heritage created a collective DNA, a defense mechanism that still sets off alarm bells when Jews are confronted even by respectful missionaries. For some Christian groups, Jews still remain primary targets for religious conversion, or, as Paul wrote, "to the Jew first" (Romans 1:16). However slick the missionaries' modern bottles of conversionary wine may appear, the containers still hold the old wine of Christian triumphalism, a combined attack on both Jewish history and the validity of the covenant made with God.

A Free Gift for Jews

I remember one up-close and personal encounter with a Christian missionary during my first week as a rabbinical student in New York City. I was then twenty years old, a freshly minted college graduate who had come from my Virginia home to study in exciting Manhattan. To use Alfred Kazin's book title, I quickly became "a walker in the city," a habit that remains to this day.

One autumn afternoon, I was on East Forty-second Street near Grand Central Terminal when a man approached me carrying a large hand-painted sign advertising an offer I could not refuse: "A Free New Testament for Any Jewish Person." I was intrigued with the proposal because it provided a new volume for my then meager theological library.

I happily took the book but was disappointed to discover the tiny letters of the text were poorly printed on cheap paper. Almost by rote I uttered the three words of politeness I was taught as a child to say when someone gives you a gift: "Thank you, sir."

The "sir" was clearly a mistake. The missionary thought I was interested in receiving more than a badly printed book. As I walked away, he shouted, "Wait a minute. I haven't told you what's in the New Testament!" I turned to him and yelled, "I know very well what's in the book. And no thank you."

Not satisfied with my abrupt answer, he pursued me on one of New York City's busiest streets, and I wondered if the Christian missionary had a daily quota of shabbily printed New Testaments he needed to distribute to Jews. "Let me share my Jesus with you," he pleaded. I replied, "Leave me alone. Your Jesus has already done enough damage to my people." Thus ended that long-ago inter-religious encounter.

It was not a favorable beginning for a rabbi who devoted most of his career to developing better relations between Jews and Christians. But the interaction on that long-ago day near Grand Central Terminal tersely captured much of the historical record of Christian missionary activity and the equally historical Jewish response to such efforts.

"Mission" is used by both Jews and Christians in their "religionspeak." However, they interpret the term in different ways. For Jews, "mission" means extending the message of the one God of the universe—ethical monotheism—to the entire world. "On that day the Lord shall be One and God's name shall be One" is a well-known synagogue prayer that is based on Zechariah 14:9. Jews are commanded to be a "light unto the nations" (Isaiah 42:6).

However, because of the religious disputations of the past, Jewish mission precludes coercion, religious triumphalism, or any sense of spiritual "victory."

Jews Are Already with the Father

People may be unfamiliar with German-Jewish Franz Rosenzweig (1888–1929) and his complex theological volume *The Star of Redemption* (1921), one of the twentieth century's most influential Jewish works of theology. As a young man, Rosenzweig was influenced by Eugen Rosenstock (1888–1973), a German Jew who converted to Christianity as a teenager. The two exchanged a series of letters that focused on the relationship between Judaism and Christianity. In 1911, the twenty-three-year-old Rosenzweig contemplated converting to Christianity, but before being baptized, he gave Judaism a final look by attending a Yom Kippur service in the city of Kassel. Profoundly moved by the Day of Atonement experience, he turned to Judaism with dedication and intensity: "It [conversion to Christianity] seems unnecessary and for me impossible now. I remain a Jew."

Even though he was a devout Christian, Rosenstock had to flee Germany in the 1930s for the United States, because under Nazi law he was still considered a Jew. His conversion offered no protection from the Nazi anti-Semitic campaign. Rosenstock later became a professor, first at Harvard and later at Dartmouth.

In a now-famous letter to a cousin, Rosenzweig expressed his perspectives of both Judaism and Christianity:

> We agree on what Christ and his Church mean in the world: no one comes to the Father but through him (John 14:6). No one comes to the Father—but it is different when somebody does not have to come to the Father because he is already with him. And this is so for the people of Israel.[7]

It was Rosenzweig's way of describing the permanency of the Sinai covenant between God and the Jewish people. On October 31, 1997, Pope John Paul II affirmed that covenant from a Christian perspective, calling it "a supernatural fact":

> The fact of divine election is at the origin of this small people situated between the great pagan empires whose brilliant culture overshadowed them. This people was gathered together and led by God, the Creator of heaven and earth. Thus its existence is not a mere fact of nature or culture, in the sense that through culture man displays the resources of his own nature. It is a supernatural fact. This people perseveres in spite of everything because they are the people of the Covenant, and despite human infidelities, the Lord is faithful to his Covenant.[8]

When Pope Benedict XVI spoke in Rome's Great Synagogue in 2010, he reaffirmed the Jewish covenant and the achievements of the Second Vatican Council:

> [Today there are] increasingly close relations between Catholics and Jews.... [I]n the course of my Pontificate, [I] have wanted to demonstrate my closeness to and my affection for the people of the Covenant.... It is in pondering her own mystery that the Church, the People of God of the New Covenant, discovers her own profound bond with the Jews, who were chosen by the Lord before all others to receive his word (cf. *Catechism of the Catholic Church*, 839). "The Jewish faith, unlike other non-Christian religions, is already a response to God's revelation in the Old Covenant. To the Jews 'belong the sonship, the glory, the covenants, the giving of the law, the worship, and the promises; to them belong the patriarchs and of their race, according to the flesh is the Christ' (Rom[ans] 9:4–5), 'for the gifts and the call of God are irrevocable!' (Rom[ans] 11:29)."... The [Second Vatican] Council gave a strong impetus to our irrevocable commitment to pursue the path of dialogue, fraternity and friendship, a journey which has been deepened and developed in the last forty years, through important steps and significant gestures.[9]

Meanings of "Mission"

However, Christians perceive "mission" differently than Jews do. It is the focus of the "Great Commission," that is, bringing the message of Jesus to the entire world. The genesis of that missionary effort is found in Matthew, when Jesus in a kind of "farewell address" spoke to his disciples:

> All authority has been given to Me in heaven and on earth. Go therefore and make disciples of all the nations, baptizing

them in the name of the Father and the Son and the Holy
Spirit, teaching them to observe all that I commanded you.
                                    —Matthew 28:18–20, NASB

But a few chapters earlier in Matthew, Jesus told his dozen closest
followers to focus their attention not on the Gentiles, the "outside
world," but upon the "House of Israel":

> Do not go in the way of the Gentiles, and do not enter any
> city of the Samaritans; but rather go to the lost sheep of the
> house of Israel. And as you go, preach, saying, "The king-
> dom of heaven is at hand."
>   —Matthew 10:5–7, NASB

The continuing tension between Christian missionaries and Jews is
inherent in those few words. Jews have never believed they are religious "lost sheep." On the contrary, they believe in the eternal
validity of their covenant with God. In addition, for Jews the "kingdom" of God is not "at hand." To achieve that blessed but still distant goal requires the combined efforts of men and women of
goodwill throughout the world. Christians, however, read the
words of Jesus as a mandate to seek converts everywhere, but especially among Jews, the alleged "lost sheep."

As noted above, Jews have usually experienced mission or the
Christian "Great Commission" throughout the centuries as a bitter
and theologically insulting experience. Today they are still confronted by Christian missionaries who perceive Jews as primary targets for conversion. "Christian mission," whatever its earliest
meaning, has become a pejorative, an attack upon Jewish history
and upon a covenanted people of God.

Hebrew Christian Deceptions

A divisive issue between some Christians and Jews is the existence
of Hebrew Christian groups in the United States, Israel, and other
countries. Such missionary groups combine the basic Christian

message that Jesus is the Messiah with traditional Jewish cultural, religious, and ethnic elements, including food, music, dance, and even humor.

They use the Hebrew language and Torah scrolls at worship services, give Christological meanings to Jewish holidays, bestow their clergy with the unearned title of "rabbi," and distribute a deceptive missionary version of the Jewish religious calendar. At the same time, Hebrew Christians publicly support the security and survival of the State of Israel, and they backed the Soviet Jewry movement during the 1970s and 1980s. But such activities have not insulated them from receiving criticism for their misleading conversionary tactics.

Hebrew Christians assure Jews that baptism and accepting Jesus as the Messiah do not mean renouncing Judaism or severing ties with the Jewish people. Instead, they become so-called completed Jews.

Hebrew Christians use Jewish symbols in distorted forms. They falsely identify the three pieces of unleavened bread—matzah—used at the Passover Seder as a symbol of the Trinity. Jews link the matzah to the three categories of ancient Jews: the *Kohanim*, the priestly leaders of the Holy Temple in Jerusalem; the Levites, who ministered within the Temple; and the Israelites, or "common folk." At every Seder, the middle matzah is split in two, and one part is hidden so youngsters at the meal can search for it and return the missing piece to the Seder leader. That broken piece of unleavened bread is required to complete the ritual of the Seder. But the Hebrew Christians have given the three pieces of unleavened bread a false Christological meaning: the middle broken matzah represents the broken crucified Jesus.

Hebrew Christians have distorted the meaning of the starter candle on the Hanukkah menorah, the *shamash*. For them, Jesus is the Great Candle of humanity, the light to the world. Their duplicity is also evident in their abuse of the religious meanings of the Jewish High Holy Days of Rosh Hashanah (the New Year) and Yom Kippur (the Day of Atonement).

The distribution and use of an ersatz Jewish calendar is another deceptive act. It is estimated that nearly one hundred thousand Hebrew Christian calendars are distributed annually. The months of the year feature conversion messages printed along with Sabbath candle-lighting times on Friday evenings and the Torah portions read each week in synagogues.

Hebrew Christians speak of "completed" or "fulfilled Jews," terms insinuating that today's Jews and those of the past two thousand years constitute religiously incomplete Jews who lack the "truth" in their spiritual beliefs. The true intention of one Hebrew Christian group, "Jews for Jesus," is revealed in a supposedly "confidential" report:

> We define ourselves as evangelical fundamentalists and we seek the cooperation of individuals and Christian bodies meeting this description.... We believe in affiliation with a local church and being accountable to the church for service and discipline. We will uphold the local church wherever we can.
>
> We consider ourselves an arm of the local church. We are primarily evangelists and we are mindful that we should not usurp the authority of the local pastor. As we win and disciple [convert] Jewish people, we urge them either to take their place in a local evangelistic church or establish a congregation and call their own minister. Our duty is to aid the church at large and we work as an arm of that body to gather in the Lost Sheep of the House of Israel.[10]

The Jews for Jesus "Mission Statement" is a single aggressive sentence: "We exist to make the messiahship of Jesus an unavoidable issue to our Jewish people worldwide." The word "unavoidable" smacks of Christian missionary tactics used for the past two thousand years, an "in-your-face," intrusive, coercive campaign that insults the personal integrity of individual Jews and the theological validity of Judaism.

Although the group claims to be part of the Jewish people and its traditions, the Jews for Jesus "Statement of Faith" reveals its permanent rupture with Judaism: "We recognize the value of traditional Jewish literature, but only where it is supported by or conformable to the Word of God. We regard it as in no way binding upon life or faith."

The Jews for Jesus in their Christian missionary zeal replicate Paul's break with the Torah two thousand years ago. The group dismisses the "value of traditional Jewish literature," that is, the *halacha* (Jewish religious law, faith, rituals, and observances), which is rooted in the Bible and the Talmud, the Rabbinic sages of the past and present, the teachings of Maimonides and other religious philosophers, and many additional essential components of Judaism.

But the Jews for Jesus group, in an egregious act of chutzpah, sets itself up as the true arbiter of whether the vast array of Jewish literature is "supported by or conformable to the Word of God." With their own words, they have removed themselves from Jewish life, faith, history, and experience. At least Paul was more honest when he broke with the Judaism of his day. The Jews for Jesus are not.

The Jews for Jesus and other Hebrew Christian groups are not Jews, but are converts to Christianity. That is their right, but they do not have the right to distort and twist authentic Judaism and claim Hebrew Christianity is its rightful heir and legitimate successor. Gross deception takes place when invalid claims are made, and the internal documents cited above and similar examples of distortion and duplicity make clear exactly who and what Hebrew Christians represent: old conversionary wine in new bottles.

There are "truth in labeling" laws in the United States. Hebrew Christians need to obey a religious version of such legislation. While everyone has the right to join other faith communities, religious groups do not have the right to conceal or disguise their true intentions or to deliberately distort the beliefs of another faith in a crass attempt to gain converts. Deception, misrepresentation, and distortion are not part of the Christian Great Commission.

Witnessing to one's faith must be transparent, open, and honest and must never include coercion or false labeling of any kind.[11]

When a Christian church or institution offers Hebrew Christians a platform or venue, when Christians make financial contributions to such groups, or when Christians condone the duplicity of Hebrew Christians, such actions poison the integrity of interreligious dialogue. After two thousand years of history, Christianity is recognizable in all its many forms. Even the missionary on Forty-second Street was clear in his intentions. Judaism is also recognizable in all its many forms. But the Hebrew Christians pose as Jews when in fact they are Christian missionaries; their actions are offensive to both faith communities.

There are always individual acts of conversion; people move from Judaism to Christianity, and the reverse process also takes place. But Jews resent and are angered by Christian efforts, whatever their source or motive, that target Jews qua Jews as potential converts.

However, a growing number of theologians are emphasizing the Jewish roots of their Christian faith and questioning the validity of missionary activities aimed at Jews. In 1973 during the Evangelical-sponsored "Key '73" conversion campaign in the United States, Billy Graham, the world's most prominent evangelist, criticized such actions:

> I believe God has always had a special relationship with the Jewish people…. In my evangelistic efforts, I have never felt called to single out Jews as Jews…. Just as Judaism frowns on proselytizing that is coercive, or that seeks to commit men against their will, so do I.[12]

Creating "Holy Envy"

The former Harvard Divinity School dean and Lutheran bishop Krister Stendahl spoke about making others "jealous" of one's own spiritual life and faith. Stendahl urged Jews and Christians to create "holy envy" by competing with one another in developing the quality of their family lives, personal ethics, social justice concerns, and prayer life. Stendahl felt that is the best form of missionary activity.[13]

Despite the Jewish aversion to Christian missionary activity, many respected rabbis have believed Christianity has a necessary role in the divine economy. This is perhaps surprising given the unhappy, often lethal history of Christian behavior toward Jews. No less an authority than Moses Maimonides perceived Christianity in somewhat positive terms.

Scholars, however, point out that Maimonides (also known as the Rambam, an acronym of his name, Rabbi Moshe ben Maimon) lived much of his life among Muslims and had limited contact with Christians. That may be why he wrote more positively about Christianity than about Islam, the religious group that forced his family to flee from his native Spain. Even Maimonides' exalted status as the court physician to the Egyptian caliph in Cairo did not significantly soften Maimonides' perception of Islam.

The Rambam was aware of the pain and bitterness Jews experienced as Christianity and Islam, each in its own manner, attempted to supersede Judaism. But despite this, Maimonides viewed Jesus and Muhammad (570–632) as teachers whose task was to prepare the world for the coming of "King Messiah." Put in philosophical language, Maimonides believed Christianity and Islam were necessary elements but not sufficient by themselves to bring about the era of the Messiah. Specifically referring to Jesus, he wrote:

> Even Jesus the Nazarene who imagined that he would be Messiah was killed ... is there a greater stumbling-block than this one [Jesus]? So that all of the prophets spoke that the Messiah redeems Israel, and saves them, and gathers their banished ones, and strengthens their commandments. And this one caused [nations] to destroy Israel by sword, and to scatter their remnant, and to humiliate them, and to exchange the Torah, and to make the majority of the world err to serve a divinity besides God.

Maimonides continued:

> But the human mind has no power to reach the thoughts of
> the Creator, for his thoughts and ways are unlike ours. And
> all these things of Jesus the Nazarene, and of [Muhammad]
> the Ishmaelite who stood after him—there is no (purpose)
> but to straighten out the way for the King Messiah, and to
> restore all the world to serve God together. So that it is said,
> "Because then I will turn toward the nations (giving them) a
> clear lip, to call all of them in the name of God and to serve
> God (shoulder to shoulder as) one shoulder" (Zephaniah
> 3:9). How is this? The entire world had become filled with
> the issues of the anointed one and of the Torah and the
> Laws, and these issues had spread out unto faraway islands
> and among many nations uncircumcised in the heart, and
> they discuss these issues and the Torah's laws.... But when
> the anointed king will truly rise and succeed and will be
> raised and uplifted, they all immediately turn about and
> know that their fathers inherited falsehood, and their
> prophets and ancestors led them astray.
>
> —*Mishneh Torah, Hilchot Melachim* 11:4

In a later era, Rabbi Jacob Emden (1697–1776), who lived near
Hamburg, Germany, had another explanation for the rise of
Christianity and its role in history: while the 613 divine command-
ments or *mitzvot* are only for Jews and do not apply to Gentiles,
Emden believed the latter group is obligated to follow the seven
Noachide Laws, named for the biblical Noah who lived before the
Hebrew patriarch Abraham. For Emden, Noah represents a kind
of universal human being who is described as "a righteous man ...
blameless in his age" (Genesis 6:9, JPS), that is, he lived before the
development of Judaism with its set of divine commandments.
Noah's three sons became the prototypes of Asia (Shem), Europe
(Japheth), and Africa (Ham).[14]

Seven Noachide Laws

The seven Noachide Laws, developed by the Talmudic Rabbis, were for people who were not Jewish. The Noachide Laws are required to ensure a "righteous and wholehearted" society, and it was taught that if non-Jews carried out those seven principles, they merited the worthy title of "righteous Gentile." Nowhere in the development of the Noachide Laws or within the laws themselves is the admonition or expressed need for people to convert to Judaism as a necessary step to achieve religious salvation. Indeed, a Mishnaic teaching is that "all the righteous of the world shall have a share in the world to come" (*Tosefta, Sanhedrin* 13).

The Noachide Laws contain several provisions that also appear in the biblical Ten Commandments:

1. Prohibition of idolatry
2. Prohibition of murder
3. Prohibition of theft
4. Prohibition of sexual promiscuity, including adultery, incest, bestiality, and homosexuality
5. Prohibition of blasphemy against God or the Divine Name
6. Dietary law that prohibits eating flesh taken from an animal while it is still alive
7. The establishment of a lawful society with courts of justice

But Emden went further in his understanding of Jesus and Paul. The eighteenth-century rabbi asserted that the initial goal of Jesus, and especially of Paul, was to reach out to and teach only Gentiles and not Jews. In Emden's view, Christians, whose religion emerged from Judaism, were to leave Jews alone—a religious form of "benign neglect"—allowing them to observe the traditional laws and practices of Judaism in peace and security.

A contemporary American Jewish theologian, Irving Greenberg, writing two centuries after Emden, presents a post-Shoah interpretation of Christian-Jewish relations. Greenberg believes interreligious dialogue is an imperative, with members of each faith community acknowledging the spiritual legitimacy of the "Other" and developing mutual respect and understanding. Instead of seeking converts, Greenberg urges Christians to join with Jews in building together the just world that is needed after the catastrophic events of the Holocaust.

Greenberg echoes Rosenzweig in asserting that Christianity, "an outgrowth of Judaism," can bring a message of God and a commitment to human life to places and people that Judaism is not able to achieve by itself. He also hopes that Islam, another global monotheistic faith, will, as another "outgrowth" of Judaism, participate in the divine task of affirming life and peace.

Mission or Witness?

Today many Christians define "mission" and "witness" differently than in the past. They stake out a distinction between the two terms; for them, mission is frequently an act of insensitivity, even coercion, that is directed toward adherents of another faith community, while witness is the actual living out of a person's religious beliefs without attempting to proselytize another human being, a child of God. There are no hidden agendas, no subliminal messages in witnessing as defined by such Christians. Instead, they cite the biblical verse "You are My witnesses, saith the Lord" (Isaiah 43:12).

Aiding this effort at recasting and redefining mission and witness is the Jewish concept of *teshuvah* (Hebrew for "turning" or "repentance"). *Teshuvah* is open to all people who have made a sincere effort to mend their unethical ways and seek atonement for errors of judgment and action. *Teshuvah* is free of religious triumphalism, with no spiritual "winners" or "losers."

Christians and Jews will continue to discover opportunities for future dialogue, but that can only happen when they address the critical themes of mission, witness, conversion, and *teshuvah* without the overt or covert aim of converting the "Other."

9 O Jerusalem!

Three Faiths but Only One Jerusalem

A new high-speed, multilane highway has replaced the twisting narrow road that millions of visitors to Israel used in past years to reach Jerusalem after their flights had landed at Israel's sprawling Ben-Gurion International Airport.

The airport, with its collection of runways, cargo hangars, parking lots, connecting roadways, and passenger terminals, is less than ten miles from the modern Mediterranean coast city of Tel Aviv, founded in 1909. The airport, named in memory of Israel's first prime minister following his death in 1973, was an act of remembrance similar to the tributes other countries have bestowed upon national heroes: John F. Kennedy in New York City, Charles de Gaulle in Paris, and Leonardo da Vinci in Rome.

But after landing at Ben-Gurion airport, first-time visitors to Israel do not usually make Tel Aviv their immediate destination. The first place they want to visit is one of the world's oldest cities—Jerusalem. The once heavily traveled road from the airport to Israel's capital snakes its way upward and eastward for thirty-one miles until it reaches the Holy City, which sits atop a plateau twenty-five hundred feet above sea level.

The old winding road was the scene of bitter fighting during the Jewish state's War of Independence in 1948–49. As a permanent memorial, Israel lined the route with some of the burned-out trucks and armored cars that were destroyed during the first of Israel's wars with its Arab neighbors.

My first visit to Jerusalem came a few weeks after the 1967 Six-Day War, and I recall the slow ascending drive past the rusting shattered vehicles from the late 1940s. They remain a reminder of the high price Israel paid to break the Arab siege in a costly, but ultimately successful effort to supply Jerusalem's beleaguered civilian population with food, fuel, water, medical provisions, and other urgently needed supplies. Each subsequent trip going up to Jerusalem was a reminder that the City of Peace, the traditional meaning given to the Hebrew word *Yerushalayim*, has been the center of armed conflicts, political controversies, and religious rivalries.

Just east of Jerusalem the hills fall sharply into the forbidding Judean wilderness and the Dead Sea. Since ancient times the area has been the hiding place for political and religious refugees. Young David hid from a jealous King Saul at the watering spring of Ein Gedi. Nine hundred years later, the puritanical Jewish Essene group, weary of sinful urban Jerusalem, fled to the Qumran caves near the Dead Sea and established an austere religious community. A century later, Jesus confronted temptation for forty days on a lonely hill in the same Judean wilderness.

Five Famous Mountains

Jerusalem's famous mountains, actually small hills, bear names that have stirred the souls and fired the imaginations of millions of people. Mount Zion, south of the walled Old City, is the biblical synonym for Jerusalem and is, according to Jewish tradition, the burial place of King David. The modern Jewish national movement, Zionism, bears the mount's name.

The Mount of Olives, east of the Old City, has the largest and oldest Jewish cemetery in the world with graves dating back three thousand years. For Jews, the Messiah will come from the Mount of Olives and enter Jerusalem in glory through the Golden Gate on the eastern side of the Holy City. To prevent that messianic event from happening, Muslims, when they controlled the city under the rule of Suleiman (1494–1566), physically sealed up the gate with stones, a condition that still exists today.

In Christian tradition, Jesus will arise from the dead on the Mount of Olives, the long-awaited Second Coming. During the Jordanian occupation of Jerusalem between 1948 and 1967, Jewish gravestones on the mount were "expropriated" and used for commonplace building purposes, including latrines and roadways.

Mount Scopus, on the northeast side of Jerusalem, derives its name from the Latin, meaning "observation point." This site is a vital military approach to the city, and Roman legions encamped on Mount Scopus before they captured Jerusalem in 70 CE. In 1967 the Israelis used the same hill as a staging area in their successful campaign to unify the divided city.[1]

Mount Scopus was the original home of the Hebrew University, founded in 1925, as well as the first site of the Hadassah Hospital. Between 1948 and 1967, following Israel's War of Independence, the Israelis retained possession of the Mount Scopus enclave, while Jordan occupied the surrounding area. During those nineteen years, Jordanians did not permit Israeli use of the Mount Scopus facilities—neither the university nor the hospital. It was a violation of the 1949 armistice agreement between Jordan and Israel.

Jordan's refusal to honor its commitment compelled Israel to build a new Hebrew University campus and Hadassah Medical Center in the western part of Jerusalem. Since 1967, the original Scopus facilities have been restored to use, and new buildings have been added. Today the institutions of Mount Scopus are again a vital part of the Israeli educational and medical systems.

Mount Herzl in western Jerusalem is named for modern Zionism's founder, Theodor Herzl, an Austrian Jew, who was first buried in Vienna. But Herzl, confident of his dream of a "Zion restored," stipulated in his will that his remains be brought to the new Jewish state after its independence had been achieved. In 1949, less than a half century after his death, Herzl's wish was honored, and today his grave occupies a prominent place on the mount that bears his name. The four Hebrew letters that spell out "Herzl" are the only markings on his grave.

Prominent Israeli leaders, including former prime ministers Golda Meir and Yitzhak Rabin, are buried nearby. However, most of the cemetery contains the graves of soldiers who lost their lives in Israel's wars.

It is only a few miles in distance and a short drive in time from Mount Zion and King David's burial place to Mount Herzl and the grave of the founder of modern Zionism, but the two hills span more than three thousand years of Jewish history. The Israeli military cemetery, similar to Arlington National Cemetery near Washington, D.C., marks the continuing human cost of maintaining and defending Israel's national freedom and independence.

Mount Moriah, within the Old City, contains the large rock where, as described in the book of Genesis, Abraham offered his son Isaac to God as a sacrifice. Mount Moriah was the site of the two Jewish Holy Temples.

Islam and Jerusalem

The Islamic tradition has spiritually and physically integrated Mount Moriah into its own religious tradition. The Hebrew name for the Temple Mount area, *Beit HaMikdash* (the House of the Sanctuary), became one of the Arabic names for Jerusalem: *Beit al-Makdis*. Omar, the Muslim caliph, captured Jerusalem in 638, and a half century later the Dome of the Rock was erected directly atop the ruins of the two Temples. Shortly thereafter, the al-Aqsa Mosque, the "remote one," was built on the mount not far from the Dome of the Rock.[2]

The three faiths—Judaism, Christianity, and Islam—connect themselves with Jerusalem, but each religious community has a different perspective on the city's role in divine and human history. A mistake frequently made in the interests of religious or political correctness is to equate the Jewish, Christian, and Islamic links with Jerusalem as synonymous and equal with one another. The groups relate to the city in distinctive ways, and their responses to

Jerusalem need to be honored and not reduced to the lowest common denominator.

Islam, influenced by both Judaism and Christianity, has ranked Jerusalem only behind Mecca and Medina in sanctity, although it is not mentioned in the Qur'an. While Islam's birth and early development are linked to the latter two cities in today's Saudi Arabia, Muslims believe the Prophet Muhammad was miraculously transported on his winged steed al-Baraq (Lightning) from Mecca to Jerusalem, and then Islam's founder was lifted to the heavens in a nocturnal ascent.

The Christian attachment to the city results from the key events in the life and death of Jesus within Jerusalem. It was the site of his death, resurrection, and ascension, and Jerusalem contains holy places associated with Jesus that have attracted Christians to the city for nearly two thousand years: the Garden of Gethsemane, the Via Dolorosa, the Stations of the Cross, Golgotha, Calvary, the Church of the Holy Sepulchre, and the Garden Tomb.

In past centuries, Christians called Jerusalem *axis mundi*, "the center of the world." It is where Passion events took place and where salvational events unfolded. Jerusalem was the scene of Pentecost, the birthday of the Christian church, and Christian communities have existed in the Holy City continuously for nearly two thousand years.

Because Jerusalem occupies a central role in much of Christian devotional poetry, hymns, and prayers, many Western Christians came to the Holy City as pilgrims. They wanted to walk in the steps of Jesus, to visit the places associated with his life and death, and to pray. But for many other Christians, no pilgrimage was required or needed, since they were born in the Holy City as members of Eastern Orthodox churches.

But sometimes the visitors were bellicose invaders who brought conflict with them. The Crusades, with their sordid record of rape, pillage, destruction, and bloodshed, is one of Christianity's darkest chapters. In the twelfth century, the Crusaders dominated Jerusalem, and during that time, they massacred thousands of Jews and Muslims.

Earthly and Heavenly Jerusalem

Despite the historical attachment to physical Jerusalem, Christian thinking has often focused on the heavenly Jerusalem, an abstract and spiritual concept devoid of specific territoriality and flesh-and-blood reality.

Professor R. J. Zwi Werblowsky of the Hebrew University has observed:

> To the extent that Jerusalem also has a terrestrial, geographical dimension as a holy city (for Christians), it is mainly in its quality as a memento of holy events that occurred at certain places—"holy places" therein.[3]

The emphasis on the heavenly city at the expense of the earthly Jerusalem has created a deep Christian ambivalence toward the city. Werblowsky added:

> A "de-territorializing" tendency has asserted itself, and many of the great spiritual figures in the history of Christianity expressed doubts ... about undertaking an actual journey to Jerusalem.[4]

The Christian saint Augustine (354–430) wrote, "When we thirst, then we should come—not with our feet, but rather with our feelings.... It is one thing to wander with the body, a different thing to wander with the heart." Jerome (347–420), another saint, was blunter: "The heavenly sanctuary is open from Britain, no less than from Jerusalem, for the Kingdom of God is within you." The English poet John Milton (1608–74) sarcastically describes the paradise of fools: "Here pilgrims roam, that stray'd so far to seek / In Golgotha him dead, who lives in Heav'n."[5]

Christian ambivalence toward the two Jerusalems remains unresolved to this day. It has resulted in political consequences that are expressed in contemporary Christian hostility to Israel's control of, and the Jewish ardor for, the flesh-and-blood, earthly

Jerusalem. Many Christians prefer the ethereal heavenly city instead.

Jewish Passion for Jerusalem

However, the Jewish passion for *Yerushalayim* differs from both the Islamic and the Christian connections to Jerusalem. The city decisively entered into Jewish self-consciousness when King David made it the political and religious capital of the Israelites around 1000 BCE.

For the past three thousand years there has been an unbroken link between the city and the Jewish people. For Jews, Jerusalem is no mere collection of holy places; instead, the entire city is sacred. Krister Stendahl has written:

> For Christians and Muslims that term [*holy sites*] is an adequate expression of what matters. Here are sacred places, hallowed by the most holy events, here are the places for pilgrimage, the very focus of highest devotion. But Judaism is different.... The sites sacred to Judaism have no shrines. Its religion is not tied to sites, but to the land, not to what happened in Jerusalem, but to Jerusalem itself.[6]

Jerusalem appears often in the *Tanach*, especially in the prophetic writings and the psalms. The city became the symbol and the reality of the people and God. Jerusalem is mentioned in the Hebrew Bible 750 times, and Zion 150 times. Nor did Jerusalem lose its transcendent importance when the Holy Temples and the entire city were destroyed first by the Babylonians and later by the Romans.

Since the days of David, Jews have always lived in Jerusalem, except for the times when outside forces such as the Roman Empire expelled them by force. Jews tenaciously maintained a community in Jerusalem despite the many foreign conquests.

Jerusalem plays a central role in Jewish liturgy, poetry, and religious writings. One particular psalm describes the inextricable bond between the Jewish people and the Holy City:

> *By the rivers of Babylon,*
> *there we sat down, yea, we wept,*
> *when we remembered Zion....*
>
> *If I forget thee, O Jerusalem,*
> *let my right hand forget her cunning.*
> *If I do not remember thee,*
> *let my tongue cleave to the roof of my mouth;*
> *if I prefer not Jerusalem*
> *above my chief joy.*
> —Psalm 137:1, 137:5–6, King James Version

The Passover Seder concludes each year with a prayer of hope and expectation: "Next year in Jerusalem!" The daily prayer of thanksgiving after meals speaks of "rebuilding Jerusalem speedily and in our day." A midrash says, "For sheer love of the earthly Jerusalem, God made one above" (*Esther Rabbah* 1:17). A Jewish teaching declares God created ten portions of beauty, and nine of them are in Jerusalem (Babylonian Talmud, *Kiddushin* 49b).

The Jewish tradition even has God declaring, "But I will not enter the heavenly Jerusalem until I have entered the earthly one first."[7] There is no Jewish ambivalence about the two Jerusalems. The earthly, flesh-and-blood, real city has absolute primacy; it is a theological position at odds with the classic Christian formulation.

The story of Jerusalem has been told through the ages in almost every language of the world, but the *Tanach* remains the primary source of Jerusalem's early history. Four decades after David established the city as his Israelite capital, his son, Solomon, built the First Temple, which was the people's religious center until its destruction about four hundred years later when Babylonians conquered the city in 586 BCE.

But seventy years later, the Second Temple was rebuilt under the leadership of Ezra and Nehemiah when Persian king Cyrus granted the exiled Israelites permission to return to Zion. It was the start of a recurring pattern in Jewish history: construction, destruction, expulsion, return, rebuilding, and ultimately restoration of Jewish sovereignty in the Land of Israel, with Jerusalem as its capital.

In 332 BCE Alexander the Great captured Jerusalem, but his large Hellenistic empire broke apart following his death ten years later. One of the post-Alexander factions was led by Antiochus IV, who attempted to eliminate all Jewish religious practices from Jerusalem and the entire Land of Israel. Ritual circumcision was banned, along with the study of Torah, and in an act certain to enrage many Jews, a statue of the Greek god Zeus was placed inside the Holy Temple.

A Jewish armed rebellion began that was led by Judah Maccabee, a member of a priestly family. The guerilla warfare against Emperor Antiochus IV and his army began in 168 BCE and lasted three years until Judah recaptured the Temple and rededicated it to the service of the God of Israel. That insurgency campaign and the rededication (*hanukkah*) are celebrated annually as the eight-day holiday Hanukkah in late November or December. Judah's military success was the start of the second independent Jewish Commonwealth; David's reign was the first.

The Second Commonwealth reached its peak during the controversial rule of King Herod. He embellished the Temple and constructed a royal winter retreat/fortress south of Jerusalem on Masada. Herod was a master builder, but many Jews of his day abhorred his leadership, believing he was not faithful in his personal religious beliefs and practices.

The Roman destruction of the Second Temple occurred in 70 CE, but somehow overlooked by the Romans in their razing of Jerusalem was a western rampart Temple wall built by Herod. It escaped destruction and remained intact, and in time the massive wall of huge beige stones became the focal point of Jewish yearning for a return to Jerusalem, a restored independent commonwealth and an end to dispersion and exile.

The Western Wall

According to one mystical interpretation, God, like the Jews, was also "exiled" from the Holy City. The divine presence dwelt in mourning within the wall itself, waiting for the Jewish people to return. Jewish sadness was expressed by shedding tears at the wall, and in time, the term "Wailing Wall" was given to the Herodian stones. Today in Israel the vast structure is correctly called *Ha-Kotel ha-ma'aravi*, the Western Wall. It remains the most sacred place on earth for Jews because of its historical bond with the destroyed Holy Temple.

In 363 CE, Byzantine Christians controlled Jerusalem. Led by Julian the Apostate and following Emperor Constantine's conversion fifty years earlier, Jews were permitted to return to the city, although many had lived there in secret. The Arabs, under Omar, came to Jerusalem in 638, and the European-based Christian Crusaders held Jerusalem from 1099 until their defeat by Saladin in 1187. In 1517 the Ottoman Turks captured the prized city, and in 1540 Suleiman the Magnificent, an Ottoman ruler, built the Old City walls. Those walls have now survived more than 450 years of weather and warfare, not to mention the visits of millions of pilgrims and tourists.[8]

During Ottoman Turkish rule, Jews returned to Jerusalem in increasing numbers to join the community already there. They came to pray at the Wall, to study at one of the many yeshivot (Jewish religious studies academies), to be near the graves of loved ones on the Mount of Olives, and simply to reside in the precincts of the Jewish Quarter of the Old City, the oldest Jewish community in the world. By 1844 Jews were the largest single religious group in the city, and in 1872 they outnumbered the Christians and Muslims combined. Indeed, the Jews were the majority in Jerusalem a quarter century before Herzl convened the first Zionist Congress in Basel in 1897.

In 1860 Jerusalem's Jewish population had grown so large that a new residence area had to be built outside the Old City for the first time in history, and the past 150 years have seen the growth of many new Jewish neighborhoods in Jerusalem. But the Western Wall inside the ancient Jewish Quarter remains the focus of reverence, and worshippers in synagogues throughout the world face east toward Jerusalem.

"Modern" Jerusalem history began in 1917, when British general Edmund Allenby captured the city from the Turks during World War I. The British occupation and the League of Nations Mandate that followed lasted until 1948, a tumultuous and significant three decades. As Jewish and Arab nationalisms emerged in those years, Jerusalem became the center of conflict.

Anti-Jewish riots spurred on by Arab leaders erupted in the 1920s and 1930s. An August 1929 Arab attack in the biblical city of Hebron, south of Jerusalem, killed sixty-seven Jews, a number that today seems insignificant when measured against the Holocaust. But the Hebron murders, especially of women, children, and yeshiva students, stunned the global Jewish community. One result of the 1929 Hebron riots was the formation of a Jewish self-defense force, the *Haganah*, which later became the nucleus of the Israel Defense Forces.

Some of the attacks on Jews in the years before World War II were inspired by the Muslim Grand Mufti of Jerusalem, Haj Amin al-Huseini (1895–1974), who collaborated with the Nazis during the war. A famous picture taken in November 1941 shows the Grand Mufti in Berlin conferring with Adolf Hitler about "the Jewish problem" in the Middle East.[9]

The British Mandate period was filled with charges and counter-charges. Jewish leaders accused the British of aiding and arming the Arabs, while the latter were convinced Great Britain favored the Jews. The British administration, headquartered in Jerusalem, was frequently inept, malicious, and insensitive (an Arab was appointed mayor, ignoring the Jewish majority in the city), and at its end in May 1948, was morally and politically bankrupt.

Despite Arab opposition and the British White Paper, which limited Jewish immigration to Palestine during the Holocaust years of the 1930s and 1940s, the Jewish population of Jerusalem had reached one hundred thousand when Israel achieved its independence.[10]

When the British Union Jack was lowered in Jerusalem for the last time, it was not replaced by a flag of another foreign occupying power, but rather by the blue and white Star of David ushering in the "Third Jewish Commonwealth," the modern State of Israel.

The Arab Siege of Jerusalem

During the fighting in 1948–49, the Jews of Jerusalem were almost starved to death by an Arab blockade of the city. The siege was broken, but at a high cost; about fifteen hundred Israelis, men and women, died to save the city. Based on the 1948 Jewish population of Israel, it was the equivalent of the United States today losing nearly seventy thousand people in a single campaign. When the 1949 armistice ended the fighting, a new ordeal faced Jerusalem.

For the first time in history, Jerusalem was physically divided between two adversaries: Israel and Jordan. The latter held the Old City and eastern Jerusalem with the important exception of Mount Scopus, while Israel controlled the western parts of the city.

It was an intolerable situation for any city, and the physical rupture in Jerusalem remained until the June 1967 war. Between 1948 and 1967, fifty-five synagogues were destroyed in the Jordanian sector of Jerusalem, and the Western Wall area became a slum. Like Berlin of the time, Jerusalem was severed by barbed wire, minefields, and concrete walls. Every year innocent civilians in the city were victims of the sporadic shooting that erupted across the jagged truce lines.

Maimonides' Face in the Ruins

During my July 1967 visit to Jerusalem immediately after the Six-Day War and the Israeli victory that reunified the city, I was shocked by the wrecked condition of the Jewish Quarter, and my photos reveal synagogues and schools in rubble, with some former Jewish institutional buildings serving as stables for donkeys.

My most poignant moment was walking through the Jewish Quarter and discovering children's school notebooks written in Hebrew in 1948 shortly before the Old City was captured by the Jordanians. The face of Maimonides was on the covers of some of the notebooks scattered under the debris and animal feces that had accumulated in the nearly twenty years of neglect.

Today, the once-abandoned Jewish Quarter is rebuilt, a model of careful historical restoration and new construction. Jews once again live amid many academies, synagogues, and community institutions. On each visit to Israel, I take photos of the same scenes I first recorded on film in 1967. The extraordinary changes are startling and represent one more chapter in the long story of Jerusalem.

Between 1948 and 1967, Jordan violated Article Eight of the armistice agreement, which provided free access to the Jewish holy places and cultural institutions under its control as a result of the war. During the period of a divided city, Jews were forbidden to visit the Western Wall, the Mount of Olives Cemetery, Rachel's Tomb in Bethlehem, and the Tomb of the Patriarchs in Hebron.

All Jews in the world, not just Israelis, were barred from their holy places, a total disregard of the armistice provisions. Muslims living in Israel were not permitted to visit the Old City, the site of the Dome of the Rock and the al-Aqsa Mosque. Christians in Israel received a slight concession. Twice a year—on Christmas and Easter—they were allowed to enter the Old City to pray at their holy places, most notably the Church of the Holy Sepulchre and the Garden of Gethsemane. Israel abolished all restrictions to Jerusalem's holy places in 1967.

Once Israel gained control of the entire city of Jerusalem, a nagging demand soon arose: calls for the "internationalization" of the city. When the United Nations General Assembly voted in November 1947 to partition Palestine into a Jewish and an Arab state (the original "two-state solution"), the UN also called for the city to be placed under international control as a *corpus separatum.* However, in the years when the city was divided, the calls for internationalization were muted or nonexistent. They were heard again only after the 1967 war and the reunification of Jerusalem under Israeli sovereignty.[11]

In 1947, the Jewish leadership reluctantly accepted the internationalization plan in the hope that the Holy City, sacred to three great religious faiths, might be spared conflict. However, the Arab states not only rejected the UN partition plan, but they also said no to any hint of internationalization, claiming instead the entire city was Arab. That position changed after Israel secured western Jerusalem and Mount Scopus in 1949. Every Arab state except for Jordan, which held eastern Jerusalem, supported international governance of the entire city, but Jordan's displeasure, a de facto veto, guaranteed the scheme was buried for nineteen years. With the passage of time since 1967, talk of internationalization has faded, but it is instructive to briefly review why the plan attracted attention from a coalition of political and religious supporters.

Internationalization of Jerusalem: Dead on Arrival

To Western ears, the internationalization of Jerusalem seemed a sensible approach, although the not-so-hidden condescending assumption was that neither Israelis nor Arabs—Jews and Muslims—were capable of or even deserved to have sovereignty over a city as precious as Jerusalem.

For many years, the Vatican supported internationalization, but beginning in 1967 the Holy See modified its position. The Holy See owns only 17 percent of the Christian holy places and sites in Jerusalem; the majority of the religious properties are owned by various Greek Orthodox, Greek Catholic, Coptic, Armenian, and Ethiopian church bodies—all of which opposed internationalization. They feared internationalization would give greater control of Jerusalem's Christian sites and institutions to the

Roman Catholic Church, which has significant influence in Europe and the Western Hemisphere.

When the Vatican and Israel signed the Fundamental Agreement on December 30, 1993, which established full and formal diplomatic relations, there was no mention of Jerusalem's status in the document's fifteen separate articles.[12] The Vatican's position, one shared by many other nations, is that Jerusalem's status must be the result of negotiations between Israel and its Arab partners in the peace process. It cannot be imposed from the outside—not by the UN, the Vatican, the United States, or any combination of international players.

In addition to Israel's positive policies relating to holy places, there is another reason internationalization of the city has been relegated to the dustbin of history. The world has seen that divided or internationalized cities are not stable or successful arrangements. Berlin following World War II is the prime example of the failure of internationalization, even when only *four* nations were involved: the United States, Britain, the former Soviet Union, and France.

That same quartet gave up international control of Vienna in 1955, and Berlin, at first broken up into four zones in 1945, became a bitterly divided city that included the infamous Berlin Wall, which finally came down in 1989. Many believe the "Free City" of Danzig, another failure of international control, contributed to the start of World War II.

An internationalized city cannot be effectively governed by an outside consortium or committee. Every new road, sewage plant, school, hospital, water system, roadway, electric power station, or municipal tax policy requires approval from either a cumbersome UN bureaucracy or a fragile coalition of nations. Such a dismal project is destined to fail.

Israel has shown that it is willing to make significant compromises to preserve Arab autonomy in the city. The plans for Jerusalem presented by former Israeli prime minister Ehud Barak in late 2000 to U.S. president Bill Clinton and Palestine Liberation

Organization leader Yasser Arafat were so sweeping that much of Israeli public opinion was opposed to the prime minister's proposal. But even the Barak plan, with its major concessions regarding Jewish sovereignty in Jerusalem, was not acceptable to Arafat, who wanted Palestinian control of the entire city.[13]

Only the Jewish people and their independent commonwealths have made Jerusalem their capital throughout thousands of years of history, beginning with King David. On the two occasions in history when Arabs had the opportunity to select the city as a capital, they failed to do so. In the Middle Ages, they chose Ramla, a town near the Mediterranean coastline, and in 1948 the Jordanians opted for Amman instead of Jerusalem.[14]

10 Why There Is Only One Holocaust

S*hoah,* a Hebrew biblical term, is increasingly being used instead of the Greek word *holocaust* to describe Nazi Germany's mass murder of six million Jews between 1933 and 1945. The word *holocaust* is derived from two Greek terms: *holos,* or "whole," and *kaustos,* or "burnt"; that is, a burnt sacrifice offered to God.

The word *shoah* appears three times in the *Tanach:*

> Evil is coming upon you.... Disaster is falling upon you which you will not be able to appease; coming upon you suddenly is ruin [*shoah*] of which you know nothing.
>
> —Isaiah 47:11, JPS

> Let disaster [*shoah*] overtake them unawares.
>
> —Psalm 35:8, JPS

> Wasted from want and starvation, they flee to a parched land, to the gloom of desolate [*shoah*] wasteland.
>
> —Job 30:3, JPS

The Vatican, one of the first Christian bodies to use "Shoah" in its documents instead of the better-known "Holocaust," believes the Hebrew word more accurately describes that singular horrific event. *Shoah* means death by calamitous devastation, and its contemporary

149

usage connects the biblical term to the twentieth-century crematoria of the Nazi German death camps. The Nazis and their accomplices burned the bodies of many Jewish victims after first murdering them by poison gas, bullets, hanging, drowning, strangulation, beatings, medical experimentation, dehydration, starvation, or disease. Because of its scriptural roots and its modern meaning, "Shoah" can never describe any other human or natural disaster.

Krister Stendahl attempted to make "Holocaust" a distinctive historical term as well. He insisted that after World War II, no plural ending could be added to the word and it must always be spelled with the capital letter *H.* For him, the term can only relate to the Nazi mass murder of Jews. But Stendahl was unsuccessful in his efforts.

If Everything Is a Holocaust ...

Unfortunately, the word has become commonplace and is today routinely used as a convenient label for almost any horrendous event. But if every hurricane, fire, tsunami, tornado, earthquake, mudslide, flood, coal-mine collapse, avalanche, and even recent examples of genocide are all described as "holocausts," the word loses any unique or potent meaning. Calling every natural or human calamity a "holocaust" minimizes the horror of each disaster. The victims of such events are entitled to more than a handy "one size fits all" term that cheapens and discounts the particular catastrophe.

When I meet Holocaust survivors (their number decreases each year as they die natural deaths), I am at first humbled in their presence, unable to comprehend their experiences. But soon I become filled with dread. That is because I was born during the 1930s, and had my birthplace been Transylvania in Europe instead of Pennsylvania in the United States, I, too, would likely have been one of the six million murdered Jews. I am a "geographical survivor," along with other Jews of my generation.

I can never forget that mass murder was the official government policy of a modern nation-state. Indeed, it was a primary goal of Nazi Germany. As we move further away from that terrible period of history, it is important to remember the Shoah was not the work of freelance "rogue" anti-Semites who acted independently from the Nazi German regime in Berlin.

The Ultimate Source of the Shoah

The oft-heard excuse expressed by many Germans after the Shoah that "I was only following orders" is filled with profound moral and ethical questions. The "orders," whether written or oral, to murder millions of people, especially Jews, came from the highest level of the German government—Adolf Hitler.

Richard J. Evans, in his *The Third Reich at War*, writes, "It is clear that the mass murder of ... Jews ... was above all, a reflection of Hitler's own personal desires and beliefs, repeatedly articulated both in public and in private."[1]

On February 14, 1942, Hitler told Josef Goebbels, his propaganda minister: "[I am] determined to clear up the Jews of Europe without compunction.... We must accelerate this process with cold ruthlessness."[2]

Nor was the Shoah carried out by a few pathological and mentally deranged Nazi leaders who seduced an entire nation of eighty million people to support and take part in radical evil. To believe that is to shun moral responsibility and to engage in historical amnesia. It is a cop-out that excuses too many people and elevates wishful thinking into a simplistic, false explanation of the Shoah.

The mass murders were not an aberration. Rather, as recent scholarly studies have shown, "ordinary people" repeatedly engaged in heinous lethal crimes. Personal diaries, photographs, letters, and other primary source materials from the Holocaust period document the widespread belief among Germans and others that killing Jews was an essential step required to rid the world of a human pestilence.

Another belief is that only Nazi elite SS units and the Gestapo carried out the mass murders. In this view, the German army, the

Wehrmacht, and the various police forces did not participate in the "final solution" to the so-called Jewish question. Such a belief is a lie.

Christopher R. Browning's 1992 book *Ordinary Men: Reserve Battalion 101 and the Final Solution in Poland* is a description of how a group of five hundred men from Hamburg formed Reserve Police Battalion 101 and relentlessly killed thousands of Jews in German-occupied Poland. Many in the Battalion were not members of the Nazi party, the Gestapo, the SS, or the German army. They were "ordinary" policemen.

But because of the latent anti-Semitism that existed in Germany prior to 1933, and especially as a result of Nazi anti-Jewish indoctrination after Hitler gained power, the Hamburg policemen were conditioned to the mass murder of Jewish civilians. Jews were considered a biological threat to the purity of the *Herrenvolk,* or "Master Race."[3]

Another explanation for the Battalion's bloody behavior can be credited to the peer pressure found in every military or police unit. There was the insistence to "carry out the mission," even if that mission meant the slaughter of innocent people.

But in 1996 Daniel Jonah Goldhagen, a former associate professor of political science at Harvard, criticized Browning's work, believing there were serious inadequacies in *Ordinary Men.* In response to Browning, Goldhagen published *Hitler's Willing Executioners: Ordinary Germans and the Holocaust,* in which he asserted there was a long-standing embedded "eliminationalist anti-Semitism" that conditioned the German people to commit genocide once the Nazi government made it legal, imperative, and a fundamental national policy.[4]

It is beyond the scope of this book to enter into the Browning-Goldhagen controversy, but both books, written a half century after the Shoah, are proof that the Holocaust and the disturbing questions it raises will not soon go away and that historians have not "moved on" to explore more recent topics. The opposite is true. Scholarly and popular interest in the Holocaust is increasing, not decreasing.

Nazi Collaborators in Europe

I cannot forget that the Shoah was aided and abetted by fervent Nazi collaborators who were not Germans. They resided through-out the continent that Pope John Paul II called "Christian Europe." Europe may have produced great art, literature, music, science, medicine, architecture, and other achievements, but dur-ing the twentieth century, it was both the source and the scene of genocide, vile hatreds, and the terrifying use of political power by three totalitarian systems—Fascism, Nazism, and Communism—whose collective crimes against the human race resist adequate words of description and condemnation.

As the years slip by and personal memories of the Shoah become more distant, our feelings and emotions can become inured to the radical evil of that era. The brutal events tend to become a blurry statistic—six million—devoid of the fact that each victim, as Pope Benedict XVI declared in May 2009 at the Yad Vashem Holocaust memorial, had a name, a family, a life filled with dreams, aspirations, achievements, failures, setbacks, and loves—the stuff of human existence. The victims, the pope warned, must never become a number, an abstraction.[5]

Three years earlier during a visit to Auschwitz-Birkenau, Benedict said:

> The rulers of the Third Reich wanted to crush the entire Jewish people.... [B]y wiping out this people, they intended to kill the God who called Abraham, who spoke on Sinai and laid down principles to serve as a guide for mankind, prin-ciples that remain eternally valid. "It is in pondering her own mystery that the Church, the People of God of the New Covenant, discovers her own profound bond with the Jews, who were chosen by the Lord before all others to receive his word" [cf. *Catechism of the Catholic Church*, 839]. The Jewish faith, unlike other non-Christian religions, is already a response to God's revelation in the Old Covenant. To the Jews "belong the sonship, the glory, the covenants, the

giving of the law, the worship, and the promises; to them belong the patriarchs and of their race, according to the flesh is the Christ" [Romans 9:4–5], "for the gifts and the call of God are irrevocable!" [Romans 11:29].[6]

A Teenager's Immortal Diary

A young girl's diary written during World War II, when two Jewish families and a friend hid in an Amsterdam attic in a desperate effort to escape arrest and death, has permanently captured the imagination of millions of readers. The first diary entry of Anne Frank (1929–45) was on July 6, 1942, and her writing abruptly ended on August 1, 1944, just days before she and the rest of the hidden Jews were arrested and deported from Holland to Nazi death camps. Anne and her older sister, Margot, died of typhus in the Bergen-Belsen camp in Germany during March 1945, two months before the end of the war in Europe.

Since it was first published in the original Dutch in 1947 and in English five years later, *The Diary of Anne Frank* has been translated into many other languages. A long-running Broadway stage play and a Hollywood film dramatized Anne's story in the 1950s. For millions of people, the play and the movie, both award winners, were their initial encounters with the Holocaust, and *The Diary of Anne Frank* still remains for many their sole reference point about the Shoah.

Critics have charged the drama and the movie were deliberately "sanitized" to downplay Anne's Jewishness and to focus instead on the universal message of the *Diary*, especially this well-known quotation, which was written on July 15, 1944, just three weeks before Anne and the others were discovered and deported to Nazi death camps:

> That's the difficulty in these times, ideals, dreams and cherished hopes rise within us, only to meet the horrible truth and be shattered. It's really a wonder that I haven't dropped all my ideals, because they seem so absurd and impossible to

carry out. Yet I keep them, because in spite of everything I still believe that people are really good at heart.[7]

Lillian Hellman, an American Jewish playwright and author, assisted with the final wording of the play's script. She has been accused of changing Anne Frank's original diary entry in an effort to make it more "universal." Anne originally wrote, "Perhaps through Jewish suffering the world will learn good."[8] Hellman changed that diary entry to "Jews were not the only ones who suffered from the Nazis."[9]

Often overlooked is this specific Jewish reference in the *Diary* that was written on April 11, 1944:

Who has inflicted this upon us? Who has made us Jews different from all other people? Who has allowed us to suffer so terribly until now? It is God that has made us as we are, but it will be God, too, who will rise up again. If we bear all this suffering and if there are still Jews left, when it is over, then Jews, instead of being doomed, will be held up as an example. Who knows, it might even be our religion from which the world and all peoples learn good, and for that reason and that reason only do we have to suffer now. We can never be just Netherlanders, or just English, or representatives of any country for that matter, we will always remain Jews, but we want to, too.[10]

Six million is an overwhelming statistic, but one teenage girl is a reminder that Jews died one by one by one. The Italian chemist and novelist Primo Levi, who survived Auschwitz and the Shoah wrote:

One single Anne Frank moves us more than the countless others who suffered just as she did but whose faces have remained in the shadows. Perhaps it is better that way; if we were capable of taking in all the suffering of all those people, we would not be able to live.[11]

To overcome the irreversible chronological problem of moving further away from the horrid events and the natural deaths of the dwindling number of Holocaust survivors, Christians and Jews need to connect themselves spiritually and emotionally, difficult as that is, with those who actually confronted an evil that had never been seen before. Christians and Jews need to link themselves with the men and women who faced what we can only begin to comprehend. It is and will always be a painful but necessary exercise.

Victims, Victimizers, and Onlookers

The majority of European Christians during the Holocaust were either victimizers or passive onlookers, perhaps tacitly approving of the cruelty that was taking place in their midst. However, some Christians did become victims themselves, including Gypsies, homosexuals, the mentally ill, the physically infirm, jailed criminals, and a few political and religious dissidents who opposed Nazism and paid with their lives for their bravery.

But for Jews there was no choice. Elie Wiesel has put the Nazi period in perspective: "Not every victim was a Jew, but every Jew was a victim."[12]

Just as Anne Frank, one person, is symbolic of individual victims, likewise the fate of the large Nazi-created Jewish ghetto in Lodz, Poland, a city southwest of Warsaw, represents the hideous situation Jewish community leaders, especially those appointed by their sadistic Nazi oppressors, faced during the Shoah.

The Lodz Ghetto merits attention because it presents an important aspect of the Holocaust that is unknown or long forgotten by Jews and Christians. The Lodz tragedy reaches across the decades and asks haunting questions many people try to avoid thinking about, much less answering: How would we have acted during the Shoah? Would we have "gone along to get along" in the hope of surviving a dangerous, frightening situation? What influences, if any, would have shaped our responses? Family and parental values? Political views? Religious beliefs? Personal friendships? None of the above?

Shortly after invading Poland on September 1, 1939, the Nazis established the Lodz Ghetto. The city was an important textile-producing center of about seven hundred thousand residents, one-third of whom were Jews. In May 1940, the ghetto was physically sealed, preventing Jews from leaving, and any escape effort was a hazardous undertaking. Jews captured trying to exit the ghetto were executed. If someone did escape, there was little or no assurance that the mostly Catholic Polish population living outside the ghetto would offer any aid in the form of food, water, new clothing without the yellow Star of David Jews were forced to wear on their garments, or even a temporary hiding place.

Some Poles did save Jewish lives during the Holocaust. This was a perilous act during the five-year German occupation. Every member of a Polish household was executed if any one of them hid, fed, or even offered water to a Jew. Indeed, any assistance was a capital crime. It was the harshest Nazi decree of its type in all of occupied Europe.

Nearly 27 percent of the Righteous Gentiles were Poles. Some Christians and Jews have pointed to this statistic as "proof" that Poland was not infected with traditional anti-Semitism. However, critics, also both Christians and Jews, question that argument, claiming the high percentage of Poles is because nearly 3.5 million Jews lived in prewar Poland, the largest number in any European nation.

In 1939, Jews constituted about a tenth of Poland's total population. In addition, critics point out that many thousands of Jews from other European countries were transported to the large Nazi death camps located in Poland. Finally, they argue that a better measurement is the percentage, not the actual number, of a nation's citizens who actually saved Jews from death. Bulgaria and Denmark are cited as countries with a better record than Poland. The debate about Polish behavior toward Jews during World War II shows no signs of abating.

In 1942 more than four hundred thousand Jews from all parts of Europe were locked inside the cramped, filthy, and disease-ridden Lodz Ghetto. Imprisoned behind walls and fences, the trapped Jews had a leader, one of their own, forced upon them by the Germans: sixty-five-year-old Mordechai Chaim Rumkowski, whom his Nazi masters designated as *Judenaelteste*, "the Eldest of the Jews." In the prewar period, Rumkowski had headed a children's orphanage.

Deluded Leader or Nazi Puppet?

Historians argue whether Rumkowski was a puppet, a collaborator with the Germans, or whether he was a brave man given heart-breaking, impossible responsibilities. Because the Jewish laborers inside the ghetto supplied the German army with uniforms and other articles, Rumkowski mistakenly believed "his" Jews in Lodz could survive the war if they worked hard and provided what their Nazi tormentors desired. "You work! You live!" was his hopeful but ultimately false mantra.

To his credit, the Jewish ghetto leader set up a large number of schools, medical clinics, pharmacies, community food kitchens, and other public facilities. Rumkowski, although totally subordinate to the Germans, became an overbearing leader himself whose actions provoked hatred and contempt among many of his "constituents."

Rumkowski was wrong in his belief the ghetto residents would survive through work. By September 1944, almost every one of the four hundred thousand ghetto Jews (including Rumkowski and his family) were deported and murdered in Auschwitz, Chelmo, and other Nazi death camps. When the Soviet army captured Lodz in January 1945, only eight hundred Jews remained in the ghetto.

The German masters of the ghetto played a ghoulish game with their appointed Jewish leader, seeming to promise him and the ghetto residents physical survival and deliverance if they performed "important" tasks in support of the Nazi war effort. The Germans perpetuated this grotesque lie even when doomed Jews entered Auschwitz and other "death factories." Posted above the entrance gates was the chilling sardonic slogan *Arbeit Macht Frei,* "Work Makes for Freedom." Rumkowski believed those three words also applied to the Lodz Ghetto.

As the year 1942 unfolded, the Germans began their draconian squeeze on both the ghetto residents and Rumkowski personally. They demanded twenty thousand young Jewish children under the age of ten for "transport" to certain death in an extermination center in Poland. "The Eldest of the Jews" was assured that if that horrendous sacrifice was made, if that monstrous "quota" was met, the rest of the ghetto inhabitants would be safe. What would any of us have done in such a brutal, cynical situation? What did Rumkowski do?

"Give Me Your Children!"

On September 4, 1942, he delivered one of the most heartrending speeches uttered in human history. His address to the wretched Jews in the ghetto is mandatory reading today for anyone who is quick to judge Jewish behavior and actions during the Shoah.

The Germans demanded that Rumkowski deliver Jewish children to certain death. He was also required to surrender the ghetto's elderly and infirm—all with the Nazi "promise" that the rest of the ghetto population would survive. Rumkowski's plea to his fellow Jews captures his pain and self-delusion, just as Anne Frank's diary captures her tender hopes and unfulfilled dreams. His public anguish of yielding up children, the sick, and the elderly to his satanic masters must be an integral part of any authentic Christian-Jewish dialogue alongside the private words of a brilliant young girl "coming of age":

> The ghetto has been struck a hard blow. [The Germans] demand what is most dear—children and old people.... In my old age I am forced to stretch out my hands and to beg: "Brothers and sisters, give them to me!—Fathers and mothers, give me your children."... I was given the order to send away more than 20,000 Jews from the ghetto, and if I did

not—"we will do it ourselves."... Should we have accepted this and carried it out ourselves, or left it to others?... [H]owever difficult it [is] going to be ... I must carry out this difficult and bloody operation, I must cut off limbs in order to save the body! I must take away children, and if I do not, others too will be taken....

I have come like a robber, to take from you what is dearest to your heart. I tried everything I knew to get the bitter sentence cancelled. When it could not be cancelled, I tried to lessen the sentence.... But they would not yield.... There are many people in this ghetto who suffer from tuberculosis, whose days or perhaps weeks are numbered.... Give me these sick people, and perhaps it will be possible to save the healthy in their place. I know how precious each one of the sick is in his home.... But at a time of such decrees one must weigh up and measure who should be saved, who can be saved and who may be saved.

Common sense requires us to know that those must be saved who can be saved and who have a chance of being saved and not those whom there is no chance to save in any case.... [13]

Just as he summed up the impact of Anne Frank, it was Primo Levi who succinctly described the dilemma faced by Chaim Rumkowski, that:

we are all in the ghetto, that the ghetto is walled in, that outside the ghetto reign the lords of death, and that close by the train [traveling to a death camp] is waiting.[14]

For too long, the remembrance of the Shoah has evolved solely into Jewish victimhood, and indeed, they were victims of an unprecedented campaign of mass murder, and Christian sympathy and empathy are to be commended. Despite the attempt to make them into *umschlag*, the German word for trash or soiled goods, the six million Jews were fully human. They were and they must always remain more than victims.

But just as most Christians of the period were onlookers or observers of the tragedy, so too, many Christians today are impatient with the constant references to the Holocaust and the large number of plays, films, music, books, sculpture, literature, diaries, poetry, paintings, and dance that focus on the Shoah. Such Christians urge the Jewish community to "get over the Holocaust" and to "move on."

But when a family is murdered, do we expect the victim's relatives and friends to "get over" their tragedy and "move on"? Do we expect the African American community to "get over" the human slavery that legally existed in this land from 1619 until the end of the Civil War in 1865? Do we expect such unnatural behavior from the descendants of Native Americans who were expelled from their hereditary lands by President Andrew Jackson and forced to move westward, alone and defenseless during what has come to be called the "Trail of Tears"? Do we expect today's Native Americans to forget Jackson's 1833 speech—words that Hitler could have spoken exactly one hundred years later, not about Indian tribes in America, but about Jews in Europe:

> My original convictions upon this subject have been confirmed by the course of events for several years, and experience is every day adding to their strength. That those tribes cannot exist surrounded by our settlements and in continual contact with our citizens is certain. They have neither the intelligence, the industry, the moral habits, nor the desire of improvement which are essential to any favorable change in their condition. Established in the midst of another and a superior race, and without appreciating the causes of their inferiority or seeking to control them, they must necessarily yield to the force of circumstances and ere long disappear.[15]

And the families of loyal Japanese Americans who were rounded up from their homes in early 1942 and by presidential decree physically moved to detention camps because their ancestry instantly condemned them as disloyal Americans—do we expect them to forget?

The historian George Santayana's famous quotation may be a cliché, but even clichés are often true: "Those who cannot remember the past are condemned to repeat it."

Jews then and Jews today are more than victims. Jews whose self-identity is focused solely on suffering and persecution do themselves and their families grave harm. Yet Jews will always remember they were Hitler's primary victims, just as they do not forget their slavery in ancient Egypt or the centuries of degradation in Europe that culminated in the Shoah.

The Eternal Cavalcade

Christians and even some Jews themselves need to recognize there is more to Jewish life than recounting the catastrophe of the Holocaust, no matter how reverential the remembrance may be. At the same time, there can be no meaningful or purposeful encounter between Christians and Jews without addressing the evil of the Shoah and the continuing cancer that is anti-Semitism today. A balance must be struck between being trapped in the dismal decades of the 1930s and 1940s and blithely "moving on" without coming to terms with that past.

Since 1945 Jews have risen from the shadows of victimization and moved into the sunlight of creativity, joy, and achievement. While they recall what happened to them as a people, they must recount and represent more than victimization to their children and grandchildren.

That is difficult to do—to remember, to never forget, but always to return to the living stage of human history and participate in the cavalcade of Jewish existence, an existence that re-creates itself with each new generation because no one—not Anne Frank, not Primo Levi, and perhaps not even Chaim Rumkowski—wants that cavalcade to end.

Since its founding, the State of Israel has honored more than twenty-two thousand "Righteous Gentiles" who put their lives at risk during World War II to help save a Jewish life. The Yad Vashem Holocaust Research Center in Jerusalem contains a Hall of Remembrance, a museum, a synagogue, a research center, a library, and archives. The center develops teaching material about the Holocaust for schools not only in Israel but also throughout the world. It has placed online more than three million names of those murdered during the Shoah.

Additionally, in 1993 the United States Holocaust Memorial Museum was opened in Washington, D.C., and it contains extensive historical material, as well as exhibits and an educational program. Since its opening, it has drawn large numbers of visitors.

Christians today have an obligation that transcends remembrance. Christians are more than onlookers; they are participants with Jews, who are more than victims. They are partners in remembering, partners in building human bridges of mutual respect and understanding, partners in confronting the radical evils of today, partners in the quest for the city on the hill, and partners in creating the just society.

Being solely a victim or solely an onlooker results in paralysis. Christians and Jews cannot be trapped in ghettoes of perpetual rage and anger or in ghettoes of perpetual indifference and apathy. Unlike the bewildered and hapless Chaim Rumkowski, they are not being asked to give up their children.

Annual Holocaust commemorations are increasing in many American churches, and in April 1994 there was an official Holocaust Commemoration Concert at the Vatican, where I represented the American Jewish community. Pope John Paul II spoke that day with eloquence about the evils of the Holocaust:

We are gathered ... to commemorate the Holocaust of millions of Jews.... This is our commitment. We would risk causing the victims of the most atrocious deaths to die again if

we do not have an ardent desire for justice, if we do not
commit ourselves, each according to his own capacities,
to ensure that evil does not prevail over good as it did for
millions of the children of the Jewish people.... Do not forget us.[16]

It is impossible to minimize the Holocaust's importance in relations between Christians and Jews. We cannot understand today's
Jewish community either in Israel or in the Diaspora without confronting the Shoah. The human loss is beyond measurement, and
many believe the moral questions raised by the Shoah defy adequate comprehension or meaning.

When it became clear that hundreds of thousands of baptized
Christians had murdered the kin people of Jesus and that Christian
church bodies, their leaders and members, had been mainly silent
in the face of Nazism, it was apparent that a line of cosmic importance had been irrevocably crossed. Systemic radical evil had tri-
umphed over Christian moral teachings.

Was Nazism, as some claim, a secular pagan movement that
was also anti-Christian at its core? What roles did Christians and
their churches play during the Holocaust years? While some
Christians resisted Nazism and saved Jews from death, most did
not. And what was the role of the Vatican led by Pope Pius XII during the Holocaust and in the years immediately following World
War II? This last question remains a source of continuing controversy between Catholics and Jews and cannot be definitively settled
until all appropriate archival materials from the period are studied
by Christian and Jewish scholars.

Responsibility, Not Guilt

Today's Christians, most of whom were born after 1945, should not
feel personal guilt for the horrific events carried out in the heart
of Christian Europe. Rather, they need to take responsibility to
educate themselves and church members about the Shoah and the
widespread collapse of Christian morality and ethics.

In 1995 the Alliance of Baptists in the United States issued a statement on Christian-Jewish relations recognizing that the Shoah was made possible by

> centuries of Christian teaching and church-sanctioned action directed against the Jews simply because they were Jews. As Baptist Christians we are the inheritors of and, in our turn, have been the transmitters of a theology which lays the blame for the death of Jesus at the feet of the Jews … a theology which has valued conversion over dialogue, invective over understanding, and prejudice over knowledge.[17]

The Alliance also confessed sins of "complicity … of silence … of indifference and inaction" to the horrors of the Holocaust.

Emil Fackenheim, a Jewish philosopher born in Germany, warned against granting Hitler a "posthumous victory" because of compassion fatigue, emotional indifference, spiritual apathy, or emotional lethargy. Failing to make the Holocaust a central part of every interreligious encounter would do just that.[18]

11 The Meaning of Modern Israel for Christians and Jews

Two dates involving modern Israel are etched in my mind: May 14, 1948, and June 5, 1967. The unforgettable events of those days permanently impacted me, as they did millions of other people.

The 1948 date was when David Ben-Gurion, Israel's first prime minister, read the Jewish state's Declaration of Independence in a Tel Aviv art museum. The document, signed by thirty-seven leaders of the Jewish community in British Mandate Palestine, marked Israel's rebirth, coming 1,878 years after the Roman destruction of the Holy Temple in Jerusalem.

Ben-Gurion, the first to sign the Declaration, ended the historic meeting without a rhetorical flourish; he offered neither soaring prose nor lyrical poetry. Instead, in his typical fashion, he simply said, "The State of Israel is established. This meeting is adjourned."

While the state may have been officially "established," it required a war with Israel's Arab neighbors to guarantee its existence, not unlike the eighteenth-century American War of Independence against the British.

The second date was the start of the Six-Day War, the conflict in which Israel defeated a host of hostile Arab nations and gained control of Jerusalem, the Golan Heights, the Sinai Peninsula, and the West Bank of the Jordan River. The seemingly miraculous victory was achieved only after Israel's citizens endured a fretful month filled with fears of a second Holocaust.

I recount my personal experiences on those two days not because they were in any way unique to me. On the contrary, they represent what millions of Jews throughout the world felt in 1948 and again in 1967.

An understanding and recognition of the intense emotions surrounding those two dates is necessary in encounters between Jews and Christians. That is because Christian-Jewish relations are more than scholarly articles, academic conferences, or the exchange of basic information about the two faith communities.

In 1948 I was a youngster growing up in Alexandria, Virginia, amid the comfort and security of post–World War II America and within a Jewish community that had escaped the horrors of the Holocaust. But it was also a community that recognized the new responsibilities thrust upon it following the virtual destruction of the once vibrant Jewish communities in Europe.

My father, an army lieutenant colonel, had, like many other Americans, served in the U.S. military during World War II, and as a result of that service he had come into possession of several German rifles and other weapons that he hid in our attic. One evening during the early spring of 1948, several men whom I had never seen before came to our home and waited in our living room while my father climbed up into the family attic.

The men spoke to each other in a language I easily recognized as Hebrew. My dad soon returned with the weapons; they were covered with a white bedsheet, and he carefully handed them to our visitors. One of them shook hands with my father and said, "Thank you and shalom."

After the men left, I inquired about the unusual scene I had witnessed. My father told me the weapons were for "the *Haganah* ... they need lots of help." A shiver of excitement ran through my body when I heard his words.

Although I had little knowledge of the efforts then under way to establish a Jewish state in the Middle East, I did know that the *Haganah* (the Hebrew term for "defense organization") was the underground Jewish fighting force in Palestine. I was thrilled and proud our family was supporting the *Haganah* in such a tangible way. A few weeks later things became even more spine-tingling.

Synagogue Applause for Harry Truman

Our family regularly attended Sabbath eve services at our Alexandria synagogue. However, Friday, May 14, 1948, was different. That night we traveled to the Washington Hebrew Congregation in the nation's capital. The large sanctuary was filled with apprehensive worshippers who, like my parents, were aware the British Mandate in Palestine was ending that day, and no one was certain what would happen next.

Midway through the prayers, a man ascended the bimah, the raised podium in the sanctuary, and handed the rabbi a note. After quickly reading it, the rabbi dramatically interrupted the service and announced, "President Truman has just recognized the new Jewish state that came into existence today." There was immediate applause from the congregation—the first time I had ever heard people clapping in a synagogue.[1]

As soon as the service concluded, we drove to 2210 Massachusetts Avenue, NW (it was soon to be the location of the first Israeli embassy in Washington). Many people in front of the building were singing in Hebrew and dancing in a large circle. It was a familiar hora folk dance, and someone in the crowd told me the festivities were in honor of the news coming from Tel Aviv and the president's diplomatic recognition of the new Jewish state. Truman's action came only eleven minutes after Ben-Gurion had "adjourned" the meeting in Tel Aviv.

It was, as the cliché goes, a "night to remember." Modern Israel was the fulfillment of a dream that was thousands of years old: the physical return of the Jewish people to their biblical and spiritual homeland and the regaining of national sovereignty.

Nineteen years later, on June 5, 1967, I was the rabbi of Sinai Temple in Champaign-Urbana, Illinois. The previous weeks had been an anxious time, especially when Egyptian president Gamal Abdel Nasser unilaterally closed the strategically important Straits of Tiran to Israeli ships and all other vessels destined for the Israeli Red Sea port of Eilat. Nasser preceded this hostile action by expelling the twenty-four-hundred-man United Nations peace-keeping force that had been stationed for ten years in the Sinai Peninsula as a buffer between Egypt and Israel.

At the same time, Nasser mobilized his armed forces and moved a large number of his military near the Egyptian border with Israel. On May 30 Nasser and Jordanian king Hussein signed a five-year mutual defense pact. The vise around Israel appeared to be tightening hour by hour. (In an ironic twist of history, twenty-seven years later the same Hussein signed a peace treaty with Israel. His Israeli partners in 1994 were President Ezer Weizman and Prime Minister Yitzhak Rabin, both top generals and Jordanian foes during the Six-Day War.)

"None Will Survive"

The Arabs' hostile military actions were combined with an anti-Israel public propaganda campaign filled with threats to annihilate the Jews of Israel. On May 27, 1967, Nasser declared, "Our basic objective will be the destruction of Israel. The Arab people want to fight."[2]

On June 1, 1967, Iraq's president, Abdul Rahman Aref, spoke to his nation's air force pilots: "Our clear aim [is] wiping Israel from the map."[3] On the same day, journalists asked the Palestine Liberation Organization's chairman, Ahmed Shukairy, who preceded Yasir Arafat in that position, what would happen to Israelis, including the native-born sabras, if the Arab forces were successful in their upcoming war with the Jewish state. Shukairy ominously replied, "Those who survive will remain in Palestine. I estimate that none will survive."[4]

Those threats and the Arab military mobilization came less than twenty-five years after the Holocaust. A collective depression set in among Jews throughout the world, including me and the members of my central Illinois congregation, even though we were thousands of miles from the Middle East. We were gripped by fear that a second mass slaughter of Jews might take place if the Arabs defeated Israel. Although it was the springtime of the year, an emotional and psychological chill enveloped my spirit on the morning of June 5, 1967.

"A People Dwelling Alone"

While the U.S. government, led by President Lyndon Johnson, expressed support for Israel, its actions in that regard appeared halting and even tepid. I remember feeling that much of the world, including many political and religious leaders, had deserted the Jews of Israel, just as their predecessors had abandoned the Jews of Europe during the Shoah. The silence of much of the Christian leadership in the United States and Europe before the Six-Day War reminded me of Balaam's biblical quotation that Israel is a "people dwelling alone" (Numbers 23:9). We felt deserted by many of our Christian dialogue partners, both individually and organizationally.

There were, however, some notable exceptions, whose voices shattered the sense of being "alone." A week before the war began, a group of Christian leaders that included Dr. Martin Luther King Jr. of the Southern Christian Leadership Conference, Dr. Reinhold Niebuhr and Dr. John C. Bennett, both of New York's Union Theological Seminary, and Dr. Robert McAfee Brown of Stanford University, urged "our fellow Americans ... to support the independence, integrity and freedom of Israel."[5] A few days later, three Roman Catholic prelates—Cardinal Richard Cushing of Boston, Cardinal Lawrence Shehan of Baltimore, and Archbishop Paul Hallinan of Atlanta—issued similar statements of support for Israel.

But three major American Christian "umbrella" organizations—the Protestant/Eastern Orthodox consortium, the National Council of Churches of Christ, and the National Conference of Catholic Bishops—failed to issue any clear, unambiguous declaration supporting Israel's security and survival in the tense days before June 5.

An Obscene Comparison

In a June 26 letter to the *New York Times* (more than two weeks after the hostilities ended in the Middle East), Dr. Henry P. Van Dusen, a past president of Union Theological Seminary, wrote:

> All persons who seek to view the Middle East problem with honesty and objectivity stand aghast at Israel's onslaught, the most violent, ruthless (and successful) aggression since Hitler's blitzkrieg across Europe in 1940, aiming not at victory but at annihilation—the very objective proclaimed by Nasser and his allies which had drawn support to Israel.[6]

The Protestant leader's comparison of Israel to Nazi Germany (a theme that has constantly surfaced in the years since 1967) was too much for one of Dr. Van Dusen's former students, Dr. A. Roy Eckardt of Lehigh University:

> Perhaps the only eventuality that would mutually satisfy Communist, Arab and Christian detractors of Jews for the latter's "aggression" would be for Jews to consent to lie down and be slaughtered. At least this would fulfill one side of the traditional yearning of Christendom.[7]

Judith Hershcopf Banki of the American Jewish Committee analyzed Christian reactions to the 1967 Middle East crisis—reactions before, during, and after the six days of fighting. She concluded her report with an accurate prediction:

> No doubt the interfaith dialogue will survive the tensions created by the Middle East crisis. But if it is to reach beyond surface differences to the underlying essentials separating religious groups today, clearly the ideas and feelings of Jews and Christians about Israel, both the land and the people— with all the religious, emotional and political connotations

this word carries for both traditions—will be on the dialogue agenda for some time to come.[8]

Israel's military victory electrified the world and dispelled my depression. I felt a sense of both pride and thanksgiving. In the weeks immediately following the Six-Day War, my congregants attended religious services in larger numbers than usual to offer prayers for Israel's deliverance; they contributed generously to meet Israel's emergency financial needs; and they realized how important—indeed, how central—the existence of Israel was in defining their personal Jewish identities.

In 1968, Elie Wiesel was asked how the Six-Day War and its outcome influenced his worldview. He responded, "I would say that the change was total, for it involved my very being as both a person and as a Jew."[9]

In the years since 1967 some Christian colleagues and associates said the Jewish community misinterpreted what was widely perceived at the time as Christian indifference to Israel's fate. They correctly pointed out that since 1948 the overwhelming majority of Americans have consistently supported Israel and its difficult quest for survival and security. But they also pointed out that many leading Christian denominations in the United States have deep historical ties to their coreligionists in Arab lands, ties that include missionary efforts, even though Middle East Christians consider themselves the oldest continuous church body in the world and feel no need for Western missionaries.

Historians and military experts also reminded the Jewish community that events proved the Arab threat to Israel's survival in 1967 was more rhetorical than real. The combined armed forces of Egypt, Jordan, Syria, Iraq, and Lebanon were no match for the highly motivated and well-trained Israel Defense Forces.

The various messages, whatever their source, were clear: both Jews and Israel had "overreacted" during the run-up to the 1967 war. But such chiding and criticism, even when coming from friends, was rejected by the Jewish community.

As every psychologist and psychiatrist knows, genuine emotions cannot be summarily dismissed or minimized. What a person or a community feels about an issue frequently determines behavior and action. Although more than forty years have passed since those frightening days, 1967 remains a key moment not merely in Middle East history but in Christian-Jewish relations as well. The effects of the Six-Day War are still felt in both the geopolitical and the interreligious arenas.

Between 1948 and 1967, many American Jews perceived Israel as a distant Sparta-like state that had courageously secured its right to exist. After all, the United States, Britain, France, and even the Soviet Union had established diplomatic relations with Israel. Before 1967, few American Jews had visited Israel, and even fewer had relatives or friends who lived there. While Israel was a source of public pride, it played a tertiary role in shaping personal American Jewish identity.

In those same years, Israel hardly registered on American Christians' political or religious radar. When they did consider Israel, it was generally not seen as the world's only Jewish state, but rather as the vague "Holy Land," the place of Jesus's long-ago life and resurrection, and not a part of the modern world. But many American Christians were positively influenced by *Exodus*, Leon Uris's 1958 best-selling novel about the creation of Israel. The book was later made into a film starring Paul Newman and Eva Marie Saint.

However, many Christian missionaries to Arab countries and their like-minded colleagues in the United States remained hostile to Israeli independence and the Zionist movement that brought the state into being. Their hostility was based on several factors.

For more than 150 years American Protestant denominations, especially the Presbyterian and United Church of Christ (Congregationalists), have maintained a missionary presence in the Arab Middle East. In addition, the Catholic Church has also been active in the region. It is a mistake to underestimate the connections, both professional and personal, that grew up between Western church members and Arab Christian and Muslim communities in the Middle East.

The American Protestant missionary campaign in the Middle East that began well over a century ago was instrumental in establishing the American University in Beirut, the American University in Cairo, and Bir Zeit University in Ramallah. It is no accident that the American Colony, an aptly named Jerusalem hotel, was founded in the early 1900s by Anna and Horatio Spafford, American Protestants from Chicago. Though they were not missionaries themselves, the Spaffords' hotel served as a religious center until the 1940s.

More Arab Than the Arabs

Some American Christians who served in the Arab world or who were born and raised in that region became "more Arab than the Arabs." As a result, many Western Christians shared the Arab hostility toward Zionism and the State of Israel.

When American church personnel returned home from the Middle East, they often assumed important positions within their denominations, Christian seminaries, the U.S. government, and international relief agencies. Because many leaders of American Protestant denominations saw such people as "Middle East experts," they deferred to them for analysis and, in many cases, church policy vis-à-vis the Middle East.

Some U.S. missionaries have never visited Israel, and if they have, they met few Israeli Jews in any official capacity. Some of these same missionaries have little personal contact with the American Jewish community. This lack of contact is detrimental in any Christian-Jewish encounter that focuses on Israel and the Middle East. Failure to visit the Jewish state combined with a similar failure to engage the American Jewish community vitiates the possibility of an open and knowledgeable exchange of views.

The various interreligious guides published in the United States before the Six-Day War contain almost no mention of the modern State of Israel and its place in Christian-Jewish relations. As a result, Israel and its meaning for Christians and Jews were nearly invisible until 1967.

There are several explanations for this lacuna. The excitement of a dialogue between Christians and Jews free of overt, even covert, conversionary efforts was a novelty to both communities, and that enthusiasm was a driving force in many of the pre-1967 interreligious encounters. The United States, with its long history of church-state separation, constitutional guarantees of freedom of religion, and diverse pluralistic population, provided an excellent stage for pioneering efforts in dialogue.

In the two decades after World War II and before the Second Vatican Council, much of the interreligious conversation and contact was between Protestants and Jews, but there was an understandable tentativeness as both communities made conscious efforts not to offend the "Other," settling instead for a friendly exchange of information mixed with autobiographical information from dialogue participants.

Christians and Jews were sometimes reticent to reveal their innermost beliefs about themselves to their new interreligious partners. In the early years of the post-Holocaust dialogue, the emphasis was on Jews explaining and describing their religious beliefs, customs, and ceremonies to Christians and vice versa. The mutual exchange of religious information and data was considered paramount, to the near exclusion of political (the Middle East) themes. As a result, both communities were caught off guard by the Six-Day War's tumultuous effects.

Israel: Central to the Dialogue

But today modern Israel occupies a central place in Christian-Jewish encounters, and the word "Israel" evokes intense emotion and passion. The Jewish state's rebirth challenges traditional Christian theology. How is it that God's despised and spiritually surplus people has risen from the ashes of Auschwitz and reentered history as a free and sovereign people in their biblical homeland?

The baleful images of the exiled "wandering Jew," the eternal out-sider, along with the other anti-Jewish stereotypes and canards, have collided with the reality of the dynamic State of Israel.

Despite, or perhaps because of, the constant threats to Israel's existence, Jews share an unshakable commitment to the security and survival of the modern Jewish state. Not since the days of Bar Kochba have there been such positive Jewish emotions, pride, and fervor.

Israel has compelled Christians and Jews to examine them-selves and one another in a new light, and previously held percep-tions have been eclipsed by the creation of modern Israel. But Israel still remains the cause of misunderstanding and even antag-onism between the two groups.

Many Christians confess how little they know about modern Israel—its origins, its role in world history, its diverse population, its achievements in many fields of human endeavor, its internal and external problems, and even why Israel's national anthem is called *Hatikvah*, "The Hope."

Jews often express frustration that Christians "don't get" Israel's quest for peace based upon security and justice, even though the Jewish state has never experienced a single day of true peace with its neighbors.

But the presence of Israel in the center of Christian-Jewish relations is even more complicated. The Middle East is one of the most reported subjects in the global media, but many Christians have gained limited or inaccurate knowledge of the region from authors who are either unable or unwilling to accept the legitimacy and permanence of the Jewish state or from other authors who make exclusive, apocalyptic Christian claims for Israel.

Israel's harshest critics, including those living outside Islamic societies, contend there is no Israel, only a "Zionist entity," a "for-eign" creation that guilt-ridden Western anti-Semitic countries placed in the heart of Arab nations as compensation for the Holocaust. Critics further allege that Israel's independence was based on an "original sin," a highly charged theological term that contains more than a whiff of anti-Judaism.

Some Christians see Jews as a perpetual minority in their midst, but not as a people living as a national entity in the Holy Land. It is a view filled with irony. For centuries Jews were accused of being "rootless," "cosmopolitans," "physically weak," and eternal "outsiders." As a result of Israeli independence, Jews are now accused of being "particularistic," "militarists," "fierce warriors," "narrow nationalists," or "hung up on a tiny piece of real estate at the eastern end of the Mediterranean Sea."

At the same time, fervent Christians believe the reemergence of an independent Jewish commonwealth, the ingathering of the exiles, is a prerequisite for the Second Coming of Jesus that has been long delayed.

One Christian group does not accept the reality of Israel and sometimes supports forces that seek the Jewish state's physical destruction, while the other Christian group defines Israel in apocalyptic metaphysical terms. Neither view provides a balanced or an accurate picture of modern Israel.[10]

Yet, even as these two polarizing groups argue their opposing theological positions, daily life goes on for the nearly six million Israeli Jews who are the object of such Christian attention and debate: births and funerals, marriages and divorces, loves and hatreds.

Jews share an intense passion for the biblical homeland that has been expressed for millennia in prayers, poems, odes, songs, commentaries, sermons, plays, films, and books. This record of profound attachment to *Ha-aretz, "the* Land," is well documented.

Nevertheless, Jews are aware of modern Israel's flaws and imperfections, and the venality of some of its elected leaders. In that sense, Israel is a "normal" nation-state with its heroes and scoundrels, its achievements and errors. Yet, since Israel's birth in 1948, Jews and many others have been stirred by the existence of a democratic Jewish state that has welcomed large numbers of Jews coming "home to Zion" from more than 130 countries.

Zionism: A Tent of Meeting

Unfortunately, Zionism, the national liberation movement of the Jewish people, still remains a toxic subject for people who are either unwilling or unable to accept Israel among the family of nations. Perhaps the best way to understand Zionism is to compare it to a giant *ohel mo'ed*, Hebrew for a biblical-style "tent of meeting," where the many streams and movements that exist among Jews throughout the world can meet. It is also important to remember that neither Zionism nor the state it helped create is monolithic in nature. Rather, both are diverse, dynamic, and often contradictory, as is much of human life.

Zionism cannot be limited or reduced to a single word or a catchphrase. Zionism's goal from its inception as a modern national liberation movement beginning in the late nineteenth century—although its roots are a basic part of both biblical and Rabbinic literature—was the reestablishment of an independent Jewish state in the Land of Israel. But as Herzl noted, "Before there can be a return to Zion, there must first be a return to Judaism."[11] The two are linked together.

Modern Israel has always been a challenge to certain tenets of Christian theology. For Christians who believe that Jews are eternally punished by God for "rejecting" Jesus, Israel is a sharp rebuttal to that doctrine of faith.

Marvin R. Wilson, professor of Bible at Gordon College and a leading American Evangelical scholar, describes his view of modern Israel:

> The remarkable preservation of Israel over the centuries and her recent return to the land are in keeping with those many biblical texts which give promise of her future. But my concern and support for Israel only begins with the predictive prophetic texts; it does not end there. The more

> relevant prophetic texts … are those which speak to Israel's
> present situation by calling men and nations to practice jus-
> tice, righteousness, kindness, and brotherhood in their
> dealings with one another.[12]

Nor should anyone overlook the Christian and Islamic attach-
ments to the same piece of spiritual real estate. All three religions
have links to the land, albeit different ones. For proof, we only
have to list the various names given to the land during the past
thirty-five hundred years. Each name reveals the diverse political,
religious, cultural, and social forces that have impacted that region
of the world: Canaan, Israel, Judea, Palestine, South Syria, the
Promised Land, and the Holy Land.

Few lands have had so many different names, and each time
one of them was applied, it was assumed that particular name
would trump and outlast the others, but it didn't happen that way.
Perhaps the simplest method may be to emulate the Jewish people,
who call it most simply and most profoundly *Ha-aretz*, "the Land."

Christians' Responses to Israel

Christian support for the security and survival of the Jewish state
often divides along moral and eschatological lines. One Christian
response held by many Evangelicals is rooted in the many biblical
verses that speak of a Jewish restoration in the Land of Israel. For
such Christians, Israel is God's chosen people (Deuteronomy 7:6–8),
the State of Israel is the fulfillment of prophecy (Isaiah 43:5–6;
Ezekiel 37), Israel occupies a special place in God's kingdom
(Ezekiel 36:30, 36:33–38; Amos 9:1–15; Zechariah 8:22–23; Romans
9–11), and Israel has a God-ordained right to the land (Deuteronomy 28–30; Acts 7:5).

A second major Christian response is also highly supportive,
but it is not based on biblical prophecy or eschatology. This position affirms the twin concepts of justice and morality for the Jewish
people. Solidarity with Israel is a concrete and compassionate way
to begin the Christian process of eradicating anti-Semitism and of

building a healthy and respectful relationship with the Jewish people, who have been wronged by Christians for so long.

Many prominent Protestant and Catholic leaders have articulated this position. They include Father Robert Drinan, a former U.S. Congressman from Massachusetts; Drs. Alice and Roy Eckardt; Father Edward H. Flannery; Methodist minister and professor Franklin Littell; Professor Reinhold Niebuhr; and Sister Rose Thering. Flannery wrote:

> In view of the ceaseless persecutions visited upon Jews so often by Christians throughout the centuries, and because of their scattered state throughout the world, it is the Christian, above all, who should rejoice at the upturn in the Jewish people's fortunes in our time that has brought them back to their ancient homeland. The return to Israel can only be seen as the righting of a historical wrong.[13]

A third Christian response to Israel is negative and highly critical. It combines anti-Zionism and anti-Judaism and opposes any Jewish claims to the Land of Israel because the coming of Jesus and the rise of Christianity have negated such claims. This position is a "theological displacement" that delegitimizes the Jewish state and denies it any linkage with biblical and religious promises of land, sovereignty, and peoplehood.

In 1977, the patriarch of the Syrian-based Antiochian Orthodox Church, Elias IV, in a visit to the United States told a news conference that Jews had little "historic connection" with the land that comprises modern Israel. Although Elias's words were spoken more than thirty years ago, little if anything has changed for Christians who share his beliefs:

> As far as we Christians are concerned, we are the new Israel. All the prophecies of the Old Testament were fulfilled by the coming of the Messiah.... After the destruction of the Temple, the Jews were dispersed. Those who remained

lived in peace ... until modern times when "outsiders" [modern Israelis] came into the land.[14]

But despite such anti-Israel rhetoric and theological anti-Judaism, Israel has the potential to bring Jews and Christians closer together as "peoples of God" in their shared efforts to improve the world. Israel represents one way Jews are working to maintain their distinctive identity in a challenging age of rapid travel and communication, intermarriage, religious extremism, terrorism, and economic stress. Christianity, even with its larger numbers, faces similar problems of identity, continuity, and religious indifference.

Rabbi Marc Tanenbaum, the American Jewish Committee's interreligious affairs director for more than twenty years beginning in 1960, wrote:

The way in which Judaism is seeking to engage modernity and history in the land of Israel ... may have some instruction for others who are concerned about the present spiritual crisis for the whole of mankind.[15]

Proceed with Caution

Interreligious Relations Is Now a Three-Way Intersection

12

Four diverse events unconnected to one another that took place during the first decade of the twenty-first century have exposed the uneven landscape of contemporary interreligious relations: the September 11, 2001, Islamic al-Qaeda terrorist attacks on the United States; the July 2, 2004, vote of the General Assembly of the Presbyterian Church (USA) to support a selective divestment of denominational holdings in multinational corporations doing business in Israel; Pope John Paul II's death on April 2, 2005; and the Rev. Rick Warren's plenary address at the Union for Reform Judaism's 2007 biennial meeting in San Diego on December 13, 2007.

The attacks on 9/11 fundamentally altered Islamic-Jewish relations in particular and interreligious relations in general. The public call by a major liberal church body to use financial divestment as a means of punishing Israel was a major negative shift in Protestant-Jewish relations. John Paul II's death marked the end of an extraordinary twenty-seven-year pontificate that changed Catholic-Jewish relations. The address by one of the world's most prominent evangelists before five thousand leaders of Reform Judaism marked a new chapter in the ambivalent relationship between the two religious communities.

After 9/11, it is no longer possible to limit interreligious relations to Christians and Jews; Islam, now a part of those relationships, is a latecomer to the once bilateral encounters and conversations. The emergence of Islam has revealed how little accurate information Christians and Jews sometimes have about a faith that has more than a billion followers and, equally disturbing, how little Muslims know about the two older faiths.

Only recently have some Western academics stopped using the erroneous term "Mohammedans" to describe Muslims.[1] Many Muslims still regard today's Christians as "Crusaders" and continue to describe Jews in obscene terms not heard since the Holocaust, when Nazi propaganda defamed and dehumanized Jews. But after September 11, 2001, Americans were compelled to recognize that Islam, for good or ill, is a major element in any meaningful inter-religious encounter.

Before the 9/11 attacks, the development of a budding set of Islamic-Jewish relationships was under way, especially in the United States. Well-intentioned members of both communities expressed hope that gains could be achieved between Muslims and Jews emulating the earlier achievements in Christian-Jewish relations. At least that was the hope.

The American Jewish Committee sponsored two national conferences on Muslim-Jewish relations at the University of Denver during the mid-1990s, and there were similar meetings in other U.S. cities. Jews quickly discovered that, like them, Muslims in the United States were deeply concerned about assimilation and religious continuity, the future of the family unit, indifference by young Muslims to the faith, the need for quality education, and opposition to discrimination. It all sounded familiar to American Jews, and those issues became major components of many pre-9/11 meetings.

But those encounters (I was a participant in many of them), whether conducted in public or off the record, became difficult and controversial following 9/11. Trusted Islamic colleagues in Muslim-Jewish encounters sometimes turned out to be public apologists for terrorism, or they employed "doublespeak": professing strong support for dialogue, Jews, Judaism, and Israel in English-language communications, while at the same time verbally assailing them when the same leaders spoke in Arabic, Farsi, and other "insider" languages.

The 9/11 attacks, carried out by nineteen Muslim al-Qaeda members, sapped much of the energy, enthusiasm, and commitment from Jews who had been building a constructive set of relations with their Islamic partners.

Typical of the disillusionment that set in among Jews was the fact that shortly after the terror attacks, Mohamed Gemeaha, the imam of a prominent mosque in Manhattan who had participated in earlier interreligious dialogues, fled to Cairo a few days after September 11.[2]

Once there, the Egyptian-born imam gave an interview to an Arab newspaper claiming that the U.S. government was persecuting Muslims and that Jewish doctors in New York were poisoning Muslim children. He also said Jews, not Muslims, were responsible for the attack on the World Trade Center and the Pentagon.

"Sons of Monkeys and Apes"

In Ohio, Fawaz Damra, the imam since 1991 of the state's largest mosque, the Islamic Center of Cleveland, had by 2001 emerged as a major interreligious figure and appeared to many Jewish and Christian leaders as a valued colleague and partner. But, when Damra's pre-2001 Arabic-language tape-recorded messages intended solely for his congregation, in which he called Jews "the sons of monkeys and apes," were made public after 9/11, Muslim-Jewish relations quickly soured.

In June 2004 Damra was convicted for failing to disclose his links to three Islamic terrorist organizations when he applied for U.S. citizenship, and he was recorded on FBI wiretaps discussing the distribution of funds for the families of Muslim suicide bombers. The Cleveland imam was also named an unindicted co-conspirator in the terrorism trial of Palestinian Jihad leader Dr. Sami al-Arian of the University of South Florida in Tampa. Damra was deported from the United States in January 2007, and the disgraced imam left behind a mosque whose membership was divided over his activities along with a residue of bitterness among Jews and Christians who had worked in good faith with him.[3]

Even before 9/11 it was difficult to discover an appropriate Islamic organization to participate in Muslim-Jewish meetings. Before the attacks, Islamic organizations in the United States— many controlled by religious and political extremists—never unequivocally condemned Muslim suicide bombers when they killed Israeli civilians. However, after the 2001 attacks, eleven leading Islamic and Arab groups did issue a joint declaration denouncing "the cowardly acts of terror against innocent American civilians." But the Islamic/Arab coalition failed to call for any U.S. action against the terrorists or the nations that sheltered them.

A major problem in advancing Islamic-Jewish relations is a lack of moderate Muslim leaders in the United States. Before 9/11, several organizations, including Council on American-Islamic Relations (CAIR), American Muslim Council (AMC), and Muslim Public Affairs Council (MPAC), refused to condemn by name the terrorist perpetrators of hostile actions against the United States and Israel, including the 1993 bombing of the World Trade Center, the 1996 attack on U.S. military barracks in Saudi Arabia, the 1998 attacks on two U.S. embassies in Africa, and the 2000 assault on the USS *Cole* in Yemen's harbor.[4]

Since 9/11, many Islamic religious and political leaders, including President Mahmoud Ahmadinejad of Iran and prominent imams, have unleashed a constant stream of verbal attacks on the United States, the West, Christianity, Judaism, and the State of Israel. The Iranian president has repeatedly called for the physical destruction of Israel.

Especially worrisome was U.S. Army major Nidal Hassan's November 2009 murder spree at Fort Hood, Texas, in which thirteen people were killed and dozens injured. The December 2009 arrest in Pakistan of five young American Muslims from the Washington, D.C., area raised concern that Muslims born and educated in pluralistic, democratic America were not immune to Islamic jihadism. In addition, the attempt by Umar Farouk Abdulmutallab on Christmas Day 2009 to blow up a Delta Airlines flight from Europe bound for Detroit and Faisal Shahzad's unsuccessful effort to detonate explosives in New York City's Times Square in May 2010 underscored the continued threats to the United States.

Nonetheless, some Christian and Jewish leaders in Europe, Israel, and North America have continued their encounters with Muslims, hoping to establish dialogue based upon the principles enunciated in *Nostra Aetate*: "mutual respect and knowledge."

A Trio of Difficult Issues

Before inaugurating efforts to develop constructive relations with Islam and Muslims, it is necessary to explore several key issues.

The Territorial Conflict

The Arab-Israeli conflict has significance for both Jews and Muslims. For Jews, the creation of the State of Israel is an ancient promise fulfilled—a democratic nation-state based on Jewish values that guarantees physical and spiritual security for a historically oppressed people.

Yet, for many Muslims, the existence of an independent Jewish state in the Middle East is a religious and political aberration that must be eliminated. They believe Israel is located on *dar al-Islam*, the "abode of Islam"—territory that was once under Islamic rule and law. Devout Muslims believe Islamic rule and law must be reinstated to the territory, and the Jews who may choose to live there must submit to that authority—a concept that delegitimizes Israel not only politically but theologically as well. Imposing religious inferiority on a people and continuing efforts to destroy the only Jewish state in the world are assaults upon both the core beliefs and the self-definitions of Jews.

Theological Differences

Although similarities exist between Jews and Muslims—both peoples profess monotheism, speak Semitic languages, follow prescribed rituals for daily prayer, practice male circumcision, and observe dietary laws that include the prohibition of pork—the differences in theology, custom, and religious law exceed these commonalities. Theologically, perhaps the most significant difference is the Muslim belief that Islam, through Muhammad, represents the ultimate fulfillment of both Judaism and Christianity: the "Final Seal" of the Prophet.[5]

Lack of Authentic Knowledge

I know from years of interreligious work that in many cases Muslim academics and religious leaders in the Middle East and elsewhere know practically nothing about authentic Judaism. Some years ago at a meeting in New York City, a visiting group of prominent Muslim professors of religious studies from Arab countries was asked which books or articles on Judaism they had read that were written by Jewish authors. Without exception, their startling answer was "none."

The professors admitted their perception and knowledge of the Jewish religion was derived exclusively from other Muslims, many of whom are hostile to Jews and Judaism. Using biased writings as primary source material runs counter to a fundamental principle of interreligious relations: each faith group has the right to define itself in its own terms and not to be defined by others.

A large number of Jews know little about the Islamic faith and community. How many are aware that approximately one and a half million Muslims reside in the United States? (There are no exact figures, but Islamic organizations tend to inflate the numbers to bolster their claim—for political purposes—that Muslims outnumber Jews in America. They do not.)

The Islamic community in the United States is composed of three diverse groups: African Americans (many of them converts from Christianity); Arabs; and the largest number from India, Pakistan, Southeast Asia, Indonesia, and Africa. Approximately 40 percent of Muslims living in the United States are African Americans, including the well-known sports figures Mohammed Ali, Kareem

Abdul-Jabbar, and Mike Tyson. They follow the spiritual leadership of the late Warith Deen Mohammed and his father, Elijah Mohammed. Another African American, Louis Farrakhan, the Nation of Islam (NOI) leader, is based in Chicago. He has publicly attacked Jews and Judaism in the vilest language. However, most African American Muslims in the United States are not NOI members.

Arab Muslims, most of them immigrants, are the most engaged Islamic group vis-à-vis Middle East issues, especially the Israeli-Palestinian conflict. They seek to enlist support for the Palestinian cause from non-Arab Muslims, and Arab Muslims are frequently the source of anti-Israel and anti-Jewish rhetoric within the general American society.

Exploring Three Key Phrases

When Jews and Muslims meet, the latter group usually employs several well-known phrases to highlight the positive side of relations between the two communities. Those phrases need to be analyzed as Christian and Jews have examined their own set of beliefs about one another.

Children of Abraham

Because Jews, Muslims, and Christians profess a spiritual connection to the first patriarch, all three groups consider themselves "Children of Abraham." Jews revere Isaac, the son of Abraham and Sarah, as a patriarch; Muslims trace their heritage to Ishmael, the son of Abraham and Hagar, even though Islam did not come into existence for another two thousand years.

Although Jews and Muslims jointly claim Abraham/Ibrahim as their own, including his burial place in Hebron, they symbolically and permanently part company with the births of Isaac and Ishmael—a separation that has had momentous consequences for both faith communities, since the divine covenant is linked to Isaac and his progeny. Although the Bible promises that Ishmael's descendants will be numerous and become a great nation (Genesis 17:20–21), once Sarah casts away Hagar and her son Ishmael, little more is heard from them except for the Genesis account that Ishmael's twelve sons became tribal chieftains—a parallel to Jewish history one generation later. Some Muslims use the ancient story as a biblical basis for hostility to Israel by linking Ishmael's fate with that of the Palestinian refugees.

The Golden Age in Spain

This phrase posits an earlier idyllic "Golden Age" that allegedly existed between Jews and Muslims starting in 711 with the Islamic invasion of the Iberian Peninsula. That era ended with the Christian reconquest on January 2, 1492, and the expulsion of the Jews later that year. While Jews living in Islamic Spain were frequently better off than their coreligionists residing in Christian-controlled lands, the so-called Golden Age was nevertheless very restricting for Jews.

Jews were forbidden to serve in public positions of authority (this rule was not always followed), carry weapons, or ride horses, the equivalent of driving an automobile today. The only means of transportation for Jews were mules and donkeys, from which they were required to dismount in deference to any Muslim seen walking on foot. They also were subjected to occasional violent attacks from Muslim mobs. Nonetheless, Jews in Spain produced important and enduring works in theology, poetry, philosophy, science, and philology. Classical works by Moses Maimonides, Hasdai ibn Shaprut (915–970), Yehudah HaLevi (1075–1141), and Solomon ibn Gabirol, among others, attest to the extraordinary richness of Jewish intellectual and spiritual life in Spain.

Peoples of the Book

Muslims often use this phrase to mean that Jews and Christians, monotheistic minorities living within Islamic societies, must be respected and not harmed because of their identification with sacred religious texts: the *Tanach* and the New Testament. In practice, however, Jews and Christians, the peoples of the Book, lived highly restricted lives, or *dhimmitude,* as "protected people" under

Islamic rule, beginning in the eighth century and continuing into modern times. As the nineteenth-century Jewish historian Heinrich Graetz has noted, Jews and Christians could not build new houses of worship, were required to sing in subdued tones in synagogues and churches, and had to wear distinguishable clothing while living in Islamic societies.

Each phrase—"Children of Abraham," "the Golden Age in Spain," and "peoples of the Book"—is filled with ambivalences, ironies, and paradoxes that require joint study. The history of Jews living as a minority under Islamic rule is uneven. In some places and eras, Jews were tolerated, albeit with severe restrictions; but in times of war or societal stress, Jews were mistreated and killed by Muslims. Many scholars note that the Qur'an includes both hostile references to *Yahud*, meaning the Jews of Muhammad's day, as well as favorable references to *bani Isra'il*, or the ancient Children of Israel who believed in the One God. The inconsistent realities as well as the commonalities that underlie a shared history need to be examined in interreligious dialogue.

Despite the challenges, the shattering of friendships, associations, and trust following 9/11, Islamic-Jewish relations are a key component of interreligious relations in the United States and in other parts of the world. But because of the hostile anti-Zionist, anti-Israel, and anti-Jewish rhetoric spread by Muslim leaders, future Islamic-Jewish relations will take place in an atmosphere and public arena far different from the hopeful but unrealistic high expectations expressed before 9/11. However, an authentic encounter based on reasonable goals with reliable partners is no longer a luxury, but a necessity.

No Quick Fix

Such encounters will initially require a series of small achievements that can later lead to larger gains. There is no "quick fix" in Islamic-Jewish relations for the following issues: the negative 9/11 fallout; the Arab/Iranian conflict with Israel, which is of central concern for both Jews and Muslims; the Hamas and Hezbollah foundational documents calling for the physical destruction of the Jewish state; and the justifiable sense of betrayal many Jews who were engaged in Islamic-Jewish relations experienced after the 2001 attacks.

Before the death of Pope John Paul II, many Catholic and Jewish leaders, especially in North America and Western Europe, worked together for nearly four decades in a systematic effort to reverse the sad history that has poisoned relations between those two faith communities for two millennia. Their clear goal was to replace the dismal past with sturdy new human bridges of solidarity, mutual respect, and understanding.

John Paul II's death marked the end of a forty-year period in Catholic-Jewish relations filled with gains and achievements. The era began in October 1965 at the conclusion of the three-year-long Second Vatican Council in Rome. Karol Wojtyla of Poland, the future pope, then a young bishop, attended the Council, and it had a positive influence on him and his later teachings as John Paul II.

The *Nostra Aetate* Declaration on the Relation of the Church with Non-Christian Religions called for Catholics to engage Jews in dialogue built upon "mutual respect and knowledge." *Nostra Aetate*, described in an earlier chapter, "decries hatreds, persecutions, and manifestations of anti-Semitism directed against Jews at any time and by anyone," and it rejected the deicide charge.

Sixteen Hundred Words That Changed History

Although the bishops spent many hours debating the exact wording of the Declaration before its adoption, *Nostra Aetate* is less than 1,600 words in length, and the section on Jews, Judaism, deicide, and anti-Semitism numbers only 675 carefully crafted words.

Despite its brevity, *Nostra Aetate* is not a piece of arcane or esoteric literature whose few sentences can be easily forgotten. Rather, it is one of the most important documents of the twentieth century and holds a major place within religious history. The Declaration sparked a huge number of positive contacts between Christians and Jews. There have been more constructive Catholic-Jewish encounters since 1965 than there were in the first twenty centuries of Christianity.

Catholic-Jewish relations since 1965 were on a "fast track" spurred on by a series of Vatican and other church statements and declarations, and especially by John Paul II's leadership. Many of the post-1965 documents focused on Christianity's roots within Judaism; self-critical examinations of Catholic teaching materials that related to Jews, Judaism, and the Holocaust; official repudiation of all forms of anti-Judaism and anti-Semitism; admissions that the Shoah took place within "Christian Europe"; and especially after Egypt and Jordan signed peace treaties with Israel, a more sympathetic perception and appreciation of Israel as a source of Jewish self-understanding and a necessary component of interreligious dialogues.

One example of positive Catholic-Jewish developments after the Second Vatican Council is the 1994 Fundamental Agreement between the Vatican and the State of Israel, which formalized diplomatic relations. That document calls upon both parties to oppose anti-Semitism, language not found in other diplomatic agreements and treaties.

Yet, that relationship became more complex and difficult with the death of John Paul II, a larger-than-life world religious leader who made the improvement of Catholic relations with Jews and Judaism a centerpiece of his pontificate. Before the mists of legend (and possible sainthood) envelop the late pope, it is important to recall why his reign was the catalyst for and a crowning achievement of Catholic-Jewish relations.

The Surprising Polish Pope

Because Karol Joseph Wojtyla was Polish-born, his election as pope on October 16, 1978, was met with skepticism within parts of the Jewish community. There was concern the new pope would reflect the traditional anti-Semitism that marked much of Jewish life in Poland. But John Paul II proved the skeptics wrong. His extraordinary contributions to building mutual respect and understanding between Catholics and Jews are historic in nature, and he will be remembered as the "best pope the Jews ever had."

Wojtyla was born in Wadowice, and as a youngster, a quarter of young Karol's schoolmates were Jews. On the eve of World War II in 1939, when the future pope was nineteen, the Polish Jewish community of 3.5 million was a center of rich spiritual, intellectual, and cultural resources and represented 10 percent of the country's total population.

He was a young man during the German occupation of Poland and was a personal witness to the Shoah. Poland was the Nazis' chief killing field, and the monstrous Auschwitz-Birkenau death camp was not far from Wojtyla's hometown. By war's end, more than three million Polish Jews had been killed.

John Paul II needed no academic seminars or scholarly papers to instruct him about the radical evil of the Holocaust. The tragedy was indelibly etched in his mind and his heart. During his first papal visit to Poland in June 1979, John Paul II knelt in prayer before the stone marker at Auschwitz-Birkenau, a marker placed there to remember the large number of Jews murdered in that infamous death camp. In later years he called the Shoah "an indelible stain on the history of the [twentieth] century."[6]

In his travels, the pope sought meetings with the Jewish communities in many lands, and he repeatedly condemned anti-Semitism as a sin against God. John Paul II's visit to Rome's Great Synagogue on April 13, 1986, was the first time a pope had entered a Jewish house of worship since the days of the apostle Peter. In his address that day, the pope reminded Catholics that Jews are "our elder brothers in faith" and that the Jewish covenant with God is "irrevocable." He declared:

> The Jewish religion is not "extrinsic" to us, but in a certain way is "intrinsic" to our own religion. With Judaism, therefore, we have a relationship which we do not have with any other religion. You are our dearly beloved brothers and, in a certain way, it could be said that you are our elder brothers.[7]

In 1994 the Holy See and the State of Israel had established diplomatic relations. This important action, combined with the pope's public denunciations of anti-Semitism and his reverential remembrance of the Holocaust, changed the initial Jewish perception of John Paul II. His personal intervention in 1995 resolved the decade-long crisis over the location of a convent in Auschwitz. As a result, the Carmelite nuns left the death-camp building where the Germans had stored the poison gas used to kill Jews, and the sisters moved a short distance to a newly constructed convent.

On March 16, 1998, the Vatican released "We Remember: A Reflection on the Shoah." Although there was criticism from both Catholics and Jews about sections of the document, John Paul II's introductory letter was praised. In it, the pope urged Catholics to "examine themselves on the responsibility which they too have for the evils of our time."[8]

In March 2000 the pope visited Israel, and I was present at that significant event in his pontificate. Unlike Pope Paul VI's brief visit to Israel in the mid-1960s, when the pontiff never once mentioned the name of the Jewish state, John Paul II was an honored guest at the official residence of the Israeli president and in the offices of the Chief Rabbinate. The pope's sorrowful visit to Yad Vashem, the Israeli Holocaust memorial, where he met with Polish Jewish survivors, was televised around the world.

The most lasting image of the entire pilgrimage—perhaps of his entire pontificate—was John Paul II's slow walk to the Western Wall in Jerusalem, Judaism's holiest site, and his insertion of a prayer of reconciliation into one of the Wall's many crevices:

> *God of our fathers,*
> *you chose Abraham and his descendants*
> *to bring your Name to the Nations:*
> *we are deeply saddened by the behaviour of those*
> *who in the course of history*
> *have caused these children of yours to suffer,*
> *and asking your forgiveness we wish to commit ourselves*

to genuine brotherhood
with the people of the Covenant.
Amen.[9]

Flash Points Overcome

Although there were serious Catholic-Jewish flash points during John Paul II's reign, most of them were overcome or solved because neither side wanted to vitiate the positive gains achieved since 1965.

One controversy occurred in June 1987, when Austrian president and former United Nations secretary general Kurt Waldheim was accorded full diplomatic honors during a state visit to the Vatican. At the time, the United States had placed Waldheim on its "watch list" and had forbidden him entry into the United States because of his wartime activities in the Balkans.

After years of hiding his military record during World War II, Waldheim was accused of participating in war crimes against Jews and other groups. The negative reaction to Waldheim's Vatican visit nearly caused the cancellation of the pope's scheduled meeting a few months later with American Jewish leaders in Miami.

But the meeting took place, and the pope electrified his audience by declaring, "Never again!" in his reference to the Shoah. John Paul II had another successful encounter with Jewish leaders during his visit to the United States in October 1995.

Toward the end of his pontificate, however, some serious problems arose in Catholic-Jewish relations around the question of making the wartime records of the Vatican available to an appropriate team of Catholic and Jewish historians who sought to examine the Vatican's role during the Holocaust, especially the actions or inactions of Pope Pius XII. It is an issue John Paul II's successors must confront, especially because the wartime pope is being considered for sainthood.

While the Vatican document *Dominus Iesus*, issued in 2000, primarily focused on Catholic relations with other Christian groups and did not specifically mention Jews or Judaism, questions were raised whether the Holy See had abandoned the pope's strong commitment to positive interreligious relations.[10]

In late 2003, there was another flash point when the pope appeared to offer an endorsement for Mel Gibson's controversial film *The Passion of the Christ.* John Paul II was reported to have seen it at a private screening and commented, "It is as it was." Vatican sources denied any papal approval of the film, but the contretemps remained.[11] About a year later the pope's book *Memory and Identity: Conversations between Millenniums* drew criticism from some European Jewish groups. They charged that John Paul II unfairly compared the "evil" of abortion with the horrors of the Shoah. Vatican officials claimed this was a misinterpretation of the pope's words.[12]

But despite these issues, the Catholic-Jewish encounter became stronger when it became clear that Pope John Paul II was leading his church, and by extension all of Christianity, into a new historic relationship with Jews that began at the Second Vatican Council. When he died in 2005, he had earned an imperishable place in Jewish history, because his leadership had strengthened Christianity's reconciliation with its Jewish "elder brother."

There is concern that John Paul II and his achievements in interreligious affairs and the high priority he placed upon them may weaken or fade as the Catholic Church faces new challenges and issues, many of them internal. Catholics face many serious problems—a shrinking number of seminarians in the West and in Australia, the growth of secularism in Europe and North America, continuing clergy sexual-abuse scandals, a resurgent ultraconservative element that seeks to mitigate or even negate the reforms of the Second Vatican Council, a complicated relationship with Islam and Muslims—and all of them demand the time, talent, and attention of any pope.

Some Catholics believe the task of developing positive relations with Jews and Judaism is nearly complete, thus allowing the church's energy and attention to be turned elsewhere. Other Catholics differ, asserting instead that the joint efforts have just begun. Nearly two thousand years of religious anti-Judaism cannot be eradicated in less than a half century. The Christian "teaching of contempt" toward Judaism and its adherents took hundreds of years to develop, and it will require a serious and systematic effort lasting many more years to overcome the tragic legacy of the past.

John Paul II's successor, Benedict XVI, reaffirmed his strong support for the Catholic-Jewish enterprise, but some Jewish and Catholic observers believe those interreligious relations, while highly personal and meaningful to the pope, do not have the same sense of urgency as they did during the previous pontificate.

While he lacks his predecessor's enormous charisma and compelling personality, Benedict XVI has, however, publicly reinforced John Paul II's achievements in regard to Catholic-Jewish relations, anti-Semitism, the Shoah, and the commitment to the security and survival of Israel. His visits to synagogues in his native Germany, the United States, and Rome, combined with several meetings with Jewish leaders at the Vatican and in the United States, were widely reported and welcomed by the Jewish community. During Benedict's visit to Israel in May 2009, attention was paid to his youth—growing up in an anti-Nazi German family during the Shoah—and his personal biography is also a part of the pope's outreach to Jews.

Benedict XVI's Good Friday Prayer

On Ash Wednesday 2008, *L'Osservatore Romano*, the official Vatican newspaper, published a revised text of a 1962 Latin-language prayer that was declared permissible for use on Good Friday. Normally, such an article would attract little attention, despite its placement in the Vatican paper. But this was no ordinary prayer; its Latin title is *Pro Conversione Iudaeorum*, "For the Conversion of the Jews." And Pope Benedict XVI, the author of the new prayer text that still retains the prayer's original title, is no ordinary liturgist.

The original Latin prayer the pope revised was used during Good Friday services in Catholic churches before 1970, and it urged the conversion of the Jewish people to Christianity. The prayer contains negative descriptions of both Jews and Judaism:

Let us pray also for the Jews.... May our God and Lord remove the veil from their hearts; that they may also acknowledge our Lord Jesus Christ.... Almighty God ... you drive not even the Jews away from your mercy, hear our prayers, for the blindness of that people, that acknowledging the light of your truth, which is Christ, they may be rescued from their darkness.[13]

Benedict eliminated much of that offensive language, including "the veil from their hearts," "the blindness of that people," and the "darkness" of the Jews. But the pope's new version, while an improvement, was disappointing to many Catholics and Jews because of its retained title and because it still seeks the conversion of the Jews to Christianity, although it will come only at the "End of Days." The pope's revised prayer reads:

Let us also pray for the Jews: That our God and Lord may illuminate their hearts, that they acknowledge Jesus Christ is the Savior of all men. (Let us pray. Kneel. Rise.) Almighty and eternal God, who want that all men be saved and come to the recognition of the truth, propitiously grant that even as the fullness of the peoples enters Thy Church, all Israel be saved. Through Christ Our Lord. Amen.[14]

The pope's modification of the old pre–Vatican Council II text was mystifying to many observers because he ruled it could be used instead of the Good Friday prayer Pope Paul VI had introduced in 1970, three years after the conclusion of the Second Vatican Council. Benedict's new wording is different in substance and tone from the forty-year-old prayer that had replaced the traditional *Pro Conversione Iudaeorum*. The post–Vatican Council prayer strikes a positive tone about Jews and affirms the Jewish religious vocation:

Let us pray for the Jewish people, the first to hear the word of God, that they may continue to grow in the love of his name and in faithfulness to his covenant. (Prayer in silence. Then the priest says:) Almighty and eternal God, long ago you gave your promise to Abraham and his posterity. Listen to your Church as we pray that the people you first made your own may arrive at the fullness of redemption. We ask this through Christ our Lord. Amen.[15]

Also dismaying was the new wording about Jews and Judaism in the adult Catholic catechism. The 2006 United States Catholic *Catechism for Adults* declares:

> The covenant that God made with the Jewish people through Moses remains eternally valid for them.[16]

But two years later, the American bishops voted 231–14 to delete that wording from the next printed edition of the catechism. They were concerned the prayer might be interpreted to mean the Jewish people have their own path to salvation that does not require the church, Jesus, or Christianity. In August 2009 the Vatican approved this revised text in the catechism:

> To the Jewish people, whom God first chose to hear his Word, belong the sonship, the glory, the covenants, the giving of the law, the worship and the promises; to them belong the patriarchs, and of their race, according to the flesh, is the Christ.[17]

However, drawing the most attention was Benedict's January 2009 action in lifting the ban of excommunication on the followers of the late Bishop Marcel Lefebvre (1905–1991).

A Holocaust-Denying Bishop and a Vatican Apology

In 1988 Pope John Paul II had excommunicated Lefebvre and members of his Sacred Society of Pius X (SSPX), an ultraconservative theological group soaked with anti-Jewish and anti-Semitic teachings, some of them stemming back to the French Revolution and the Dreyfus Affair. One of the four Lefebvre bishops whose ban of excommunication was lifted by Benedict was Richard Williamson, a public denier of the mass murders that took place during the Holocaust.

Benedict's actions in lifting the excommunication ban on SSPX members created a sense of bewilderment mixed with anger among many Jews and Catholics. The negative reaction to the pope's action and Williamson's denial of the Shoah was both swift and fierce, much of it coming from Catholic clergy and laity. Critics charged Williamson's Holocaust denial record was easily available on the Internet, but the pope and others in Rome had not availed themselves of online documentation. As a result of the backlash, in March 2009 the pope was compelled to write an unprecedented letter of apology to the world's bishops explaining the mistakes he and other Vatican officials had made regarding the SSPX.

Benedict's straightforward language in the letter and his specific reference to the Internet was a first in Vatican history. Benedict's apology to his bishops also linked himself to the interreligious efforts of his predecessor:

> An unforeseen mishap for me was the fact that the Williamson case ... momentarily upset peace between Christians and Jews, as well as peace within the Church; [it] is something which I can only deeply deplore. I have been told that consulting the information available on the Internet would have made it possible to perceive the problem early on. I have learned the lesson that in the future in the Holy See we will have to pay greater attention to that source of news. I was saddened by the fact that even Catholics who, after all, might have had a better knowledge of the situation, thought they had to attack me with open hostility. Precisely for this reason I thank all the more our Jewish friends, who quickly helped to clear up the misunderstanding

and to restore the atmosphere of friendship and trust which—as in the days of Pope John Paul II—has also existed throughout my pontificate and, thank God, continues to exist.[18]

Despite the Pope's positive statements and policies, several central questions remain to be answered: Will John Paul II's historic achievements and teachings about Jews and Judaism be strengthened, or will they be deemphasized, perhaps weakened as the Catholic Church confronts its own internal problems and a nettlesome encounter with the world's Muslims? Will sufficient attention be paid to Catholic-Jewish relations? Or will a sense of exhaustion or worse, ecclesiastical atrophy, set in after the exuberance and extraordinary advances since 1965?

Since 1965, several major Protestant church bodies both in North America and in Europe have followed the lead of the Roman Catholic Church and adopted statements, policy positions, and declarations that denounced anti-Semitism, recognized Christian culpability for the Shoah, acknowledged the Jewish roots of Christianity, affirmed the need for Israeli security and survival, and supported and called for improved relations with Jews built on mutual respect and understanding.

For more than two hundred years, the tall-steeple "mainstream" churches—Presbyterian, Congregational, Episcopalian, Methodist, Lutheran, Northern Baptist, and Disciples of Christ—represented the American religious establishment: white Anglo-Saxon Protestants. Every U.S. president except for John Kennedy and Barack Obama came out of that tradition, including two Christian mavericks, Thomas Jefferson and Abraham Lincoln.

The National Council of Churches of Christ, an organization of thirty-five church bodies—mostly Protestant and Eastern Orthodox—headquartered in its "God box" building on Manhattan's Riverside Drive, was once *the* dominant voice of American Christianity. That is no longer true; there is no one voice representing U.S. churches.

Protestants—mainstream, Evangelical, and black—today number only 51 percent of the general U.S. population; less than 20 percent of Americans identify as a member of a mainstream church; and one in four Protestants—26 percent—is Evangelical. Indeed, the national percentage of all Christians has shrunk to 78.4 percent, the first time in U.S. history it has dropped below 80 percent, a result of smaller families, church membership losses, and religiously indifferent young people.[19] Protestants, liberal and conservative, black and white, will soon become a minority faith community in the United States. Clearly, for them, the future will not be what their past was.

Surveys indicate a growing number of Americans are turning away from organized religion and opting for a nebulous "spirituality," creating serious problems for all faith communities. As a result, economically stressed clergy and laypeople are concerned with basic questions of institutional survival, and they view Christian-Jewish relations as a "luxury" best pursued by a few professional "ecumaniacs."

Mainstream Protestants and Jews in Coalition

In the decades after the end of World War II, the American Jewish community was often a coalition partner with liberal Protestant denominations as well as the National Council of Churches of Christ on a series of domestic social-justice concerns. Those shared issues included support for the principle of church-state separation and opposition to anti-Semitism, racism, ageism, sexism, Christian conversion campaigns aimed at Jews, mandated prayers and Bible reading in public schools, South African apartheid, and the American "Religious Right's" agenda including efforts to legally define the United States as a "Christian nation."

Mainstream Protestant church bodies and American Jews generally supported a pro-choice position on abortion and backed gun control, universal voting rights, immigration reform, and other progressive domestic issues.

At the same time, Jews and Evangelical Christians inaugurated a wary but important relationship beginning in the late 1960s and early 1970s. Jews quickly perceived the strongest Christian public support for the survival and security of Israel consistently came from Evangelicals. During the decades-long campaign to free Soviet Jewry, the Evangelical community was a strong ally of the American Jewish community. Yet, most American Jews differed with the public policy positions held by many Evangelicals, including opposition to gun control, abortion, the Equal Rights Amendment, embryonic stem cell research, and gay rights, while supporting mandated prayer and Bible reading in public schools.

A Delicate Balancing Act for Jews

The American Jewish community intensified its contacts and its agenda of shared concerns with both liberal and conservative Protestant church bodies. It was a delicate balancing act fraught with pitfalls and conflicting responses to specific issues: joining with liberal Protestants against Evangelicals on church-state issues, but also welcoming Evangelical support for Israel while many liberal Christian leaders were cool, at best, or hostile, at worst, toward the Jewish state. Zionism was never looked on favorably by most mainstream Protestant leaders before 1948, and the State of Israel, Zionism's creation, has been a constant target of criticism and hostility from the same Protestant leadership cadre.

However, the proverbial men and women in the pews of mainstream churches have viewed Israel favorably since its independence in 1948. A February 2010 Gallup poll indicates American public support for Israel is at a twenty-year high, with 63 percent of Americans supporting Israel and only 15 percent backing the Palestinians.[20]

This split between national leaders and their flocks is not limited to Israel; it reflects the grassroots rejection of many public positions taken by denominational leaders that were the creation of their professional staffs. That tension is real and is one reason, among others, for the continuing decline in mainstream membership.

There have been other recent controversies between liberal Protestants and Jews. However, efforts made by leaders in both communities mitigated or overcame many of those difficulties.

Church Divestment from Israel

But one major controversy could not be papered over or ignored. It began on July 1, 2004, in Richmond, Virginia, when the General Assembly of the Presbyterian Church (USA) voted to "initiate a process of phased selective divestment in multinational corporations doing business in Israel." The vote was 413–62. Criticism of divestment came quickly from many Presbyterians, including clergy and laypeople, progressives and conservatives. Some critics of the divestment plan labeled it "anti-Semitic," a charge church leaders denied.[21]

Three months after the General Assembly's divestment vote, a twenty-four-person Presbyterian delegation visited Lebanon and met with Sheikh Nabil Qaouk, a prominent Hezbollah leader. The U.S. government and others have officially designated Hezbollah a terrorist organization. It is publicly committed to the destruction of Israel and is supported by Iran.

Following the meeting in Lebanon, Dr. Ronald Stone, a retired Pittsburgh Presbyterian Seminary ethics professor, appeared on Hezbollah's al-Manar satellite television network and declared, "We treasure the precious words of Hezbollah and your expression of goodwill towards the American people…. Relations and conversations with Islamic leaders are a lot easier than dealings and dialogue with Jewish leaders."[22]

Stone's statement ignited a firestorm of criticism, and Presbyterian leaders issued a damage-control statement making clear that Stone's views "do not reflect the official position of the Presbyterian Church."[23]

Subsequently, the United Methodist Church and the Episcopal Church also explored divestment from Israel as a means of "promoting peace" in the Middle East. The Christian divestment controversy exploded at a time when many universities in America rejected similar calls to empty their investment portfolios of corporations doing business with Israel.

Bashing Israel, the Middle East's only democracy, through divestment is unfair and ineffective. Since Israel achieved independence, some political and religious leaders have falsely believed Middle East peace could be achieved by applying one-sided pressure on Israel through boycotts, embargoes, diplomatic isolation, or divestment.

"If Israel Would Only ..."

Another dangerous idea suggested by some Protestant leaders is to link the Israeli-Palestinian conflict to other Middle East problems—that is, if only Israel, the strongest power in the Middle East, satisfied Arab demands, the problems confronting the United States in the region would evaporate. Such thinking smacks of old-time anti-Semitic scapegoating: Jews are the "root problem," and if they ceased making aggressive demands related to Israeli security and survival, other problems would go away, leaving America with a peaceful Middle East and an unhindered flow of Arab oil.[24]

All divestment efforts were ultimately thwarted and, in some cases, rescinded because of the dedicated leadership of many Presbyterian, United Methodist, and Episcopal clergy and laypeople. But enormous damage was done, and after decades of coalitional efforts between mainstream Protestants and Jews, the 2004 Presbyterian divestment vote shattered that coalition and increased the complexities and difficulties of an already ambivalent relationship. But because so much is at stake for both groups, mainstream Protestant-Jewish relations will continue, but with less enthusiasm than before. The halcyon days when all things seemed possible between the two communities are over.

Rick Warren is the pastor of the evangelical Saddleback Church in Lake Forest, California, one of the largest Christian congregations in America. Warren's book *The Purpose Driven Life* has sold more than thirty million copies, and he was one of the clergypersons who offered a prayer at President Barack Obama's inauguration in 2009.

While Warren's plenary address at the Reform Jewish convention in 2007 focused on how to create exciting, "worship-friendly" congregations, his appearance was a milestone in Evangelical-Jewish relations because it brought together the national leaders of progressive Judaism and a prominent Christian evangelist.[25] Warren is considered the new face and voice of the American Evangelical movement.

Because the term "Evangelical" is widely used and often misunderstood, a basic working definition is needed. The word stems from the Greek *evangelion*, meaning "good news." All Christians and their churches, by definition, are "evangelical"; they are commanded to bring the "good news" of their faith to the entire world.

But in modern parlance, and particularly within the United States, the term is usually applied to Protestant Christians who tend to interpret biblical texts literally. The term used to describe this belief is "inerrancy"—the Holy Scriptures are literally true and without any error.

A second defining characteristic of Evangelicals is a personal conversion experience. That experience can be sudden in nature, similar to Paul on the ancient road to Damascus, or it can occur gradually over a period of time. Evangelicals generally call such a spiritual transformation "being born again." It involves accepting Jesus as one's personal Savior and Messiah.

A third feature of Evangelicals is the imperative to evangelize, or convert, the world's population to their faith. Many liberal or "mainstream" Protestants have rejected or even abandoned active missionary activities, especially those aimed at Jews. Leading this effort was the American Protestant theologian Reinhold Niebuhr, who condemned Christian attempts to convert Jews. He believed such activity was theologically unnecessary and incompatible with Christianity, as well as spiritually insulting to Jews.[26]

A Late Arrival at the Dialogue Table

Evangelical-Jewish relations came rather late to the American interreligious scene. As mentioned above, for nearly twenty years after the end of World War II, meetings in the United States between Christians and Jews usually involved members of mainstream Protestant churches. But even those early contacts were generally limited to joint Thanksgiving services in a synagogue or church and rabbi-minister contacts involving local community issues, including fair employment and housing, church-state issues, and especially civil rights.

In February 1964 I spent a week in Hattiesburg, Mississippi, marching in front of the Forrest County courthouse in support of voting rights for African Americans, who, in that era, were denied their constitutional right to cast ballots. I was joined in those demonstrations by rabbinical colleagues and Christian clergy. The marches were led by the national Presbyterian Church. It was a challenging, frightening time filled with threats of bodily violence and possible imprisonment. But thanks to the Presbyterian leadership, the marchers were well protected both physically and legally.

But in the mid-1960s the building of serious and constructive Evangelical-Jewish relations was not yet part of the interreligious mix. The reasons were both geographical and theological. Until recently, most American Jews lived in the major urban centers of the Northeast or the upper Midwest: New York City, Philadelphia, Boston, Hartford, Providence, Baltimore, Pittsburgh, Cleveland, Chicago, and Detroit. The Christian groups Jews encountered in those cities were often Catholics with family roots in Italy, Ireland, and Poland, and Eastern Orthodox Christians from Greece, Russia, Romania, and the Balkans. Evangelicals, mainly the descendants of immigrants to the United States from Great Britain and other Western European countries, were the religious majority in the South and Southwest, areas with small Jewish populations until recently.

Ships That Pass in the Night

Those demographic patterns meant the formative American experiences for both Jews and Evangelicals took place in different sections of the country. I have written elsewhere that until the early 1970s, members of the two faiths were similar to the proverbial "ships that pass in the night," barely aware of one another and never truly encountering one another as vibrant and unique spiritual communities.

Geographical and emotional distance that bordered on an abyss was why many Evangelicals and Jews dealt in caricatures and stereotypes with the unknown "Other." Each group hurled verbal hand grenades at one another. Jews perceived Evangelicals as unenlightened "Elmer Gantrys," even bigoted anti-Semites. Conversely, Evangelicals defined Jews as "Christ killers," "deniers of Jesus," and "scribes and Pharisees."

Two initial encounters between Evangelicals and Jews took place in 1969 at the Southern Baptist Seminary in Louisville, Kentucky, and six years later in New York City. The American Jewish Committee cosponsored both conferences with several institutional Christian partners. In the early years of Evangelical-Jewish dialogue, I wrote that it "was as if decades of pent-up energy among Jews and Evangelicals were released,"[27] two communities that had been distant from one another, but who soon discovered they had much in common.

Participants at the two conferences addressed the meaning of Messiah, biblical theology, the impact of modern Israel, conversion, witness, mission, and the long-held negative images each group had of the other. Also on the joint agenda was the plight of Jews and Evangelicals in the Soviet Union, the quest for global human rights, the roots of religious anti-Semitism, the Holocaust, church and synagogue polity, the shared American principle of church-state separation, and the role of religion in American life. Participants from both communities felt they were spiritual pioneers pressing forward on a new interreligious frontier.

Today, the strengthening of Evangelical-Jewish relations shows no sign of easing, even though ambivalences, ambiguities, and differences still remain. Overarching those relations are several important issues. The Jewish community rejects all Evangelical efforts to convert Jews to Christianity. The term "completed Jews," used by many Evangelicals to describe a converted Jew, is odious because it implies Judaism is an "incomplete" religion, a belief Jews deny.

At the same time, the two religious communities are linked together as international partners; both are committed to the survival and security of the State of Israel and the enhancement of human rights and religious liberty throughout the world.

Major Issues for Evangelicals and Jews

Whenever Evangelicals and Jews encounter each other, the following issues are key parts of such conversations: anti-Semitism, the State of Israel, the Shoah, mission, witness, *teshuvah*, conversion, and the Religious Right in American politics.

The recent surge in anti-Semitic acts and language, especially in parts of Europe and within many Islamic nations, is a cause of concern that hopefully will bring Evangelicals and Jews closer as part of a broad-based interreligious coalition that opposes hatred of Jews and Judaism and all other forms of religious bigotry and prejudice. Because Evangelical missionaries are active in many regions of the world, it is imperative that Evangelicals speak out against what the Vatican Council in 1965 called "hatreds, persecutions, and manifestations of anti-Semitism."

In the last decades of the twentieth century, Evangelicals and Jews were active partners as they demanded religious liberty and freedom of conscience for Jews and Christian believers—often Evangelicals—residing within the former Soviet Union. Evangelicals were highly supportive of the public campaign to allow Soviet Jews to immigrate to Israel, the United States, and other lands of freedom.

It was a successful effort. During the past twenty years, more than one million Jews have left the former USSR. However, many others have chosen to remain, especially in the three Baltic republics of Estonia, Latvia, and Lithuania as well as Russia, Belarus, and Ukraine.

While their situations are much improved from the grim days of the former USSR, Jews remain victims of anti-Semitism and discrimination. Today, another coalition of Evangelicals and Jews is required to monitor and actively oppose the continued persistence of anti-Semitism in Europe and in Muslim nations.

Another area of partnership between Evangelicals and Jews is working to protect Israel. The creation of the Jewish state has placed Evangelicals and Jews in new theological and psychological territory. Neither community regards modern Israel as simply another nation. Marvin Wilson has written:

> The concepts of "land of promise" and "return to Zion" are deeply grounded in biblical literature. The very last word in the Hebrew Bible (2 Chronicles 36:23) is a call to "go up" to Zion.... I also believe that the remarkable preservation of Israel over the centuries and her recent return to the land are in keeping with those many biblical texts which give promise of her future.[28]

Millions of Evangelicals are aware that the Land of Israel was where Jesus taught, was executed by the Roman Empire, and, they believe, was resurrected. For them, modern Israel is a powerful combination of biblical landscape combined with a sense that Israel reborn is part of a divine economy that calls for a Jewish ingathering of exiles as a prerequisite for the Second Coming of Jesus.

The emergence of the Religious Right in the United States has important implications for the Evangelical-Jewish encounter. My studies show it is the white Evangelical community that supplies much of the religious and political ideology as well as the "foot soldiers"—the voters—who fuel the current "culture war."

In my book *The Baptizing of America: The Religious Right's Plans for the Rest of Us,* I note:

Evangelicals do constitute the largest group of Christians who are actively involved in politics and piety, and they lead the current effort to baptize America. But not all evangelicals seek to permanently alter the historic communal fabric of American life. Such evangelicals may, in fact, be devout Christians, but they do not want to shatter or even weaken the long-held American principle of church-state separation, nor do they desire the legal establishment of any religion, even their own, in today's America.[29]

Evangelicals and Jews need to recognize that the Religious Right believes America has lost its moral compass as a nation. There are some Religious Right leaders who continually invoke "divine authority" to validate their own political policies and partisan platforms, and who characterize their opponents as "sinful" or "ungodly."

Behind the catchy rhetoric of "family values" and "moral tradition," the Religious Right remains committed to changing the America we have known since its creation in the late eighteenth century. Some zealots speak of establishing a "Christian America" that will embody the Religious Right's particular and exclusivist theological beliefs.

Nor should anyone be deceived that many Religious Right leaders are strong public supporters of Israel. Evangelical-Jewish relations, indeed interreligious relations in general, is not a quid pro quo game in which Jews overlook the disturbing domestic agendas of the Religious Right in return for support of the Jewish state. Because the Evangelical-Jewish agenda is broad, support on one key issue does not guarantee agreement or consensus on other vital questions. Authentic dialogue presupposes both agreement and disagreement.

Instead, Jews and Evangelicals should continue their efforts to build mutual respect and understanding while fully recognizing that the Religious Right seeks to impose its restrictive agenda at a time in our nation's history when population studies indicate the

United States is increasingly a multireligious, multiethnic, and multiracial society. Americans are becoming more, not less, diverse in their religious identities. The attempt—so far unsuccessful—by the Religious Right to create an exclusive and constricted "Christian America" flies in the face of these facts.

In 1984 during an Evangelical-Jewish meeting at Gordon College, Marvin Wilson and I jointly issued a ten-point "Conference Call." More than a quarter century has passed since then, but the words of the original "Call" remain relevant and still form a basis for continued Evangelical-Jewish cooperation:

1. We are united in a common struggle against anti-Semitism. We are outraged by the continued presence of this evil and pledge to work together for the elimination of anti-Semitism and all other forms of racism. We are committed jointly to educate this present generation and future generations about the unspeakable horror of the Holocaust.

2. We categorically reject the notion that Zionism is racism. Zionism, the Jewish people's national liberation movement, has deep roots in the Hebrew Scriptures, no less than in the painful history of the Jewish people.

3. We are committed to support Israel as a Jewish state, within secure and recognized borders. We also recognize that Palestinian Arabs have legitimate rights. We pledge our joint efforts in behalf of a just and lasting peace not only between Jews and Arabs but among all peoples of the Middle East.

4. No government is sacred, and no government's policies are beyond criticism. But we strongly object to the practice of holding Israel to a different standard of conduct and morality from that applied to all other nation-states, especially those committed to Israel's destruction.

5. We affirm the eternal validity and contemporary relevance of the Hebrew Scriptures as a primary source of moral, ethical, and spiritual values. And we pledge to work together

to uphold and advance these biblical values in our society and throughout the world.

6. We pledge to uphold the precious value of religious pluralism in our society. We strongly condemn those who would use unethical, coercive, devious, or manipulative means to proselytize others. Witness to one's faith must always be accompanied with great sensitivity and respect for the integrity of the other person lest religious freedom and pluralism be threatened.

7. We will seek to overcome any popular stereotypes, caricatures, and images that may contribute to one faith community falsely perceiving the other. To further this end, we pledge to continue to examine the rich spiritual legacy that Judaism and Evangelicalism hold sacred together as well as their profound differences of belief.

8. We share a common calling to eliminate inhumanity and injustice among all humankind. We also jointly resolve to work together to prevent nuclear annihilation and to pursue the path of world peace.

9. We share a joint commitment to uphold the principle of separation of church and state in the United States.

10. We pledge to deepen our joint involvement in the struggle to achieve human rights and religious liberty for our co-religionists in the Soviet Union and elsewhere in the world.[30]

Pessimists who worry about the future of the interreligious enterprise might paraphrase Bette Davis's famous line in the 1950 award-winning film *All About Eve*: "Fasten your seat belts, it's going to be a bumpy night." But Hollywood does not have the final word. That honor goes to Robert Browning, the author of the poem "Rabbi Ben Ezra." Browning wrote, "Grow old along with me! The best is yet to be...."

13 We Are Prisoners of Hope

One of the most compelling biblical phrases is the prophetic challenge, especially in a turbulent society and era like our own, to become "prisoners of hope" (Zechariah 9:12). Though uttered more than twenty-six hundred years ago, it is a fitting description of how today's Christians and Jews need to relate to one another and to the world.

For too long, these two communities have been prisoners of despair. For much of their shared history, each group eyed the other through the distorted prisms of mutual suspicion, fear, and contempt that locked Christians and Jews into separate spiritual and emotional prisons. And all too often, Christian religious or political leaders confined Jews to physical ghettoes of segregation and persecution.

Over the centuries, that lamentable situation drained precious psychic energy and prevented both communities from working together to build God's Kingdom on earth, a task the two religious traditions affirm.

Today, thanks to the recent gains in interreligious relations, there is an opportunity to do what few other generations have achieved: reverse an old and negative history and build something new and positive. Critics charge that attempts to reconcile the two ancient faith communities with one another will create a squishy spiritual pabulum, a watered-down symbiotic relationship that says

215

Christians and Jews, Christianity and Judaism are basically the same. They are not.

Nor is that the aim of authentic dialogue. Instead, there is an opportunity today to overcome mutual distrust and hatred, replacing it instead with mutual respect, knowledge, and understanding. This generation has been provided the historical incentive, the moral imperative, and the theological tools to achieve that goal.

Those tools include a plethora of positive and constructive statements that various Christian and Jewish bodies have issued during the past fifty years. As detailed in earlier chapters, those documents and declarations address the relationship of Christianity to Jews and Judaism, anti-Judaism and anti-Semitism, the uses and abuses of biblical interpretation, the Holocaust/Shoah, the security and survival of the State of Israel, Jerusalem, and a host of other interreligious concerns.

Christian-Jewish Studies on Campus

During the same half century, hundreds of U.S. colleges and universities have offered courses in Jewish studies that attract students of all spiritual persuasions and those with no religious preferences. These schools include both public and private institutions of higher learning as well as colleges and universities sponsored by Christian bodies and churches.

Since the conclusion of the Second Vatican Council in 1965, nearly forty interreligious centers have been established in the United States, and most are members of the Council of Centers on Jewish-Christian Relations (CCJR).[1] Many centers and institutes are located on college, university, or seminary campuses, including Auburn Seminary, Boston College, Catholic Theological Union, Fairfield University, Florida Atlantic University, General Theological Seminary, Iona College, Kings University, Merrimack College, Muhlenberg College, University of Notre Dame, Sacred Heart University, College of Saint Elizabeth, Saint Leo University, Saint Joseph's University, University of Saint Thomas, Seton Hall University, Seton Hill College, Siena College, Spring Hill College, and Xavier University.

The centers provide information, programming, websites, publications, and public arenas for in-depth study and contact for students, rabbis, Christian clergy, and laity from both communities.

But because religious bigotry, stereotypes, and caricatures are akin to a deadly cancer, addressing that pathology requires much more than courses for credit, interreligious studies, or simply goodwill or eloquent words that come "trippingly off the tongue." It requires one of the hardest things a human being can do: to replace biased beliefs and belligerent behavior with mutual knowledge and respect.

A Great Success Story

The beginning of healing and reconciliation between two ancient faith communities is one of the great success stories in recent intergroup history. But that vital task has not been easy and will demand continued hard work to reverse a tragic legacy. Future historians will not be kind to our generation if we fail in that effort. For that reason men and women of goodwill must be "prisoners of hope."

A first step for Jews is to recognize that significant differences exist among Christians. Many Jews mistakenly lump Christians together by calling them ether "Gentiles," "non-Jews," or sometimes *Goyim*, a biblical Hebrew word meaning "nations." While the modern usage of the last term is derogatory and offensive, "non-Jew" is an inadequate and ethnocentric definition. The first designation does not take into account the differences many Christians make between "Gentiles" and those individuals who have experienced a personal religious experience with God and/or Jesus.

The overwhelming majority of Christians throughout the world fall into three major classifications: Roman Catholic, Eastern Orthodox, and Protestant/Anglican. There has been a long quest for Christian unity that has resulted in a number of unsuccessful attempts to end the divisions and bring the followers of Jesus into a unified religious body. Because of a complicated and competitive religious history, it is difficult to fully describe all the streams of contemporary Christianity. But the overwhelming majority of Christians continue to stress classic creedal declarations and affirmations along with liturgical and sacramental ceremonies.

Both Roman Catholics and Eastern Orthodox Christians declare they are members of the "first Church" and trace their origins as ecclesiastical bodies to the first century. A schism occurred between the two communities in 1054, and it has never been healed despite recent fraternal relations between the Roman Catholic pope in Rome and the Eastern Orthodox patriarch in Constantinople (today's Istanbul).

It has been nearly five hundred years since King Henry VIII of England in 1534 declared royal supremacy in religious matters, actions that created the Anglican Communion. Seventeen years earlier, in 1517, the German Catholic priest Martin Luther broke with the Catholic Church and became a leading figure in the Protestant Reformation.

It seems unlikely that Christian unity will soon, if ever, be achieved. Today Christians differ from one another in a host of ways, including church polity, theological belief, language, ritual and liturgy, biblical interpretation, geography, married or celibate clergy, a hierarchy of bishops or "the priesthood of the laity," the role of women, ordination of gay clergy, evangelization, social-justice concerns, and racial/ethnic differences.

There are global relief agencies supported by various church bodies, and there are also a vast number of Christian colleges, universities, seminaries, orphanages, convents, monasteries, medical centers, electronic and print media, and in some parts of the world, including Germany and Italy, "Christian"-based political parties. There are also a host of modern Christian movements that press for social justice; human liberation; pacifism; sexual, racial, and gender equality; arms limitation; world peace; environmentalism; and public advocacy on a variety of issues that cover the entire political spectrum.

So, too, it is equally important for Christians to recognize the many significant differences that exist among Jews in the areas of spiritual beliefs, which may include the concept of a future personal Messiah versus the coming of a messianic age; the divine or human authorship of the *Tanach* (the Jewish Scriptures); the place of *halacha* (Jewish religious law) in liturgy, ritual, customs, and ceremonies, including Sabbath and holiday observance; the necessity of maintaining the dietary laws of kashrut; the role of women in religious life and their ordination as rabbis and cantors; modern Israel's influence in shaping Jewish identity; attitudes toward intermarriage; and the Reform movement's adoption in 1973 of the nontraditional principle of patrilineal descent, which asserted the father is equal to the mother in defining the Jewish identity of a child.

Christians would do well to follow the teachings of the Vatican's "Guidelines and Suggestions for Implementing the Conciliar Declaration *Nostra Aetate* (no. 4)" issued on October 22, 1974, by the Holy See's Commission on Religious Relations with the Jews. The document's introduction includes these points regarding authentic dialogue:

> These links and relationships [between Catholics and Jews] render obligatory a better mutual understanding and renewed mutual esteem. On the practical level in particular, Christians must therefore strive to acquire a better knowledge of the basic components of the religious tradition of Judaism; they must strive to learn by what essential traits the Jews define themselves in the light of their own religious experience.

The best advice for both Jews and Christians when attempting to describe one another is: beware of generalizations.

There are many Jewish organizations involved in interfaith relations. Among them, the major ones include the American Jewish Committee (AJC), which was founded in 1906 by a group of prominent American Jews, many of whom traced their family roots to Germany. The committee's establishment was in reaction to the

1903 deadly anti-Jewish pogroms in Kishinev, Moldavia, a region of czarist Russia.

From its inception, the committee has worked with a wide range of American and international government, political, and religious leaders to support democratic, pluralistic societies and human rights. Today the AJC, a membership organization, is a global advocacy group that fights bigotry and prejudice and for many decades has made interreligious, interethnic, and interracial programs a key part of its agenda.

B'nai B'rith (Hebrew for "Children of the Covenant"), the oldest Jewish service organization in the world, was founded in New York City in 1843, and seventy years later it created the Anti-Defamation League (ADL) as a means of combating anti-Semitism and "the defamation of the Jewish people" as well as securing "justice and fair treatment for all people." Like the American Jewish Committee, the ADL is now an independent organization and carries out a series of interreligious activities.

In 1918, during World War I, Stephen S. Wise (1874–1949), America's most prominent and influential rabbi of his generation, formed the American Jewish Congress, another membership group. Among its founders were two future United States Supreme Court justices: Felix Frankfurter and Louis Brandeis. Over the years, a major priority of the congress has been its involvement in many court cases involving separation of church and state, discrimination, and other civil rights issues.

Confronted with the rise of Nazism, in 1936 Wise founded the World Jewish Congress (WJC) in Geneva, Switzerland, to act as a representative of Jews throughout the world. Its membership is composed of both individuals and Jewish communities in many countries; like the AJC, the ADL, and the American Jewish Congress, it, too, engages in interreligious work.

Because Jews often define themselves as a people, the various organizations dedicated to the welfare, education, spiritual life, and security of Jews are not "ecclesiastical" in nature as the term is usually understood by many Christians. While this is true of the groups described above, there are synagogue-based associations, including the Union for Reform Judaism, founded in 1873; the United Synagogue of America, established in 1913, composed of Conservative congregations; the Union of Orthodox Jewish Congregations, created in 1898; and the Jewish Reconstructionist Federation, founded in 1955. These religious streams of Judaism have their own rabbinical associations and seminaries. Many of the religious groups within the American Jewish community actively engage in interreligious efforts on both the national and the local levels, and the Reform movement even maintains an interfaith Washington, D.C., presence through its Religious Action Center and Commission on Interreligious Affairs.

This plethora of organizations sometimes confuses Christian and Islamic groups who seek to work with the Jewish community. It is important for them to recognize that unlike some Christian bodies, there is no religious hierarchy, "central address," or designated leader for American Jews. As a result, there are many other organizations and associations that carry out a variety of interfaith and other activities, including Hadassah, the women's Zionist organization that supports medical facilities and research in Israel; the Jewish Federations of North America, the major fund-raising group for both domestic and international charities; and community relations bureaus in many cities that are represented nationally by the Jewish Council for Public Affairs. These groups, associations, and organizations are components of the total Jewish community. Central to positive interreligious relations is the right of each group to define itself in its own terms and to create the specific instrumentalities, institutions, and programs required to ensure its continuity, including engaging in interreligious relations with other faith communities.

An Unfair Comparison of Christianity and Judaism

Because Christians belong to no specific ethnic group, nation, or people and because their faith is not rooted to one land or language, they often portray themselves as "universalistic" in their concerns when compared with "particularistic" Jews. However, this is a false analogy and a dangerous dichotomy. Christianity, with its extraordinary emphasis on the life and death of one Jewish person at a specific time and place in history, is actually a "particularistic" faith, and Judaism contains a robust, well-defined "universalistic" tradition. But the harmful canard lingers on and damages relations between the two communities.

Christianity and Judaism, with their varied schools of thought, belief, and practice, constantly interact with the powerful political, social, cultural, and economic forces of contemporary society. Christians and Jews are continually sorting out and debating what must be preserved, enriched, and adapted from the past while attempting to relate their religions to the problems of the modern human situation. It remains a necessary but often divisive process for Christians and Jews.

Religion on the Changing World Stage

Perhaps one source of the tension is the fact that both communities are concerned about their future survival as viable religions in a contradictory world where secularism collides with religious extremism. During the past century, some historians termed our era "post-Christian," and Christians were told by several of their theologians that "God is dead." At the same time, a series of modern Jeremiahs regularly predict "the end of the Jewish people."

But neither prediction seems to be true. For better or worse, all religions are playing major roles on the world stage, but that stage is rapidly shifting for Christians and Jews. Beginning in the fifth century and continuing until the present time, Europe and, more recently, North America have been the major centers of Christian population, thought, and theology. Today most of the world's Christians reside in South America, Africa, and Asia, a demographic trend that is accelerating even as the number of Christians is declining in Europe and North America. This shift in global population will influence both Christianity and Judaism in the twenty-first century as well as Christian-Jewish relations.

Could Europe and North America, longtime centers of Christianity and Judaism, be losing their dominance and influence? We do not know the answer to that question, because human existence is much more than a series of demographic statistics and trends, but several examples are perhaps indicative of things to come.

Significant Demographic Changes for Christians and Jews

The Anglican Church was established by English king Henry VIII in the sixteenth century; the break with Rome came in 1534. As the colonial British Empire expanded throughout the world, Anglican overseas missionaries established "mission churches" in colonial possessions in Africa, Asia, the Caribbean, and South America. It was a classic example of faith following flag—in this case, the Union Jack.

Today the Anglican Church in the United Kingdom and its American counterpart, the Episcopal Church, are suffering continuing losses in membership, but the younger, formerly colonial Anglican Church bodies are increasing in size and are politically and theologically more conservative than their ecclesiastical mentors. It is an old story: the child has grown up and broken from the views, opinions, and beliefs of its parent.

Pope Benedict XVI has repeatedly expressed his concern about the shrinking number of active Catholics on the European continent. The causes for the falloff are many, including the clergy sexual-abuse scandal, the "secularization" of the so-called first world, and the decreasing Catholic birth rate in North America and Europe.

These factors have created a growing shortage of priests and sisters on both sides of the Atlantic Ocean. As a result, priests from Latin and South America, Africa, and Asia are leaving their homes and assuming new pastoral duties in what was once the spiritual and population center of Catholicism. It is a trend likely to continue.

Following the expulsions of Sephardic Jews from Spain and Portugal in the late fifteenth and early sixteenth centuries, the influence of that group declined while that of Jews of central and eastern Europe (the Ashkenazim) increased. Poland, Germany,

Lithuania, Hungary, Romania, and Russia became large and important centers of Jewish life. When the anti-Semitic persecutions intensified in that part of the world, especially in the nineteenth and twentieth centuries, new Ashkenazic Jewish centers grew in size and influence: modern Israel and the United States.

But one unanticipated result of Israel's creation in 1948 was the arrival of 850,000 non-Ashkenazic Jews from Arab and Muslim countries. Some members of these groups were descendants of the expelled Spanish and Portuguese Jews, but most stemmed from ancient Jewish communities in Iraq, Iran, Egypt, Morocco, Yemen, and Ethiopia that existed for more than a thousand years. Not surprisingly, because of their critical population mass, they are changing the dominant Ashkenazic image and reality of modern Israel.

For two thousand years, the majority of Jews lived in the Diaspora outside of Israel, their biblical homeland. However, a major population change is currently under way, and in the near future, more than half the world's Jews will live in Israel, a nation that many people forget is located in southwest Asia.

The times, they are a-changin'.

14 A User's Guide to Christian-Jewish Relations

Developing constructive relations between Christians and Jews is not the sole domain of rabbis, Christian clergy, or academics. Indeed, the strength of those relations ultimately depends on the efforts of laypeople who actively seek to change the troubled history of the past. The following suggestions and guidelines are the result of decades of interreligious programming and have been "kitchen tested" for their effectiveness in achieving positive results.

Laypeople often approach interreligious encounters with anxiety and even fear. They do not want to be embarrassed by either their faith commitments or their lack of knowledge about their own religion or the religion of the "Other." It is necessary to stress that dialogue is a conversation, not a test or an exam, nor is it a device to openly or covertly seek religious conversions.

Based on my experience, here are "ten commandments" for successful Christian-Jewish dialogues:

1. *Be there.* Show up. As that great American philosopher, Woody Allen, once said, showing up is 80 percent of life.
2. *Don't try to defend the indefensible regarding your own faith.* Dialogue participants frequently become sidetracked and backed into a corner. It is important to acknowledge errors and mistakes that members and leaders of your faith

225

community have made. Then move on. Keep the discussion focused on subjects that can be supported and defended.

3. *Listen.* Frequently, dialogue participants are poor listeners. It is important to hear what those of another religion are saying. It is counterproductive to interrupt someone to challenge a specific remark. Do not talk over each other; it's rude. Sometimes waiting until the end of a presentation will allow you to pick and choose the points to which you'll respond.

4. *Focus.* You can't cover everything in Christian-Jewish relations. Focus on two or three points and develop them firmly. Don't spread yourself all over the interreligious map.

5. *Avoid simply preaching Bible texts, history, or law.* Don't concentrate solely on historical, scriptural, and legal perspectives or rationales; if you do, your audience's eyes will glaze over as you speak. Provide authentic information, but remember that theology is not counting "angels on the head of a pin"; it is autobiographical.

6. *The person with the most words usually loses.* You are not participating in a word contest or a court case. In short, less is often more.

7. *Know your audience.* Are they academics? Attorneys? Businesspeople? Politicians? Homemakers? Religious leaders? Elderly? Educators? A particular presentation of a religious tradition may be inappropriate for one audience, but on the mark for another.

8. *Journalists may sometimes be inadequately informed, but they are usually interested in religious matters.* Journalists cover many different subjects on deadlines or on short notice. Often they don't know what to ask when covering an interreligious encounter. Try to get them to focus on a few points and emphasize context, context, context.

9. *Seek areas of solidarity and mutual respect.* Emphasize the "values we share"; don't merely cite "what you have done to us."

10. *Don't try to change people's minds; concentrate on enlightenment, explanation, and clarification.* A Christian-Jewish dialogue is not a contest with winners or losers.

Organizing Interreligious Programs

All programs should be respectful, reciprocal, and constructive in both substance and tone. Participants need to be reminded that true dialogue is a lifelong process, not a "quick fix." Pope John Paul II accurately described Christian-Jewish relations as a "culture of dialogue … a harmony of differences."

How should an interreligious program be organized?

1. Interreligious engagement should lead to mutual respect and understanding between religious groups. It is also possible for the dialogue process to produce joint action on specific problems or themes, including public statements, educational materials, the interpretation of key issues for public officials, or domestic and overseas study missions. In all cases, there must be no hidden agendas on the part of the participating individuals or groups.

2. There should be adequate joint planning by both Jewish and Christian participants in any interreligious engagement. This planning includes not only the various logistical details of a program but the specific themes and topics as well. The planning process is an integral part of the total dialogue experience and should not be minimized. A bad or an inadequate planning process can doom the entire program.

3. Appropriate cosponsorship from both faith communities is required. The cosponsors can be a local house of worship, a clergy/rabbinical association, seminary, religious or community organization, college/university, or institute.

4. The precise number of sessions should be announced at the beginning of the program so participants will know exactly how much time they are expected to give to the

undertaking. An open-ended program is a recipe for failure. For example, if the Christian and Jewish participants agreed on six sessions, each session should be structured to cover specific topics or themes.

5. If possible, there should be an equal number of participants from each community, and women from the involved religious communities must be adequately represented.

6. An appropriate balance is needed between clergy and laypeople among the participants. Obviously, this does not apply if the program is for clergy only or for laypeople only. It is always important to ensure that clergy members do not dominate an interreligious encounter when laypeople are present. While the clergy are professionally involved with their religion and may be "experts," the laity constitutes the membership of every religious community.

7. While some programs may take place in a home setting, it is better to house an interreligious dialogue in a synagogue, church, school, or similar public location. The programs can be rotated from one location to another.

8. Two discussion leaders should be selected in advance, one from each community. These leaders should meet prior to the formal program so they can jointly develop the project and decide on ground rules, themes, reading assignments, and so forth.

9. Ideally, basic reading materials or audiovisual materials from both communities should be sent to all participants in advance of the program. Experience has shown, however, that participants frequently do not read articles and papers before dialogue sessions. But once the dialogue is under way, participants often turn in great interest to the printed or visual materials they have received. All participants should receive the same materials to ensure a successful program.

10. Once a dialogue project has started and matured, it may be useful to feature guest speakers or specialists who can

focus on a specific issue or theme. However, this should not take place until the participants themselves have had an opportunity to bond and to establish their own identities in the dialogue process.

11. Caution should be exercised regarding interreligious services, to ensure that the character and sensitivities of each religion are respected. The danger in interreligious services is that, no matter how well intentioned, they can result in reducing the particular faith commitments of the participants to the lowest common denominator. Preferably, each religious community should be encouraged to conduct its own authentic service. Christian participants should be invited to attend a Jewish service, and vice versa, as a way of developing mutual understanding and respect. Let each group do what it does best: genuine worship services. Artificially created services frequently satisfy no one.

12. The presence of Hebrew Christians in interreligious activities usually skews the dialogue and creates unnecessary and unneeded dissonance and polarization.

13. Once the specific programs are formally concluded, contact should be maintained with the participants by the sponsoring groups. Such alumni are useful in developing future programs; relating to the general and religious media in a community; and encouraging friends, associates, and family members to become involved in Christian-Jewish relations.

14. A final word of caution: Christian-Jewish programs must not be used as either individual or group therapy sessions that may center on such topics as intermarriage, intrafamily conflicts, or anger directed at various clergy.

Specific Projects for Christians and Jews

Christian and Jewish participants in the dialogue process, especially laypeople, can undertake "doable" joint projects that will strengthen relationships. As always, careful advance planning is necessary to ensure success. Some projects might include:

1. Joint visits to local churches and synagogues to attend religious services or to tour the facilities with an emphasis on learning about the sacred objects found in the various houses of worship.

2. Researching family trees with special attention paid to the religious identities, practices, and beliefs of previous generations. Building religious histories of families is easy to do thanks to the many technological tools currently available.

3. Joint visits to a local Holocaust museum or, if possible, to the United States Holocaust Memorial Museum in Washington, D.C. A shared study mission to both Israel and the Vatican has proved to be life changing for both Christians and Jews.

4. Contributing appropriate books, periodicals, CDs, DVDs, and other educational material to local public libraries or schools.

5. Writing op-ed articles or letters to the editor for the general and religious press. It is especially helpful when a Christian composes a piece for a Jewish newspaper and vice versa. Such articles can also be useful to condemn racist, anti-Semitic, and anti-Christian articles if they appear in a local community or region.

6. Swift and strong joint denunciation of any hate crime, cemetery desecration, or vandalism of houses of worship. These responses to bigotry should appear in the print, electronic, and Internet media.

7. Development of community-wide services to commemorate both the *Kristallnacht* pogrom of 1938 and Yom HaShoah (Holocaust Remembrance Day). Many churches and dioceses already conduct such annual remembrances in various houses of worship.

8. Organizing a four-person lay panel—two members from each faith community—that can address local service club meetings (e.g., Rotary, Kiwanis, Lions, Elks, B'nai B'rith, Knights of Columbus) to highlight Christian-Jewish relations and to enlist new participants.

9. Useful interreligious community social-action projects, which may include regional and local issues (e.g., religious/racial profiling; discrimination in employment, education, housing). A strong Christian-Jewish voice frequently carries more weight than a single religious community's action.

10. Publicly acknowledging the men and women who make significant contributions to authentic dialogue. Such recognition can include annual awards that honor leaders in building interreligious relations.

The most pressing task in Christian-Jewish relations today is the need to develop an authentic religious foundation for the principle of religious pluralism. Achieving a theology of pluralism will not be easy, but it is needed at this moment in world history. It will require people of faith to explore their spiritual traditions to discover a theological anchor for pluralism.

It is no longer enough for faith communities to simply live side by side in a kind of de facto coexistence. That is not an acceptable situation today as we experience the harsh winds of religious bigotry and violent extremism mixed with political, demographic, and economic upheavals. It is easy to affirm religious pluralism when such negative elements are absent from the world stage, but it is not sufficient in today's turbulent world.

That is why dialogue is not a luxury, but rather a necessity that provides a spiritual mooring on the planet, so billions of people who believe differently can reside together in peace. A theological girding of religious pluralism will guarantee its permanence and will replace the facile sense of toleration that currently exists among religious groups.

Finally, Christians and Jews, because of their long shared history, must be the ones to take the lead and become the model for other world religions to emulate. Developing a theology of pluralism is not surrendering to the contemporary age nor is affirming religious pluralism a white flag waving in submission to the siren song of modernity. It is, rather, a clear recognition and a firm belief that there is and will continue to be an extraordinary plurality of spiritual expressions, beliefs, and actions all operating under a universal God.

As a Jew who has lived during the era of Fascism, Communism, and Nazism, World War II, the Shoah, and endless ethnic and religious conflicts, and seen the use of religion to justify violence and terrorism, I believe a strong religious pluralism rooted to profound and genuine faith commitments is a necessary antidote, a counterforce. Christians and Jews can agree upon this kind of mission; it is our generation's destiny to achieve that goal.

Discussion Guide

This discussion guide focuses on the major issues in Christian-Jewish relations within three broad historical eras: the biblical period and the early years of Rabbinic Judaism and Christianity, the medieval/premodern time span, and the contemporary period.

Each study session should have a fixed time frame, and the discussion leader must make sure there are no lengthy speeches or time-consuming two-person debates that do not involve the entire group. Participants in an interreligious study group should receive the questions and issues to be discussed in advance of the actual sessions.

Ideally, Christians might analyze a specific Jewish theme, and similarly, Jewish participants might study a specific Christian theme. This "crossover" procedure is an excellent method for enhancing Christian-Jewish discussion. In addition, shared visits to churches and synagogues along with explanations of various sacred objects and religious holidays strengthen interreligious encounters.

The questions for study listed below are intended to inaugurate a fruitful conversation and dialogue. If these questions are used in a more formal educational setting, it is important that teachers not dominate the conversations because of their expertise or knowledge of the subject matter.

Often the most dynamic and fruitful discussion sessions occur when participants speak in autobiographical terms and use questions as a "launching pad" for authentic dialogue.

The Biblical Period

1. Why did the early Christians call themselves the "New Israel" even though the majority of church membership just a few decades after Jesus's death was Gentile and not Jewish? What implications did the "Gentile church" have for future relations between the two faith communities?
2. Why do you think Paul was so adamant for followers of Jesus to abandon Jewish dietary laws and ritual circumcision? Why did the leaders of the Jerusalem church retain them as religious obligations?
3. Why did the church make the *Tanach* a part of its sacred canon?
4. Compare and contrast the Jewish and Christian views of the Messiah.
5. If the early Christians were part of the Jewish people, what caused the parting of ways?
6. Why do some scholars believe that without the Maccabean victory in 165 BCE (the Hanukkah story), there might not have been either Judaism or Christianity?
7. If you were a Jew living in ancient Israel during the Roman occupation, would you have identified with the Sadducees, Pharisees, Essenes, or Zealots?
8. Can a Christian Passion play be free of anti-Jewish themes and images, especially the deicide charge? Discuss the roles of Pontius Pilate and Joseph Caiaphas in the death of Jesus.
9. How has biblical typology affected Christian-Jewish relations?

The Medieval/Premodern Period

1. Describe the intellectual cross-fertilization between major Jewish and Christian philosophers during the medieval period. How was Aristotle a bridge between the two religious communities?
2. Did the Crusades significantly change relations between Christians and Jews?

3. What role, if any, do the seven Noachide Laws play in interreligious relations?

4. Is there a difference between what has been called the "Jewish Jesus" and the "Christian Christ"? Is there a difference between anti-Judaism and anti-Semitism?

5. Why did many church leaders attack the Talmud while revering the *Tanach*, or "Old Testament"?

6. What caused the rabbis to discourage messianic speculation among Jews as well as "turning inward" in the medieval period? How did the Protestant Reformation affect Christian-Jewish relations?

7. Why was the conversion of the Jews so important to church leadership?

8. Describe the status of Jews living in Muslim Spain during the eleventh century and those who lived in Christian France or Germany at the same time.

9. Salo Baron wrote that "suffering is part of the destiny of the Jews, but so is repeated joy as well as ultimate redemption." Do you agree with his rejection of what he has called the "lachrymose concept" of Jewish history?

The Contemporary Period

1. How did the Age of Enlightenment impact Christians and Jews?

2. Do Jews and Christians have different expectations about dialogues with one another?

3. What should be the relationship between religion and state in the United States?

4. Some Christian leaders make a direct connection between the church's "teaching of contempt" and the Holocaust. Others disagree and believe the Shoah was an expression of paganism, not Christianity. What is your opinion on the origins of the Holocaust?

5. Define what is meant by "religious pluralism."

6. How has the creation of modern Israel in 1948 affected Christian-Jewish relations? What has been the influence of the Second Vatican Council, which concluded in 1965?

7. What is your opinion of joint Christian-Jewish worship services?

8. Are Christian-Jewish-Muslim "trialogues" valid interreligious programs?

9. How are the two patriarchal traditions of Christianity and Judaism dealing with the role of women in their respective faith communities?

Notes

1. What's in a Name? Hebrews, Israelites, or Jews?

1. While there is no specific biblical reference to *ivrim* as slaves in Egypt, there are five references in Exodus to "the God of the Hebrews" in the description of the slavery status of the Israelites (3:18, 5:3, 7:16, 9:1, 10:3).

2. University of Haifa news release, January 7, 2001. According to Gershon Galil of the University of Haifa, who deciphered the inscription, "It indicates that the Kingdom of Israel already existed in the tenth century BCE and that at least some of the biblical texts were written hundreds of years before the dates presented in current research."

3. James A. Shapiro, review of *Trials of the Diaspora: A History of Anti-Semitism in England*, by Anthony Julius, *Financial Times*, February 20, 2010: "But Jew-hatred is only part of a larger set of prejudices explored in this dark play. Shakespeare is not obsessed with Jews ... so much as drawn to questions of Jewish difference that enabled Elizabethan play-goers to confront issues of English racial, national and religious identity." See also Harold Bloom, "The Jewish Question: British Anti-Semitism," *New York Times Book Review*, May 9, 2010, p. 10: "As an old-fashioned bardolator, I am hurt when I contemplate the real harm Shakespeare has done to the Jews for some four centuries now.... Yet nothing mitigates the destructiveness of the portraits of Shylock and Fagin."

4. Eric H. Yoffie, Union of American Hebrew Congregations Board of Trustees address, December 14, 2002, Phoenix, Arizona: "The first problem with our current name is that it is anachronistic. When the Union was founded in 1873, the word 'Jewish' was disliked, and the word 'Hebrew' was considered a genteel substitute that was far more acceptable in Christian society. But such apologetics are unacceptable

to us now. We are Jews, and proud of it, and surely our name should proclaim, in the most unmistakable tones, who we are."

5. Nazi Germany required name changes for Jews on August 17, 1938. See David J. Hogan, ed., *The Holocaust Chronicle* (Lincolnwood, Ill.: Publications International, 2000), 133–34.

6. Patrick F. O'Hare, *The Facts about Luther* (Cincinnati: TAN Books, 1987), 202. Luther is quoted as saying: "The book of Esther, I toss into the Elbe. I am such an enemy to the book of Esther that I wish it did not exist, for it Judaizes too much and has in it a great deal of heathenish foolishness." For a Lutheran perspective on the Great Reformer's anti-Jewish beliefs, see Helmut T. Lehmann, gen. ed., *Luther's Works*, vol. 47, *The Christian in Society IV*, ed. Franklin Sherman (Philadelphia: Fortress Press, 1971). Sherman, editor of volume 47 of the American edition of *Luther's Works*, rejects the claim that "Luther's antipathy towards the Jews was religious rather than racial in nature." Luther's writings against the Jews, he explains, are not "merely a set of cool, calm and collected theological judgments. His writings are full of rage, and indeed hatred, against an identifiable human group, not just against a religious point of view; it is against that group that his action proposals are directed." Sherman argues that Luther "cannot be distanced completely from modern anti-Semites."

7. Jacob Neusner, *Jews and Christians: The Myth of a Common Tradition* (New York: Trinity Press International, 1990), 28.

2. The Ancient Big Three: Jews, Greeks, and Romans

1. Charles Lentheric, *The Riviera: Ancient and Modern*, trans. Charles West (London: T. F. Unwin, 1895; Chicago: Ares, 1976), 209: "In the maritime towns of antiquity, the seaport was frequently separate from the city proper, and at some distance from it. In early times, there were very few artificial harbors, surrounded by quays, divided into basins, and protected by jetties, breakwaters, and fortifications, as in many modern seaports.... The ancients chose as a rule, for their ports, a small natural gulf or inlet, sheltered from the fury of the open sea, and provided with a gently inclined beach, upon which their vessels could be drawn up." Citation is to the Ares edition.

2. Qur'an, *Sura Al-Isra* 17:1.

3. Eric H. Cline, *Jerusalem Besieged: From Ancient Canaan to Modern Israel* (Ann Arbor: University of Michigan Press, 2004), table 1.2.

4. Thucydides, *History of the Peloponnesian War*, ed. and trans. M. I. Finley and Rex Warner, rev. ed. (New York: Penguin Classics, 1972).

5. Jeremy Cohen, ed., introduction to *Essential Papers on Judaism and Christianity in Conflict: From Late Antiquity to the Reformation* (New York: New York University Press, 1991).

6. There are significant differences between the Septuagint Greek translation and the Hebrew Bible; see Jerome, *Apology*, book 2; and Henry B. Swete, *An Introduction to the Old Testament in Greek*, rev. R. R. Ottley (Peabody, Mass.: Hendrickson, 1989).

7. See George Finlay, *History of the Greek Revolution* (London: W. Blackwood and Sons, 1861; London: Zeno, 1971).

8. T. P. Wiseman, *Remus: A Roman Myth* (New York: Cambridge University Press, 1995).

9. Julian Bennett, *Trajan, Optimus Princeps: A Life and Times* (Bloomington: Indiana University Press, 1997).

10. Peter Heather, *The Fall of the Roman Empire: A New History* (New York: Oxford University Press, 2007), 227–29.

11. Bannister Fletcher, a prominent architectural historian, calls St. Peter's "the greatest of all churches of Christendom" in his book *History of Architecture*, 20th ed. (London: Architectural Press, 2001), 719.

12. E. J. Dionne Jr., "Pope Speaks in Rome Synagogue, in the First Such Visit on Record," *New York Times*, April 14, 1986.

13. Saul Friedlander, *Nazi Germany and the Jews: The Years of Extermination, 1933–1945* (New York: HarperCollins, 2007), 561.

3. The World's Longest Running Religious Debate Begins

1. Robert Wilken, "John Chrysostom," in *Encyclopedia of Early Christianity*, ed. Everett Ferguson (New York: Garland, 1997), xiv; John Chrysostom, "Eight Homilies against the Jews: Homily 1," *Internet Medieval Source Book*, www.fordham.edu/halsall/source/chrysostom-jews6.html.

2. Salo W. Baron, "Ghetto and Emancipation: Shall We Revise the Traditional View?" *Menorah Journal*, June 14, 1928, 526. Baron, the twentieth century's most prominent Jewish historian, who taught at Columbia University for many years, challenged the "lachrymose concept" of Jewish history. He believed "medieval Jews possessed more rights than the great bulk of the population ... and enjoyed full internal autonomy," but in modern times Jews became a religious confessional group only.

3. Philip A. Cunningham, *Education for Shalom: Religion Textbooks and the Enhancement of the Catholic and Jewish Relationship* (Collegeville, Minn.: Liturgical Press, 1995); Eugene J. Fisher, *Faith without Prejudice* (New York: Paulist Press, 1977); Bernhard E. Olson, *Faith and Prejudice: Intergroup Problems in Protestant Curricula* (New Haven: Yale Universit

Press, 1963); John T. Pawlikowski, *Catechetics and Prejudice: How Catholic Teaching Materials View Jews, Protestants, and Racial Minorities* (New York: Paulist Press, 1973); Gerald S. Strober, *Portrait of the Elder Brother: Jews and Judaism in Protestant Teaching Materials* (New York: American Jewish Committee, 1972); Rose Thering, *Jews, Judaism, and Catholic Education* (New York: Anti-Defamation League, 1986).

4. Amy-Jill Levine, *The Misunderstood Jew: The Church and the Scandal of the Jewish Jesus* (San Francisco: HarperCollins, 2006), 20, 51.

5. Raymond E. Brown, *An Introduction to the New Testament* (New York: Doubleday, 1997), 333–82.

6. Donald Senior, *The Passion of Jesus in the Gospel of John* (Collegeville, Minn.: Liturgical Press, 1991), 155–56.

7. See Michael J. Cook, *Modern Jews Engage the New Testament: Enhancing Jewish Well-Being in a Christian Environment* (Woodstock, Vt.: Jewish Lights, 2008).

8. *Encyclopaedia Judaica*, 2nd ed., ed. Fred Skolnik (Detroit: Macmillan Reference USA, 2007), s.v. "crucifixion."

9. Flavius Josephus, *The Great Roman-Jewish War: A.D. 66–70 (de Bello Judaico)*, trans. William Whiston, rev. D. S. Margolioth, ed. William R. Farmer (New York: Harper, 1960), bk. 5, chap. 11.

10. Ellis Rivkin, "Defining the Pharisees: The Tannaitic Sources," *Hebrew Union College Annual* (1970): 40–41, 205–49; see also Ellis Rivkin, *A Hidden Revolution: The Pharisees' Search for the Kingdom Within* (Nashville: Abington Press, 1978).

11. Barry Schwartz, Yael Zerubavel, and Bernice M. Barnett, "The Recovery of Masada: A Study in Collective Memory," *Sociological Quarterly* 27, no. 2 (Summer 1986): 155.

12. Lawrence H. Schiffman, *Reclaiming the Dead Sea Scrolls: The History of Judaism, the Background of Christianity, the Lost Library of Qumran* (Philadelphia: Jewish Publication Society, 1994).

13. Harold W. Attridge, "How Would All of This Have Influenced Jesus?" *Frontline*, PBS-TV, April 1998. Platonic philosophy and Stoic philosophy probably had little impact upon Jesus, unlike Jews in other areas of the Middle East, i.e., Philo of Alexandria. Early Christianity, however, was influenced by Hellenistic civilization.

14. Republican presidential hopeful and former governor of Wisconsin Tommy Thompson apologized for telling a Jewish group that making money is "part of the Jewish tradition." Thompson had told the Religious Action Center of the Union for Reform Judaism in a public address in Washington, D.C.: "You know that's sort of part of the Jewish tradition, and I do not find anything wrong with that. I enjoy that."

Associated Press, "Thompson Apologizes for Jewish Comments: Candidate Says He Meant to Compliment Success of Jewish Business," April 17, 2007.

15. Eugene J. Fisher, *Faith without Prejudice: Rebuilding Christian Attitudes toward Judaism* (New York: Crossroad, 1993), 75–76.

16. Flavius Josephus, *Antiquities*, bk. 17, chap. 4:1–2.

17. Michael Specter, "Tomb May Hold the Bones of Priest Who Judged Jesus," *New York Times*, August 14, 1992.

18. Harold Hoehner, "Pontius Pilate," in *Dictionary of Jesus and the Gospels*, ed. Joel Green, Scot McKnight, and I. Howard Marshall (Downers Grove, Ill.: Intervarsity Press, 1992), 616.

19. Ibid., p. 407.

20. Flavius Josephus, *Great Roman-Jewish War*, trans. Whiston, 80–81. The selection is from chapter IX, 4:175–177.

21. Flavius Josephus, *Jerusalem and Rome: The Writings of Josephus*, ed. Nahum N. Glatzer (New York: Meridian Books, 1960), 144–145. The selection is from *The Great Roman-Jewish War*, chapter II, 9:2–3.

22. Philo, *Legatio ad Gaium*, ed. and trans. E. Mary Smallwood (Leiden: Brill, 1961), 302.

23. Asher Finkel, "The Passover Story and the Last Supper," in *Root and Branch: The Jewish/Christian Dialogue*, ed. Michael Zeik and Morton Siegel (New York: Roth, 1973), 19–46; and Asher Finkel and Lawrence Frizzell, eds., *Standing Before God: Studies on Prayer in Scriptures and in Tradition* (New York: Ktav, 1981).

24. *Encyclopaedia Judaica*, 2nd ed., s.v. "Jesus"; see also David Flusser, "The Crucified One and the Jews," in *Judaism and the Origins of Christianity* (Jerusalem: Magnes Press, 1988).

25. *Encyclopaedia Judaica*, 2nd ed., s.v. "Jesus."

26. Schalom Ben-Chorin, *Brother Jesus: The Nazarene through Jewish Eyes*, trans. Jared S. Klein and Max Reinhart (Athens, Ga.: University of Georgia Press, 2001); see also Beatrice Bruteau, ed., *Jesus through Jewish Eyes* (Maryknoll, N.Y.: Orbis Books, 2001), 5.

4. Saul, Call Me Paul: The Controversial Apostle to the Gentiles

1. Alexander Roberts and James Donaldson, eds., *Recognitions of Clement*, in *The Ante-Nicene Fathers* (Grand Rapids, Mich.: Wm. B. Eerdmans, 1995), 8:65–66.

2. Krister Stendahl, *Paul among Jews and Gentiles* (Philadelphia: Fortress Press, 1976).

3. Sydney E. Ahlstrom, ed., *Theology in America: The Major Protestant Voices from Puritanism to Neo-Orthodoxy* (Indianapolis: Hackett, 2003), 23.

4. Levine, *Misunderstood Jew*, 84.

5. Barrie Wilson, *How Jesus Became Christian* (New York: St. Martin's Press, 2008), 114.

6. Walter Kasper, "The Commission for Religious Relations with the Jews: A Crucial Endeavour of the Catholic Church," speech delivered at Boston College, November 6, 2002. This speech represents Walter Kasper's fundamental beliefs about Catholic-Jewish relations.

7. Avery Dulles, "Covenant and Mission," *America*, October 21, 2002. See also Avery Dulles, "The Covenant with Israel," *First Things*, November 2005.

8. Marcion was excommunicated from the church in 144 CE, but his influence is still felt among some Christians; www.umass.edu/wsp/biblica/marcion/index.html.

9. John Paul II, address to the Vatican Symposium on the Roots of Anti-Judaism, October 31, 1997, www.vatican.va/holy_father/john_ paul_ii/speeches/1997/october/documents/hf_jp-ii_spe_19971031_com-teologica_en.html.

5. The Partings of the Way: Jews and Christians Take Separate Paths to God

1. Paul Johnson, *A History of the Jews* (New York: Harper & Row, 1987), 141–42.

2. Heinrich Graetz, *History of the Jews* (Philadelphia: Jewish Publication Society of America, 1956), 2:412.

3. Johnson, *History of the Jews*, 141–42.

4. Cassius Dio, *Roman History*, Loeb Classical Library (Cambridge, Mass.: Harvard University Press, 1925), vol. 8, bk. 69.

5. Robert M. Seltzer, *Jewish People, Jewish Thought: The Jewish Experience in History* (New York: Macmillan, 1980), 767.

6. James Parkes, *Whose Land? A History of the Peoples of Palestine* (Harmondsworth, U.K.: Penguin Books, 1970), 266.

6. Why "Old Testament" Is Not a Term of Endearment

1. Walter C. Kaiser Jr., "Law and Good Works in Evangelical Christianity," in *A Time to Speak: The Evangelical-Jewish Encounter*, ed. A. James Rudin and Marvin R. Wilson (Grand Rapids: Eerdmans, 1987), 132.

2. David R. Blumenthal, "The Place of Faith and Grace in Judaism," in *A Time to Speak*, ed. Rudin and Wilson, 104–05.

3. Friedrich Heer, *Gottes erste Liebe; 2000 Jahre Judentum und Christentum; Genesis des Österreichischen Katholiken Adolf Hitler* (Munich: Bechtle Verlag, 1967), 54, as translated in René Latourelle, ed., *Vatican II. Assessment and Perspectives, Twenty-five Years After, 1962–1987* (New York: Paulist Press, 1989), 317.

4. Allen S. Maller, "Isaiah's Suffering Servant: A New View," *Jewish Bible Quarterly* 37, no. 4 (2009): 243–49. See also Bernd Janowski and Peter Stuhlmacher, eds., *The Suffering ·Servant: Isaiah 53 in Jewish and Christian Sources*, trans. Daniel P. Bailey (Grand Rapids: William B. Eerdmans, 2004).

5. Harry M. Orlinsky, "The So-Called 'Suffering Servant' In Isaiah 53," in *Interpreting the Prophetic Tradition: The Goldenson Lectures, 1955–1966* (Cincinnati: Hebrew Union College Press, 1969), 227–73.

6. John Paul II, "Declaration to Europe," Santiago de Compostela, Spain, November 9, 1982.

7. *Catechism of the Catholic Church* (1993), pt. 1, sec. 1, ch. 2, art. 3, para. 110, www.vatican.va/archive/ENG0015/_INDEX.HTM.

7. Anti-Judaism and Anti-Semitism: The Poisoned Branches of Paul's "Good Olive Tree"

1. Louis L. Snyder, ed., *Encyclopedia of the Third Reich* (New York: McGraw Hill, 1976), 222.

2. Egal Feldman, "American Protestant Theologians on the Frontiers of Christian-Jewish Relations, 1922–1982," in *Anti-Semitism in American History*, ed. David A. Gerber (Urbana: University of Illinois Press, 1986), 383.

3. Adolf Hitler, *Mein Kampf* (Boston: Houghton Mifflin, 1971), 55, 121; see also Peter G. J. Pulzer, *The Rise of Political Anti-Semitism in Germany and Austria*, rev. ed. (Hoboken, N.J.: Wiley, 1988).

4. Flannery's book has drawn wide praise and influenced many outside the interreligious field; see the review by Ari Belenkiy of the physics department at Bar-Ilan University in Israel, "Edward Flannery's *The Anguish of the Jews*: A Forgotten Feat," January 2002, www.professors. org.il/docs/edward_flannery.

5. Edward Flannery, 1967 interview, quoted in Eric Pace, "The Rev. Edward Flannery, 86, Priest Who Fought Anti-Semitism," *New York Times*, October 22, 1998.

6. Graetz, *History of the Jews* 2:69–70.

7. "Father Charles E. Coughlin, The Radio Priest," *Detroit News*, July 23, 1995, http://apps.detnews.com/apps/history/index.php?id=43.

8. William Manchester, *The Glory and the Dream: A Narrative History of America, 1932–1972* (New York: Bantam Books, 1974), 176; see also Marc Dollinger, *Quest for Inclusion: Jews and Liberalism in Modern America* (Princeton: Princeton University Press, 2000), 66.

9. "Mississippi: … and to the Nation," *Time Magazine*, August 6, 1945, www.time.com/time/magazine/article/0,9171,803647,0.html. The letter was written before Israel was established in 1948.

10. Max Wallace, *The American Axis: Henry Ford, Charles Lindbergh, and the Rise of the Third Reich* (New York: Macmillan, 2005), 193.

11. Eugene J. Fisher, "Catholics and Jews Confront the Holocaust," John Courtney Murray Lecture, Fordham University, 1999, www.jcrelations. net/en/?id=811.

12. Michael J. Cook, *Modern Jews Engage the New Testament: Enhancing Jewish Well-Being in a Christian Environment* (Woodstock, Vt.: Jewish Lights, 2008), 278–79.

13. See Philip A. Cunningham, "*Nostra Aetate*: Transforming the Catholic-Jewish Relationship," October 20, 2005, www.adl.org/main_Interfaith/ nostra_aetate.htm.

14. Jeremy Cohen, *The Friars and the Jews: The Evolution of Medieval Anti-Judaism* (Ithaca: Cornell University Press, 1982).

15. Thomas Aquinas, *The Summa Theologica of St. Thomas Aquinas*, trans. Fathers of the English Dominican Province (1920), *Secunda Secundae Partis*, q. 10, art. 8, objection 4, www.newadvent.org/summa/3010.htm; see also Edward Kessler and Neil Wenborn, eds., *A Dictionary of Jewish-Christian Relations* (New York: Cambridge University Press, 2005), 29.

16. Martin Luther, "On the Jews and Their Lies," in *Luther's Works*, vol. 47, *The Christian in Society IV*, ed. Franklin Sherman (Philadelphia: Fortress Press, 1971), 267, 289, 292.

17. Helmut T. Lehmann, gen. ed., *Luther's Works*, vol. 47, *The Christian in Society IV*, ed. Sherman, iii.

18. Victoria J. Barnett, "For the Soul of the People: Protestant Protest under Hitler," *Christian Century*, April 26, 1995, 454–57.

19. Edith Stein to Pope Pius XI, 1933, www.baltimorecarmel.org/saints/ Stein/letter%20to%20pope.htm.

20. "The Unnecessary Problem of Edith Stein," *National Catholic Reporter*, February 3, 1995.

21. Paul VI, *Nostra Aetate*, October 28, 1965, www.vatican.va/archive/ hist_councils/ii_vatican_council/documents/vat-ii_decl_19651028_ nostra-aetate_en.html. Pier Franceso Fumagalli's commentary reflects the official Vatican position thirty-five years after *Nostra Aetate*'s adoption:

"*Nostra Aetate:* A Milestone," www.vatican.va/jubilee_2000/magazine/documents/ju_mag_01111997_p-31_en.html.

22. American Jewish Committee, "History & Highlights: A Timeline," www.ajc.org/site/c.ijITI2PHKoG/b.844677.

23. "Text of Cushing's Address," *New York Times,* September 29, 1964; see also John Oesterreicher, *The New Encounter between Christians and Jews* (New York: Philosophical Library, 1986), 197–98.

24. *Nostra Aetate,* no. 4.

25. Ibid.

26. General Synod 16 of the United Church of Christ, "The Relationship between the United Church of Christ and the Jewish Community," June 27, 1987, www.ccjr.us/dialogika-resources/documents-and-statements/protestant-churches/na/united-church/687-ucc87june.

27. General Conference of the United Methodist Church (USA), "Bridge in Hope: Jewish-Christian Dialogue," April 1, 1972, www.ccjr.us/dialogika-resources/documents-and-statements/protestant-churches/na/methodist/690-umc72apr.

28. United Methodist Church, "Building New Bridges in Hope," 1996, http://archives.umc.org/interior.asp?ptid=4&mid=3301.

29. John Paul II, address to representatives of the American Jewish Committee, March 16, 1990. See John Paul II, *Spiritual Pilgrimage: Pope John Paul II, Texts on Jews and Judaism, 1979–1995,* ed. Eugene Fisher and Leon Klenicki (New York: Crossroad Herder, 1995), 134.

30. The complete text of "*Dabru Emet:* A Jewish Statement on Christians and Christianity" can be found at www.jcrelations.net/en/?item=1014.

31. Jon D. Levenson, "How Not to Conduct Jewish-Christian Dialogue," *Commentary* 112 (December 2001): 31–37; David Berger, statement issued by the Institute for Public Affairs of the Orthodox Union, September 14, 2000, www.ou.org/public/statements/2000/betty25.htm.

32. Arthur Hertzberg, *The French Enlightenment and the Jews: The Origins of Modern Anti-Semitism* (New York: Columbia University Press, 1990), 10, 286.

33. Theodor Herzl, *The Jewish State* (1896; n.p.: General Books, 2010), 13.

34. Peter Steinfels, "Vatican Document Condemns All Forms of Racism as Sinful," *New York Times,* February 11, 1989.

8. Mission, Witness, and Conversion

1. "Paris 1242—The Burning of the Talmud," www.chaburas.org/paris.html.

2. The United States Holocaust Memorial Museum in Washington, D.C., has excellent resources on book burning on its website: www.ushmm.org/wlc/en/article.php?ModuleId=10005852.

3. Elinor Slater and Robert Slater, *Great Moments in Jewish History* (Middle Village, N.Y.: Jonathan David, 1999), 168.

4. Michael Prestwich, *Edward I* (New Haven: Yale University Press, 1997), 343.

5. Bice Migliau and Micaela Procaccia with Silvia Rebuzzi and Micaela Vitale, *Lazio Jewish Itineraries: Places, History, and Art*, trans. Gus Barker (Venice: Marsilio, 1997), 25.

6. Benedict XVI, address at the Synagogue of Rome, January 17, 2010, www.vatican.va/holy_father/benedict_xvi/speeches/2010/january/documents/hf_ben-xvi_spe_20100117_sinagoga_en.html.

7. Nahum N. Glatzer, *Franz Rosenzweig: His Life and Thought* (New York: Schocken Books, 1961), 341.

8. John Paul II, address to participants in the Vatican symposium "The Roots of Anti-Judaism in the Christian Milieu," October 31, 1997, www.ccjr.us/dialogika-resources/documents-and-statements/roman-catholic/pope-john-paul-ii/321-jp2-97oct318.

9. Benedict XVI, address at the Synagogue of Rome, January 17, 2010.

10. James and Marcia Rudin, "The Jews for Jesus Are Out to Get Your Kids," *Present Tense Magazine*, Summer 1977, 17–26.

11. I was interviewed on this topic in Margalit Fox, "Moishe Rosen Dies at 78; Founder of Jews for Jesus," *New York Times*, May 23, 2010.

12. "Billy Graham on Key '73," *Christianity Today*, March 16, 1973, 29.

13. Harvard Divinity School, "Krister Stendahl, 1921–2008," www.hds.harvard.edu/news/article_archive/stendahl.html.

14. Harvey Falk, "Rabbi Jacob Emden's Views on Christianity and the Noachide Commandments," *Journal of Ecumenical Studies* 19 (Winter 1982): 1.

9. O Jerusalem! Three Faiths but Only One Jerusalem

1. Linda Machaud-Emin, "Jerusalem 1948–1967 vs. 1967–2007: Comparing the Israeli and Jordanian Record," April 18, 2007, www.sixdaywar.co.uk/gloria-report-jerusalem-compared.htm.

2. See "al-Aqsa Mosque" in *Merriam-Webster's Encyclopedia of World Religions* (Springfield, Mass.: Merriam-Webster, 1999), 70.

3. R. J. Zwi Werblowsky, "The Meaning of Jerusalem to Jews, Christians and Muslims," 1978, http://christianactionforisrael.org/meaning.html.

4. Ibid.

5. John Milton, *Paradise Lost*, ed. John Leonard (New York: Penguin Classics, 2003), iii, 476–77.

6. Krister Stendahl, "Judaism and Christianity II—After a Colloquium and a War," *Harvard Divinity Bulletin*, Autumn 1967, 2–8.

7. Hayim Nahman Bialik and Yehoshua Hana Ravnitzky, eds., *The Book of Legends/Sefer Ha-Aggadah: Legends from the Talmud and Midrash* (New York: Schocken Books, 1992), 373.

8. Jacqueline Schaalje, "The Walls and Gates of Jerusalem," *Jewish Magazine*, March 2003, www.jewishmag.com/65mag/jerusalemgates/jerusalemgates.htm.

9. Ministry of Propaganda, *Die Deutsche Wochenschau* (newsreel footage), Berlin, December 10, 1941, Nr. 588, www.youtube.com/watch?v=nSUEx1cKUlg. See also "Haj Amin el-Husseini Dies; Ex-Palestine Grand Mufti," *New York Times*, July 5, 1974; and Joseph Schechtman, *The Mufti and the Fuehrer: The Rise and Fall of Haj Amin el-Husseini* (New York: Thomas Yoseloff, 1965), 307–8.

10. Marshall J. Breger, "The New Battle for Jerusalem," *Middle East Quarterly* 1, no. 4 (December 1994): 23–34.

11. Ibid.

12. "Fundamental Agreement between the Holy See and the State of Israel," December 30, 1993, www.vatican.va/roman_curia/secretariat_state/archivio/documents/rc_seg-st_19931230_santa-sede-israele_en.html.

13. Bill Clinton, *My Life* (New York: Vintage, 2005), 936–46.

14. *The Columbia Encyclopedia*, 6th ed. (New York: Columbia University Press, 2004), s.v. "Ramla."

10. Why There Is Only One Holocaust

1. Richard J. Evans, *The Third Reich at War* (New York: Penguin Press, 2009), 240.

2. Ibid., 268.

3. Christopher R. Browning, *Ordinary Men: Reserve Battalion 101 and the Final Solution in Poland* (New York: HarperCollins, 1992).

4. Daniel Jonah Goldhagen, *Hitler's Willing Executioners: Ordinary Germans and the Holocaust* (New York: Vintage, 1996).

5. Benedict XVI, address given on visit to Yad Vashem Memorial Jerusalem, May 11, 2009, www.vatican.va/holy_father/benedict_xvi speeches/2009/may/documents/hf_ben-xvi_spe_2009051 yad-vashem_en.html.

6. Benedict XVI, address given at Auschwitz-Birkenau, May 28, 2006, www.vatican.va/holy_father/benedict_xvi/speeches/2006/may/documents/hf_ben-xvi_spe_20060528_auschwitz-birkenau_en.html.

7. Anne Frank, *The Diary of Anne Frank: The Critical Edition*, trans. Arnold J. Pomerans and B. M. Mooyaart-Doubleday (New York: Doubleday, 1989), 694.

8. Ibid, 600.

9. On the controversy over dramatic adaptation of the *Diary*, see Ralph Melnick, *The Stolen Legacy of Anne Frank: Meyer Levin, Lillian Hellman, and the Staging of the Diary* (New Haven: Yale University Press, 1997). Meyer Levin, an American novelist, first brought the *Diary* to the world's attention with a *New York Times* review. He later wrote a play about Anne Frank that Broadway producers and others considered "too Jewish." The well-known stage and film *Diary* versions were written later by Frances Goodrich and Albert Hackett. Levin sued them, claiming plagiarism. Although he won the case, Levin's play is rarely presented.

10. Frank, *Diary*, 600.

11. Quoted in Joyce Apsel, "Anne's Words Still Strengthen Spirits," *St. Petersburg Times*, January 26, 2000, www.sptimes.com/News/012600/NIE/Anne_s_words_still_st.shtml.

12. "Remarks on Presenting the Congressional Gold Medal to Elie Wiesel and on Signing the Jewish Heritage Week Proclamation," transcript, April 19, 1985, www.pbs.org/eliewiesel/resources/reagan.html.

13. Yitzhak Arad, Israel Gutman, and Abraham Margaliot, eds., *Documents on the Holocaust: Selected Sources on the Destruction of the Jews of Germany and Austria, Poland, and the Soviet Union* (Jerusalem: Yad Vashem, 1981), 283–84.

14. Quoted in John Leonard, "The Drowned and the Unsaved," *The Nation*, April 9, 2001.

15. Andrew Jackson, "Fifth Annual Message," December 3, 1833; www.synaptic.bc.ca/ejournal/JacksonFifthAnnualMessage.htm.

16. Pope John Paul II, April 7, 1994, www.vatican.va/holy_father/john_paul_ii/speeches/1994/april/documents/hf_jp-ii_spe_19940407_concerto-shoah_it.html.

17. Alliance of Baptists, "Statement on Baptist-Jewish Relations," March 4, 1995.

18. Obituary of Emil Fackenheim by Avi Katzman, *Ha-aretz*, September 21, 2003. See also David Ellenson, "Emil Fackenheim and the Revealed Morality of Judaism," *Judaism* 25 (1976): 402–13; and Seltzer, *Jewish People, Jewish Thought*, 765.

11. The Meaning of Modern Israel for Christians and Jews

1. Harry S. Truman Library and Museum, May 14, 1948; www.trumanlibrary. org/whistlestop/study_collections/israel/large.
2. "Egypt and Jordan Unite against Israel," *BBC News*, May 30, 1967, http://news.bbc.co.uk/onthisday/hi/dates/stories/may/30/newsid_ 2493000/2493177.stm.
3. Michael Scott-Baumann, "The Causes of the Six-Day War," in *Conflict in the Middle East: Israel and the Arabs*, 2nd ed. (London: Trans-Atlantic, 2007), 25.
4. BICOM (British Israel Communications Centre, London), "Six-Day War Series: Quotes from Arab Leaders and Media Outlets Calling for Israel's Destruction in May and June 1967," October 9, 2008, www.bicom.org.uk/context/research-and-analysis/regional-issues/six-day-war-series--quotes-from-arab-leaders-and-media-outlets-calling-for-israel-s-destruction-in-may-and-june-1967.
5. Judith Hershcopf Banki, *Christian Reactions to the Middle East Crisis: The New Agenda for Interreligious Dialogue* (New York: American Jewish Committee, 1968), 2.
6. Henry P. Van Dusen, letter to the editor, *New York Times*, June 26, 1967.
7. Banki, *Christian Reactions to the Middle East Crisis*, 6.
8. Ibid., 19. There is an enormous amount of literature about the various Christian attitudes toward the State of Israel; see A. James Rudin, *Israel for Christians: Understanding Modern Israel* (Philadelphia: Fortress Press, 1983), 121–40.
9. Joshua Michael Zeitz, "'If I Am Not for Myself ...': The American Jewish Establishment in the Aftermath of the Six-Day War," *American Jewish History* 88, no. 2 (June 2000): 253–86.
10. Rudin, *Israel for Christians*, 172.
11. Theodor Herzl, "Address to the First Zionist Congress," August 29, 1897, http://zionism-israel.com/hdoc/Theodor_Herzl_Zionist_Congress_ Speech_1897.htm.
12. In Rudin and Wilson, eds., *A Time to Speak*, 195.
13. Rudin, *Israel for Christians*, 124.
14. Ibid., 126.
15. Ibid., 140.

12. Proceed with Caution: Interreligious Relations Is Now a Three-Way Intersection

1. H. A. R. Gibb, *Mohammedanism: An Historical Survey* (New York: Mentor Books, 1955).

2. David Harris, "In the Trenches: Self-Inflicted Wounds," *Jerusalem Post*, September 3, 2007, www.eujs.org/news/article/26.

3. *Now with Bill Moyers*, PBS-TV, January 18, 2002, www.pbs.org/now/society/imam.html. In this program Martin Plax, the American Jewish Committee's Cleveland director, said, "For me, the question is 'what's the truth?' And the ambiguity of 'I don't know that I can trust him [Damra] any longer.'"

4. A. James Rudin, "Can American Jews and Muslims Get Along?" *Reform Judaism* 30, no. 2 (Winter 2001): 29–34.

5. Qur'an, *Sura Al-Ahzab*, 033.040. Yusuf Ali translation: "Muhammad is not the father of any of your men, but (he is) the Messenger of Allah, and the Seal of the Prophets: and Allah has full knowledge of all things."

6. Pope John Paul II to Edward Idris Cassidy, March 12, 1998, www.vatican.va/roman_curia/pontifical_councils/chrstuni/documents/rc_pc_chrstuni_doc_16031998_shoah_en.html.

7. Pope John Paul II, *Pope John Paul II on Jews and Judaism: 1979–1986*, ed. Eugene J. Fisher and Leon Klenicki (Washington, D.C.: U.S. Catholic Conference, 1987), 10.

8. Commission for Religious Relations with the Jews, "We Remember: A Reflection on the Shoah," March 16, 1998, www.vatican.va/roman_curia/pontifical_councils/chrstuni/documents/rc_pc_chrstuni_doc_16031998_shoah_en.html.

9. John Paul II, "Western Wall Prayer," March 26, 2000, www.bc.edu/research/cjl/meta-elements/texts/cjrelations/resources/documents/catholic/johnpaulii/westernwall.htm.

10. Peggy Polk, "Vatican Declares Only the Roman Catholic Church Brings Salvation," Religion News Service, September 7, 2000.

11. Peggy Noonan, "'It Is as It Was.' Mel Gibson's 'The Passion' Gets a Thumbs-Up from the Pope," *Wall Street Journal*, December 17, 2003.

12. "Pope Likens Abortion to Holocaust," *BBC News*, February 22, 2005, http://news.bbc.co.uk/2/hi/europe/4288103.stm.

13. *Roman Missal* (Chicago: Canons Regular of St. John Cantius, 1920), 221–22.

14. Quoted in Christian-Jewish Dialogue of Montreal, "Resolution on the Revised 1962 Good Friday 'Prayer for the Jews,'" January 12, 2009, www.jcrelations.net/en/?item=3054.

15. Ibid.

16. *Catechism for Adults* (Washington, D.C.: U.S. Conference of Catholic Bishops, 2006).

17. The Vatican revision of the catechism on "mission" and "covenant" was reported in a U.S. Conference of Catholic Bishops news release on August 27, 2009.

18. "Letter of His Holiness Pope Benedict XVI to the Bishops of the Catholic Church Concerning the Remission of the Excommunication of the Four Bishops Consecrated by Archbishop Lefebvre," March 10, 2009, www.vatican.va/holy_father/benedict_xvi/letters/2009/documents/hf_ben-xvi_let_20090310_remissione-scomunica_en.html.

19. Pew Forum on Religion & Public Life, *U.S. Religious Landscape Survey, 2008* (Washington, D.C.: Pew Research Center, 2008), 5.

20. Lydia Saad, "Support for Israel in U.S. at 63%, Near Record High," Gallup, February 24, 2010, www.gallup.com/poll/126155/Support-Israel-Near-Record-High.aspx.

21. Alexa Smith, "Assembly Endorses Israel Divestment," July 2, 2004, http://oga.pcusa.org/ga216/news/ga04121.htm.

22. Middle East Media Research Institute, "Presbyterian Church USA & Families of 9/11 Victims Delegations Meet with Hezbollah," November 23, 2005.

23. Eric Heyl, "Presbyterian's Praise of Hezbollah Raises Ire," *Pittsburgh Tribune-Review*, October 21, 2004.

24. Mark Braverman, *Fatal Embrace: Christians, Jews, and the Search for Peace in the Holy Land* (Austin, Tex.: Synergy Books, 2010); see especially Walter Brueggermann's foreword. Also, the 2009 Palestinian Christian Kairos Document reflects similar harsh views of Israel: www.oikoumene.org/gr/resources/documents/other-ecumenical-bodies/kairos-palestine-document.html. The Central Conference of American Rabbis, the Reform rabbinical group, criticized the Kairos Document: "CCAR Resolution on the 2009 *Kairos* Document," April 15, 2010, http://data.ccarnet.org/cgi-bin/resodisp.pl?file=kairos&year=2010.

25. "Creating Community," *Union for Reform Judaism Biennial Blog*, December 14, 2007, http://blogs.rj.org/ biennial/2007/12/creating_community.html.

26. Reinhold Niebuhr, a foe of Nazism, rejected Christian attempts to convert Jews, and he supported the creation of the State of Israel. See "Jews after the War," *The Nation*, February 21 and February 28, 1942, 214–16 and 253–55; "It Might Have Been," *Evangelical Herald*, March 29, 1923, 202; "The Rapprochement between Jews and Christians," *Christian Century*, January 7, 1926, 9–11; "Germany Must Be Told," *Christian Century*, August 9, 1933, 1014–15.

27. Marc H. Tanenbaum, Marvin R. Wilson, and A. James Rudin, eds., *Evangelicals and Jews in an Age of Pluralism* (Grand Rapids, Mich.: Baker Book House, 1984), 30.
28. Rudin and Wilson, *A Time to Speak*, 172.
29. James Rudin, *The Baptizing of America: The Religious Right's Plans for the Rest of Us* (New York: Thunder's Mouth Press, 2006), 5–6.
30. Rudin and Wilson, *A Time to Speak*, xi–xiii.

13. We Are Prisoners of Hope

1. Council of Centers on Jewish-Christian Relations, www.ccjr.us.

Suggestions for Further Reading

There are thousands of books dealing with Jews, Christians, and Muslims and their relations with one another, and for that reason, the listing below hardly exhausts the vast subject. *A Dictionary of Jewish-Christian Relations*, published in 2005 and listed below, contains the single best bibliography to date. It also cites more than sixty institutional declarations and statements on the subject made since 1945.

Adelson, Alan, and Robert Lapides. *Lodz Ghetto: Inside a Community under Siege*. New York: Penguin Books, 1991.

Ahmed, Akbar. *Journey into Islam: The Crisis of Globalization*. Washington, D.C.: Brookings Institution Press, 2007.

Ariel, Yaakov. *Evangelizing the Chosen People: Missions to the Jews in America, 1880–2000*. Chapel Hill: University of North Carolina Press, 2000.

Avineri, Shlomo. *The Making of Modern Zionism*. New York: Basic Books, 1981.

Baeck, Leo. *Judaism and Christianity*. Philadelphia: Jewish Publication Society of America, 1958.

Banki, Judith H., and John T. Pawlikowski. *Ethics in the Shadow of the Holocaust: Christian and Jewish Perspectives*. Franklin, Wisc.: Sheed & Ward, 2001.

Baron, Salo W. *A Social and Religious History of the Jews*. 16 vols. Philadelphia: Jewish Publication Society of America/New York: Columbia University Press, 1952–73.

Berenbaum, Michael, ed. *Witness to the Holocaust*. New York: HarperCollin, 1997.

Berger, Alan L., and David Patterson, eds. *Jewish-Christian Dialogue: Dra Honey from the Rock*. St. Paul: Paragon House, 2008.

Berger, David, and Michael Wyschogrod. *Jews and "Jewish Christianity."* New York: Ktav, 1978.

Bishop, Claire Huchet. *How Catholics Look at Jews.* New York: Paulist Press, 1974.

Blumenthal, David R. *Approaches to Judaism in Medieval Times.* 2 vols. Decatur, Ga.: Scholars Press, 1985.

Bonhoeffer, Dietrich. *Letters and Papers from Prison.* Translated by Reginald Fuller, et al. New York: Macmillan, 1972.

Borg, Marcus. *Meeting Jesus Again for the First Time: The Historical Jesus and the Heart of Contemporary Faith.* San Francisco: Harper, 1994.

Borowitz, Eugene B. *Contemporary Christologies: A Jewish Response.* New York: Paulist Press, 1980.

Boys, Mary C., and Sara S. Lee. *Christians & Jews in Dialogue: Learning in the Presence of the Other.* Woodstock, Vt.: SkyLight Paths, 2006.

Brown, Raymond E. *The Birth of the Messiah: A Commentary on the Infancy Narratives in the Gospels of Matthew and Luke.* New York: Doubleday, 1993.

————. *The Death of the Messiah—from Gethsemane to the Grave: A Commentary on the Passion Narratives in the Four Gospels.* New York: Doubleday, 1994.

Browning, Christopher R. *Ordinary Men: Reserve Police Battalion 101 and the Final Solution in Poland.* New York: HarperCollins, 1993.

Buber, Martin. *Two Types of Faith: The Interpretation of Judaism and Christianity.* New York: Harper and Row, 1961.

Carroll, James. *Constantine's Sword: The Church and the Jews.* Boston: Houghton Mifflin, 2001.

Chanes, Jerome A., ed. *Antisemitism in America Today: Outspoken Experts Explode the Myths.* New York: Birch Lane Press, 1995.

Chazan, Robert. *Barcelona and Beyond: The Disputation of 1263 and Its Aftermath.* Berkeley: University of California Press, 1992.

————. *In the Year 1096: The First Crusade and the Jews.* Philadelphia: Jewish Publication Society, 1996.

Cohen, Jeremy. *The Friars and the Jews: The Evolution of Medieval Anti-Judaism.* Ithaca: Cornell University Press, 1982.

Cohen, Martin A., and Helga Croner. *Christian Mission—Jewish Mission.* New York: Paulist Press, 1982.

Cohn-Sherbok, Dan. *The Crucified Jew: Twenty Centuries of Anti-Semitism.* Grand Rapids: Eerdmans/Philadelphia: American Interfaith Institute, 1997.

Collins, Larry, and Dominique Lapierre. *O Jerusalem!* New York: Simon and Schuster, 1988.

Cook, Michael J. *Modern Jews Engage the New Testament: Enhancing Jewish Well-Being in a Christian Environment.* Woodstock, Vt.: Jewish Lights, 2008.

Croner, Helga, and Leon Klenicki. *Issues in the Jewish-Christian Dialogue: Jewish Perspectives on Covenant, Mission, and Witness.* New York: Paulist Press, 1979.

Cunningham, Philip. *Education for Shalom: Religion Textbooks and the Enhancement of the Catholic and Jewish Relationship.* Collegeville, Minn.: Liturgical Press, 1995.

———, ed. *Pondering the Passion: What's at Stake for Christians and Jews.* Lanham, Md.: Rowman & Littlefield, 2005.

Davidowicz, Lucy S. *The War Against the Jews: 1933–45.* New York: Holt, Rinehart & Winston, 1975.

Davies, Alan T., ed. *Antisemitism and the Foundations of Christianity.* New York: Paulist Press, 1979.

Davies, William D. *Christian Origins and Judaism.* Philadelphia: Westminster Press, 1962.

Drinan, Robert F. *Honor the Promise.* New York: Doubleday, 1977.

Eckardt, A. Roy. *Jews and Christians: The Contemporary Meeting.* Bloomington: Indiana University Press, 1986.

Efroymson, David P., Eugene J. Fisher, and Leon Klenicki, eds. *Within Context: Essays on Jews and Judaism in the New Testament.* Collegeville, Minn.: Liturgical Press, 1993.

Elon, Amos. *The Israelis: Founders and Sons.* New York: Holt, Rinehart & Winston, 1971.

Evans, Richard J. *The Coming of the Third Reich.* New York: Penguin Press, 2005.

———. *The Third Reich at War.* New York: Penguin Press, 2009.

———. *The Third Reich in Power.* New York: Penguin Press, 2006.

Everett, Robert A. *James Parkes: Historian and Theologian of Jewish-Christian Relations.* Ann Arbor: University Microfilms International, 1983.

Fackenheim, Emil. *The Jewish Bible after the Holocaust.* Manchester: Manchester University Press, 1988.

Feiler, Bruce. *Abraham: A Journey to the Heart of Three Faiths.* New York: W. Morrow, 2002.

Feingold, Henry L. *The Politics of Rescue: The Roosevelt Administration and the Holocaust, 1938–1945.* New York: Schocken Books, 1980.

Feldblum, Eric. *The American Catholic Press and the Jewish State, 1917–1959.* New York: Ktav, 1977.

Feldman, Egal. *Dual Destinies: The Jewish Encounter with Protestant America.* Urbana: University of Illinois Press, 1990.

Firestone, Reuven. *Who Are the Real Chosen People? The Meaning of Chosen in Judaism, Christianity, and Islam.* Woodstock, Vt.: SkyLight Paths.

Fisher, Eugene J., ed. *Interwoven Destinies: Jews and Christians through* New York: Stimulus Books, 1993.

Fisher, Eugene J., and Leon Klenicki. *John Paul II on Jews and Judaism, 1979–1986*. Washington, D.C.: U.S. Catholic Conference, 1987.

Fisher, Eugene J., A. James Rudin, and Marc H. Tanenbaum, eds. *Twenty Years of Jewish-Catholic Relations*. New York: Paulist Press, 1986.

Fishman, Hertzel. *American Protestantism and a Jewish State*. Detroit: Wayne State University Press, 1973.

Flannery, Edward H. *The Anguish of the Jews*. Rev. ed. New York: Paulist Press, 1985.

Fleischner, Eva, ed. *Auschwitz, Beginning of a New Era?* New York: Ktav, 1977.

Flusser, David. *Jesus*. New York: Herder, 1969.

———. *Judaism and the Origins of Christianity*. Jerusalem: Magnes Press, 1998.

Frank, Anne. *The Diary of Anne Frank: The Revised Critical Edition*. Edited by David Barnouw and Gerrold van der Stroom. Translated by Arnold J. Pomerans, B. M. Mooyaart-Doubleday, and Susan Massotty. New York: Doubleday, 2003.

Fredriksen, Paula. *From Jesus to Christ: The Origins of the New Testament Images of Christ*. New Haven: Yale University Press, 1988.

Friedlander, Saul. *Nazi Germany and the Jews: The Years of Extermination, 1933–1945*. New York: HarperCollins, 2007.

Frymer-Kensky, Tikva, David Novak, Peter Ochs, David Fox Sandmel, and Michael A. Signer, eds. *Christianity in Jewish Terms*. Boulder: Westview Press, 2000.

Gager, John G. *The Origins of Anti-Semitism: Attitudes toward Judaism in Pagan and Christian Antiquity*. New York: Oxford University Press, 1983.

Gerber, Jane S. *The Jews of Spain: A History of the Sephardic Experience*. New York: Macmillan, 1992.

Gilbert, Arthur. *The Vatican Council and the Jews*. Cleveland: World Publishing, 1968.

Goldhagen, Daniel Jonah. *Hitler's Willing Executioners: Ordinary Germans and the Holocaust*. New York: Alfred A. Knopf, 1996.

Greenberg, Blu. *On Women and Judaism: A View from Tradition*. Philadelphia: Jewish Publication Society of America, 1981.

Hay, Malcolm. *The Roots of Christian Anti-Semitism*. New York: Freedom Library Press, 1981.

Helmreich, E. C. *The German Churches under Hitler*. Detroit: Wayne State University Press, 1979.

Hertzberg, Arthur, ed. *The Zionist Idea: A Historical Analysis and Reader*. Garden City: Doubleday, 1959.

Heschel, Abraham Joshua. *Israel: An Echo of Eternity*. New York: Farrar, Straus & Giroux, 1969.

Heschel, Susannah. *The Aryan Jesus: Christian Theologians and the Bible in Nazi Germany*. Princeton: Princeton University Press, 2008.

Hogan, David J., ed. *The Holocaust Chronicle: A History in Words and Pictures*. Lincolnwood, Ill.: Publications International, 2000.

Holtz, Avraham, ed. *The Holy City: Jews on Jerusalem*. New York: W. W. Norton, 1971.

Hourani, Albert. *A History of the Arab Peoples*. Cambridge, Mass.: Harvard University Press, 1991.

Hunter, James Davison. *Culture Wars: The Struggle to Define America*. New York: Basic Books, 1991.

Idinopulos, Thomas A. *Betrayal of Spirit: Jew-Hatred, the Holocaust, and Christianity*. Aurora, Colo.: Davies Group, 2007.

Isaac, Jules. *Jesus and Israel*. New York: Holt, Rinehart, & Winston, 1971.

———. *The Teaching of Contempt: Christian Roots of Anti-Semitism*. New York: Holt, Rinehart & Winston, 1964.

Jacob, Walter. *Christianity through Jewish Eyes: The Quest for Common Ground*. Cincinnati: Hebrew Union College Press, 1974.

Jewish Publication Society. *Tanakh: A New Translation of the Holy Scriptures According to the Traditional Hebrew Text*. Philadelphia: Jewish Publication Society, 1985.

Johnson, Paul. *A History of the Jews*. New York: Harper & Row, 1987.

Katz, Jacob. *Exclusiveness and Tolerance: Studies in Jewish-Gentile Relations in Medieval and Modern Times*. London: Oxford University Press, 1961.

Kertzer, David I. *The Popes against the Jews: The Vatican's Role in the Rise of Modern Anti-Semitism*. New York: Alfred A. Knopf, 2001.

Klausner, Joseph. *The Messianic Idea in Israel*. Translated by W. F. Stinespring. New York: Macmillan, 1955.

Klenicki, Leon, ed. *Toward a Theological Encounter: Jewish Understandings of Christianity*. New York: Paulist Press, 1991.

Levensen, Jon D. *The Hebrew Bible, the Old Testament, and Historical Criticism: Jews and Christians in Biblical Studies*. Louisville: Westminster John Knox Press, 1993.

Levine, Amy-Jill. *The Misunderstood Jew: The Church and the Scandal of the Jewish Jesus*. San Francisco: HarperCollins, 2006.

Lewis, Bernard. *What Went Wrong? The Clash Between Islam and Modernity in the Middle East*. New York: Oxford University Press, 2002.

Lewy, Gunther. *The Catholic Church and Nazi Germany*. Detroit: Wayne State University Press, 1974.

Lipstadt, Deborah E. *Denying the Holocaust: The Growing Assault on Truth and Memory*. New York: Free Press, 1993.

Lockman Foundation. *New American Standard Bible.* Rev. ed. La Habra, Calif.: Foundation Publications, 1997.

Marty, Martin E. *Pilgrims in Their Own Land: 500 Years of Religion in America.* Boston: Little, Brown, 1984.

Marty, Martin E., and R. Scott Appleby, eds. *Fundamentalism and Society: Reclaiming the Sciences, the Family, and Education.* Chicago: University of Chicago Press, 1993.

————, eds. *Fundamentalisms Observed.* Chicago: University of Chicago Press, 1991.

McGarry, Michael B. *Christology after Auschwitz.* New York: Paulist Press, 1977.

Mendes-Flohr, Paul, and Jehuda Reinharz. *The Jew in the Modern World: A Documentary History.* 2nd ed. New York: Oxford University Press, 1995.

Moore, George Foot. *Judaism in the First Centuries of the Christian Era.* 3 vols. Cambridge, Mass.: Harvard University Press, 1948.

Morley, John F. *Vatican Diplomacy and the Jews during the Holocaust, 1939–1943.* New York: Ktav, 1980.

Murray, John Courtney. *We Hold These Truths: Catholic Reflections on the American Proposition.* New York: Sheed & Ward, 1960.

Nasr, Seyyed Hossein, ed. *Islamic Spirituality: Foundations.* New York: Crossroad, 1991.

O'Hare, Padric. *The Enduring Covenant: The Education of Christians and the End of Anti-Semitism.* Valley Forge: Trinity Press International, 1997.

Oliner, Samuel P., and Pearl M. Oliner. *The Altruistic Personality: Rescuers of Jews in Nazi Europe.* New York: Free Press of Macmillan, 1988.

Opsahl, Paul, and Marc H. Tanenbaum, eds. *Speaking of God Today: Jews and Lutherans in Conversation.* Philadelphia: Fortress Press, 1974.

Oren, Michael B. *The Making of the Modern Middle East.* New York: Ballantine Books/Presidio Press, 2000.

Orlinsky, Harry M. *Ancient Israel.* Ithaca: Cornell University Press, 1954.

Parkes, James W. *Antisemitism.* Chicago: Quadrangle Books, 1964.

————. *The Conflict of the Church and the Synagogue: A Study in the Origins of Antisemitism.* New York: Meridian Books, 1961.

————. *End of an Exile: Israel, the Jews, and the Gentile World.* Marblehead, Mass.: Micah, 2005.

————. *The Foundations of Judaism and Christianity.* Chicago: Quadrangle Books, 1960.

Pawlikowski, John T. *What Are They Saying about Christian-Jewish Relations?* New York: Paulist Press, 1980.

....ck, Abraham J., ed. *Jews and Christians after the Holocaust.* Philadelphia: Fortress Press, 1982.

Phayer, Michael. *The Catholic Church and the Holocaust, 1930–1965*. Bloomington: Indiana University Press, 2000.

Poliakov, Leon. *The History of Anti-Semitism*. New York: Schocken Books, 1981.

Potok, Chaim. *Wanderings: The History of the Jews*. New York: Alfred A. Knopf, 1978.

Rausch, David A. *A Legacy of Hatred*. Chicago: Moody Press, 1984.

———. *Zionism within Early American Fundamentalism, 1878–1918*. New York: Edwin Mellen Press, 1980.

Reinharz, Adele. *Befriending the Beloved Disciple: A Jewish Reading of the Book of John*. New York: Continuum, 2001.

Riegner, Gerhart M., and Johannes Willebrands, eds. *Fifteen Years of Catholic-Jewish Dialogue, 1970–1985*. Rome: Libreria Editrice Vaticana & Libreria Editrice Lateranense, 1988.

Rittner, Carol, Stephen D. Smith, and Irena Steinfeldt, eds. *The Holocaust and the Christian World: Reflections on the Past, Challenges for the Future*. New York: Continuum, 2000.

Rivkin, Ellis. *What Crucified Jesus?* Nashville: Abington Press, 1984.

Rosen, David. *Haknessiah Hakatolit, Ha'Am HaYehudi u'Medinat Yisrael* [The Catholic Church, the Jewish People and the State of Israel]. Jerusalem: Jerusalem Institute for Interreligious Relations and Research, 1996.

———. *The Impact of the Interreligious Dialogue upon Theological Thought*. Vatican City: Fermenti Nella Teologica Alle Soglie del Terzio Millenia, Pontifice della Santa Croce, 1998.

Rosen, David, and Stanislaw Dziwisz. *Brothers Reunited: Catholic-Jewish Dialogue*. Krakow: Biblioteka Centrum Kultury i Dialogu, 2009.

Rosenzweig, Franz. *Star of Redemption*. Translated by William Hallo. New York: Holt, Rinehart & Winston, 1971.

Ross, Robert W. *So It Was True: The American Protestant Press and the Nazi Persecution of the Jews*. Minneapolis: University of Minnesota Press, 1980.

Rothschild, Fritz A., ed. *Jewish Perspectives on Christianity: Leo Baeck, Martin Buber, Franz Rosenzweig, Will Herberg, and Abraham J. Heschel*. New York: Crossroad, 1990.

Rubin, Theodore Isaac. *Anti-Semitism: A Disease of the Mind*. New York: Continuum, 1990.

Rubinstein, Richard L. *After Auschwitz: History, Theology, and Contemporary Judaism*. Baltimore: Johns Hopkins Press, 1992.

Rudin, A. James. *The Baptizing of America: The Religious Right's Plans for the Rest of Us*. New York: Thunder's Mouth Press, 2006.

———. "A Fractured Friendship." *Reform Judaism* (Summer 2003): 47–50.

———. *Israel for Christians: Understanding Modern Israel*. Philadelphia: Fortress Press, 1983.

————. *A Jewish Guide to Interreligious Relations*. New York: American Jewish Committee, 1996.

Rudin, A. James, and Marvin R. Wilson, eds. *A Time to Speak: The Evangelical-Jewish Encounter*. Grand Rapids: Eerdmans, 1987.

Ruether, Rosemary Radford. *Faith and Fratricide: The Theological Roots of Anti-Semitism*. Minneapolis: Seabury Press, 1974.

Rynne, Xavier. *Vatican Council II*. Maryknoll, N.Y.: Orbis Books, 1999.

Sachar, Abram L. *A History of the Jews*. New York: Alfred A. Knopf, 1964.

Sanders, E. P. *Paul and Palestinian Judaism*. Philadelphia: Fortress Press, 1978.

Sandmel, Samuel. *A Jewish Understanding of the New Testament*. New York: Ktav, 1957. Reprint, Woodstock, Vt.: Jewish Lights/SkyLight Paths, 2005.

————. *Judaism and Christian Beginnings*. New York: Oxford University Press, 1978.

Saperstein, Marc. *Moments of Crisis in Jewish-Christian Relations*. London: SCM Press, 1989.

Sarna, Jonathan D. *American Judaism: A History*. New Haven: Yale University Press, 2004.

Schlant, Ernestine. *The Language of Silence: West German Literature and the Holocaust*. New York: Routledge, 1999.

Scholem, Gershom. *The Messianic Idea in Judaism*. New York: Schocken Books, 1971.

Seltzer, Robert M. *Jewish People, Jewish Thought: The Jewish Experience in History*. New York: Macmillan, 1980.

Shanks, Hershel, ed. *Christianity and Rabbinic Judaism: A Parallel History of Their Origins and Development*. London: SPCK, 1993.

Sherman, Franklin. *Luther and the Jews: A Fateful Legacy*. Allentown, Pa.: Institute of Christian-Jewish Studies, 1995.

Shriver, Donald W., Jr. *An Ethic for Enemies: Forgiveness in Politics*. New York: Oxford University Press, 1995.

Signer, Michael A., ed. *Memory and History in Christianity and Judaism*. Notre Dame: University of Notre Dame Press, 2001.

Silver, Abba Hillel. *Where Judaism Differed*. New York: Macmillan, 1956.

Sloyan, Gerald. *Jesus on Trial*. Philadelphia: Fortress Press, 1973.

Spiro, Melford E. *Buddhism and Society: A Great Tradition and Its Burmese Vicissitudes*. 2nd ed. Berkeley: University of California Press, 1982.

Stacpoole, Alberic, ed. *Vatican II Revisited by Those Who Were There*. Minneapolis: Winston Press, 1986.

Stendahl, Krister. *Paul among Jews and Gentiles*. Philadelphia: Fortress Press, 1976.

Synan, Edward A. *The Popes and the Jews in the Middle Ages.* New York: Macmillan, 1965.

Tal, Uriel. *Christians and Jews in Germany: Religion, Politics and Ideology in the Second Reich, 1870–1914.* Ithaca: Cornell University Press, 1975.

Tanenbaum, Marc H., Marvin R. Wilson, and A. James Rudin, eds. *Evangelicals and Jews in an Age of Pluralism.* Grand Rapids: Baker Book House, 1984.

————. *Evangelicals and Jews in Conversation.* Grand Rapids: Baker Book House, 1978.

Thoma, Clemens. *A Christian Theology of Judaism.* New York: Paulist Press, 1980.

Trachtenberg, Joshua. *The Devil and the Jews: The Medieval Conception of the Jew and Its Relation to Modern Antisemitism.* New York: Meridian Books, 1961.

Vermes, Geza. *Jesus and the World of Judaism.* Philadelphia: Fortress Press, 1983.

Werner, Eric. *The Sacred Bridge: Liturgical Parallels in the Synagogue and the Early Church.* New York: Schocken Books, 1970.

Wilken, Robert L. *Judaism and the Early Christian Mind.* New Haven: Yale University Press, 1971.

Willebrands, Johannes. *Church and Jewish People: New Considerations.* New York: Paulist Press, 1992.

Williamson, Clark M. *Has God Rejected His People? Anti-Judaism in the Christian Church.* Nashville: Abingdon Press, 1982.

Wilson, Barrie. *How Jesus Became Christian.* New York: St. Martin's Press, 2008.

Wilson, Marvin R. *Our Father Abraham: Jewish Roots of the Christian Faith.* Grand Rapids: Eerdmans, 1989.

Wolfson, Harry A. *The Philosophy of the Church Fathers.* Cambridge, Mass.: Harvard University Press, 1956.

Wyman, David S. *The Abandonment of the Jews: America and the Holocaust, 1941–1945.* New York: Pantheon Books, 1984.

Young, Brad H. *Jesus and His Jewish Parables: Rediscovering the Roots of Jesus' Teaching.* New York: Paulist Press, 1989.

Zahn, Gordon. *German Catholics and Hitler's Wars: A Study in Social Control.* New York: Sheed & Ward, 1962.

Zannoni, Arthur E., ed. *Jews and Christians Speak of Jesus.* Minneapolis: Fortress Press, 1994.

Zeitlin, Solomon. *Who Crucified Jesus?* New York: Bloch, 1964.

Zuccotti, Susan. *Under His Very Windows: The Vatican and the Holocaust in Italy.* New Haven: Yale University Press, 2000.

Index

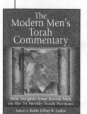

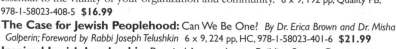

Holidays/Holy Days

Who by Fire, Who by Water—Un tanah Tokef
Edited by Rabbi Lawrence A. Hoffman, PhD
Examines the prayer's theology, authorship and poetry through a set of lively essays, all written in accessible language.
6 x 9, 272 pp, HC, 978-1-58023-424-5 **$24.99**

Rosh Hashanah Readings: Inspiration, Information and Contemplation
Yom Kippur Readings: Inspiration, Information and Contemplation
Edited by Rabbi Dov Peretz Elkins; Section Introductions from Arthur Green's These Are the Words
An extraordinary collection of readings, prayers and insights that will enable you to enter into the spirit of the High Holy Days in a personal and powerful way, permitting the meaning of the Jewish New Year to enter the heart.
Rosh Hashanah: 6 x 9, 400 pp, Quality PB, 978-1-58023-437-5 **$19.99**
Yom Kippur: 6 x 9, 368 pp, Quality PB, 978-1-58023-438-2 **$19.99**

Jewish Holidays: A Brief Introduction for Christians
By Rabbi Kerry M. Olitzky and Rabbi Daniel Judson
5½ x 8½, 176 pp, Quality PB, 978-1-58023-302-6 **$16.99**

Reclaiming Judaism as a Spiritual Practice: Holy Days and Shabbat
By Rabbi Goldie Milgram 7 x 9, 272 pp, Quality PB, 978-1-58023-205-0 **$19.99**

7th Heaven: Celebrating Shabbat with Rebbe Nachman of Breslov
By Moshe Mykoff with the Breslov Research Institute
5⅛ x 8¼, 224 pp, Deluxe PB w/ flaps, 978-1-58023-175-6 **$18.95**

Shabbat, 2nd Edition: The Family Guide to Preparing for and Celebrating the Sabbath *By Dr. Ron Wolfson*
7 x 9, 320 pp, Illus., Quality PB, 978-1-58023-164-0 **$19.99**

Hanukkah, 2nd Edition: The Family Guide to Spiritual Celebration
By Dr. Ron Wolfson 7 x 9, 240 pp, Illus., Quality PB, 978-1-58023-122-0 **$18.95**

The Jewish Family Fun Book, 2nd Edition: Holiday Projects, Everyday Activities, and Travel Ideas with Jewish Themes *By Danielle Dardashti and Roni Sarig; Illus. by Avi Katz*
6 x 9, 304 pp, 70+ b/w illus. & diagrams, Quality PB, 978-1-58023-333-0 **$18.99**

The Jewish Lights Book of Fun Classroom Activities: Simple and Seasonal Projects for Teachers and Students *By Danielle Dardashti and Roni Sarig*
6 x 9, 240 pp, Quality PB, 978-1-58023-206-7 **$19.99**

Passover

My People's Passover Haggadah
Traditional Texts, Modern Commentaries
Edited by Rabbi Lawrence A. Hoffman, PhD, and David Arnow, PhD
A diverse and exciting collection of commentaries on the traditional Passover Haggadah—in two volumes!
Vol. 1: 7 x 10, 304 pp, HC, 978-1-58023-354-5 **$24.99**
Vol. 2: 7 x 10, 320 pp, HC, 978-1-58023-346-0 **$24.99**

Leading the Passover Journey: The Seder's Meaning Revealed, the Haggadah's Story Retold *By Rabbi Nathan Laufer*
Uncovers the hidden meaning of the Seder's rituals and customs.
6 x 9, 224 pp, Quality PB, 978-1-58023-399-6 **$18.99**; HC, 978-1-58023-211-1 **$24.99**

The Women's Passover Companion: Women's Reflections on the Festival of Freedom
Edited by Rabbi Sharon Cohen Anisfeld, Tara Mohr and Catherine Spector; Foreword by Paula E. Hyman
6 x 9, 352 pp, Quality PB, 978-1-58023-231-9 **$19.99**; HC, 978-1-58023-128-2 **$24.95**

The Women's Seder Sourcebook: Rituals & Readings for Use at the Passover Seder
Edited by Rabbi Sharon Cohen Anisfeld, Tara Mohr and Catherine Spector
6 x 9, 384 pp, Quality PB, 978-1-58023-232-6 **$19.99**

Creating Lively Passover Seders: A Sourcebook of Engaging Tales, Texts & Activities
By David Arnow, PhD 7 x 9, 416 pp, Quality PB, 978-1-58023-184-8 **$24.99**

Passover, 2nd Edition: The Family Guide to Spiritual Celebration
By Dr. Ron Wolfson with Joel Lurie Grishaver 7 x 9, 416 pp, Quality PB, 978-1-58023-174-9 **$19.95**

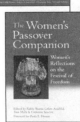

Judaism / Christianity / Interfaith

How to Do Good and Avoid Evil: A Global Ethic from the Sources of Judaism *By Hans Küng and Rabbi Walter Homolka* Explores how the principles of Judaism provide the ethical norms for all religions to work together toward a more peaceful humankind. 6 x 9, 224 pp, HC, 978-1-59473-255-3 **$19.99***

Getting to the Heart of Interfaith: The Eye-Opening, Hope-Filled Friendship of a Pastor, a Rabbi and a Sheikh
By Rabbi Ted Falcon, Pastor Don Mackenzie and Sheikh Jamal Rahman
Presents ways we can work together to transcend the differences that have divided us historically. 6 x 9, 192 pp, Quality PB, 978-1-59473-263-8 **$16.99***

Claiming Earth as Common Ground: The Ecological Crisis through the Lens of Faith *By Rabbi Andrea Cohen-Kiener*
Inspires us to work across denominational lines in order to fulfill our sacred imperative to care for God's creation. 6 x 9, 192 pp, Quality PB, 978-1-59473-261-4 **$16.99***

Modern Jews Engage the New Testament: Enhancing Jewish Well-Being in a Christian Environment *By Rabbi Michael J. Cook, PhD*
A solution-oriented introduction to Christian sacred writings that will lead Jews out of anxieties that plague them. 6 x 9, 416 pp, HC, 978-1-58023-313-2 **$29.99**

The Changing Christian World: A Brief Introduction for Jews
By Rabbi Leonard A. Schoolman 5½ x 8½, 176 pp, Quality PB, 978-1-58023-344-6 **$16.99**

Christians & Jews in Dialogue: Learning in the Presence of the Other
By Mary C. Boys and Sara S. Lee
6 x 9, 240 pp, Quality PB, 978-1-59473-254-6 **$18.99**; HC, 978-1-59473-144-0 **21.99***

Disaster Spiritual Care: Practical Clergy Responses to Community, Regional and National Tragedy *Edited by Rabbi Stephen B. Roberts, BCJC, and Rev. Willard W. C. Ashley Sr., DMin, DH*
6 x 9, 384 pp, HC, 978-1-59473-240-9 **$40.00***

Healing the Jewish-Christian Rift: Growing Beyond Our Wounded History
By Ron Miller and Laura Bernstein 6 x 9, 288 pp, Quality PB, 978-1-59473-139-6 **$18.99***

How to Be a Perfect Stranger, 4th Edition: The Essential Religious Etiquette Handbook *Edited by Stuart M. Matlins and Arthur J. Magida*
6 x 9, 432 pp, Quality PB, 978-1-59473-140-2 **$19.99***

InterActive Faith: The Essential Interreligious Community-Building Handbook
Edited by Rev. Bud Heckman with Rori Picker Neiss 6 x 9, 304 pp, HC, 978-1-59473-237-9 **$29.99***

Introducing My Faith and My Community
The Jewish Outreach Institute Guide for the Christian in a Jewish Interfaith Relationship
By Rabbi Kerry M. Olitzky 6 x 9, 176 pp, Quality PB, 978-1-58023-192-3 **$16.99**

The Jewish Approach to Repairing the World (*Tikkun Olam*)
A Brief Introduction for Christians *By Rabbi Elliot N. Dorff, PhD, with Rev. Cory Willson*
5½ x 8½, 256 pp, Quality PB, 978-1-58023-349-1 **$16.99**

The Jewish Connection to Israel, the Promised Land: A Brief Introduction for Christians *By Rabbi Eugene Korn, PhD* 5½ x 8½, 192 pp, Quality PB, 978-1-58023-318-7 **$14.99**

Jewish Holidays: A Brief Introduction for Christians *By Rabbi Kerry M. Olitzky and Rabbi Daniel Judson* 5½ x 8½, 176 pp, Quality PB, 978-1-58023-302-6 **$16.99**

Jewish Ritual: A Brief Introduction for Christians *By Rabbi Kerry M. Olitzky and Rabbi Daniel Judson* 5½ x 8½, 144 pp, Quality PB, 978-1-58023-210-4 **$14.99**

A Jewish Understanding of the New Testament *By Rabbi Samuel Sandmel;*
Preface by Rabbi David Sandmel 5½ x 8½, 368 pp, Quality PB, 978-1-59473-048-1 **$19.99***

Righteous Gentiles in the Hebrew Bible: Ancient Role Models for Sacred Relationships *By Rabbi Jeffrey K. Salkin; Foreword by Rabbi Harold M. Schulweis; Preface by Phyllis Tickle*
6 x 9, 192 pp, Quality PB, 978-1-58023-364-4 **$18.99**

Talking about God: Exploring the Meaning of Religious Life with Kierkegaard, Buber, Tillich and Heschel *By Daniel F. Polish, PhD* 6 x 9, 160 pp, Quality PB, 978-1-59473-272-0 **$16.99***

We Jews and Jesus: Exploring Theological Differences for Mutual Understanding
By Rabbi Samuel Sandmel; Preface by Rabbi David Sandmel
6 x 9, 192 pp, Quality PB, 978-1-59473-208-9 **$16.99**

*A book from SkyLight Paths, Jewish Lights' sister imprint

Spirituality

Repentance: The Meaning and Practice of *Teshuvah*
By Dr. Louis E. Newman; Foreword by Rabbi Harold M. Schulweis; Preface by Rabbi Karyn D. Kedar
Examines both the practical and philosophical dimensions of *teshuvah*, Judaism's core religious-moral teaching on repentance, and its value for us—Jews and non-Jews alike—today. 6 x 9, 256 pp, HC, 978-1-58023-426-9 **$24.99**

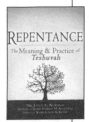

Tanya, the Masterpiece of Hasidic Wisdom
Selections Annotated & Explained
Translation & Annotation by Rabbi Rami Shapiro; Foreword by Rabbi Zalman M. Schachter-Shalomi
Brings the genius of *Tanya*, one of the most powerful books of Jewish wisdom, to anyone seeking to deepen their understanding of the soul.
5½ x 8½, 240 pp, Quality PB, 978-1-59473-275-1 **$16.99**
(A book from SkyLight Paths, Jewish Lights' sister imprint)

Aleph-Bet Yoga: Embodying the Hebrew Letters for Physical and Spiritual Well-Being
By Steven A. Rapp; Foreword by Tamar Frankiel, PhD, and Judy Greenfeld; Preface by Hart Lazer
7 x 10, 128 pp, b/w photos, Quality PB, Lay-flat binding, 978-1-58023-162-6 **$16.95**

A Book of Life: Embracing Judaism as a Spiritual Practice
By Rabbi Michael Strassfeld 6 x 9, 544 pp, Quality PB, 978-1-58023-247-0 **$19.99**

Bringing the Psalms to Life: How to Understand and Use the Book of Psalms
By Rabbi Daniel F. Polish, PhD 6 x 9, 208 pp, Quality PB, 978-1-58023-157-2 **$16.95**

Does the Soul Survive? A Jewish Journey to Belief in Afterlife, Past Lives & Living with Purpose *By Rabbi Elie Kaplan Spitz; Foreword by Brian L. Weiss, MD*
6 x 9, 288 pp, Quality PB, 978-1-58023-165-7 **$16.99**

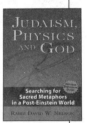

First Steps to a New Jewish Spirit: Reb Zalman's Guide to Recapturing the Intimacy & Ecstasy in Your Relationship with God *By Rabbi Zalman M. Schachter-Shalomi with Donald Gropman* 6 x 9, 144 pp, Quality PB, 978-1-58023-182-4 **$16.95**

Foundations of Sephardic Spirituality: The Inner Life of Jews of the Ottoman Empire
By Rabbi Marc D. Angel, PhD 6 x 9, 224 pp, Quality PB, 978-1-58023-341-5 **$18.99**

God & the Big Bang: Discovering Harmony between Science & Spirituality
By Dr. Daniel C. Matt 6 x 9, 216 pp, Quality PB, 978-1-879045-89-7 **$16.99**

God in Our Relationships: Spirituality between People from the Teachings of Martin Buber *By Rabbi Dennis S. Ross* 5½ x 8½, 160 pp, Quality PB, 978-1-58023-147-3 **$16.95**

The Jewish Lights Spirituality Handbook: A Guide to Understanding, Exploring & Living a Spiritual Life *Edited by Stuart M. Matlins*
What exactly is "Jewish" about spirituality? How do I make it a part of my life? Fifty of today's foremost spiritual leaders share their ideas and experience with us.
6 x 9, 456 pp, Quality PB, 978-1-58023-093-3 **$19.99**

Judaism, Physics and God: Searching for Sacred Metaphors in a Post-Einstein World
By Rabbi David W. Nelson 6 x 9, 352 pp, Quality PB, inc. reader's discussion guide,
978-1-58023-306-4 **$18.99**; HC, 352 pp, 978-1-58023-252-4 **$24.99**

Meaning and Mitzvah: Daily Practices for Reclaiming Judaism through Prayer, God, Torah, Hebrew, Mitzvot and Peoplehood *By Rabbi Goldie Milgram*
7 x 9, 336 pp, Quality PB, 978-1-58023-256-2 **$19.99**

Minding the Temple of the Soul: Balancing Body, Mind, and Spirit through Traditional Jewish Prayer, Movement, and Meditation *By Tamar Frankiel, PhD, and Judy Greenfeld*
7 x 10, 184 pp, Illus., Quality PB, 978-1-879045-64-4 **$16.95**

One God Clapping: The Spiritual Path of a Zen Rabbi *By Rabbi Alan Lew with Sherril Jaffe*
5½ x 8½, 336 pp, Quality PB, 978-1-58023-115-2 **$16.95**

The Soul of the Story: Meetings with Remarkable People
By Rabbi David Zeller 6 x 9, 288 pp, HC, 978-1-58023-272-2 **$21.99**

There Is No Messiah ... and You're It: The Stunning Transformation of Judaism's Most Provocative Idea *By Rabbi Robert N. Levine, DD*
6 x 9, 192 pp, Quality PB, 978-1-58023-255-5 **$16.99**

These Are the Words: A Vocabulary of Jewish Spiritual Life
By Rabbi Arthur Green, PhD 6 x 9, 304 pp, Quality PB, 978-1-58023-107-7 **$18.95**

Spirituality/Prayer

Making Prayer Real: Leading Jewish Spiritual Voices on Why Prayer Is Difficult and What to Do about It   *By Rabbi Mike Comins*
A new and different response to the challenges of Jewish prayer, with "best prayer practices" from Jewish spiritual leaders of all denominations.
6 x 9, 320 pp, Quality PB, 978-1-58023-417-7 **$18.99**

Witnesses to the One: The Spiritual History of the *Sh'ma*
By Rabbi Joseph B. Meszler; Foreword by Rabbi Elyse Goldstein
6 x 9, 176 pp, Quality PB, 978-1-58023-400-9 **$16.99**; HC, 978-1-58023-309-5 **$19.99**

My People's Prayer Book Series: Traditional Prayers, Modern Commentaries   *Edited by Rabbi Lawrence A. Hoffman, PhD*
Provides diverse and exciting commentary to the traditional liturgy. Will help you find new wisdom in Jewish prayer, and bring liturgy into your life. Each book includes Hebrew text, modern translations and commentaries from all perspectives of the Jewish world.

Vol. 1—The *Sh'ma* and Its Blessings
7 x 10, 168 pp, HC, 978-1-879045-79-8 **$24.99**
Vol. 2—The *Amidah* 7 x 10, 240 pp, HC, 978-1-879045-80-4 **$24.95**
Vol. 3—*P'sukei D'zimrah* (Morning Psalms)
7 x 10, 240 pp, HC, 978-1-879045-81-1 **$24.95**
Vol. 4—*Seder K'riat Hatorah* (The Torah Service)
7 x 10, 264 pp, HC, 978-1-879045-82-8 **$23.95**
Vol. 5—*Birkhot Hashachar* (Morning Blessings)
7 x 10, 240 pp, HC, 978-1-879045-83-5 **$24.95**
Vol. 6—*Tachanun* and Concluding Prayers
7 x 10, 240 pp, HC, 978-1-879045-84-2 **$24.95**
Vol. 7—Shabbat at Home 7 x 10, 240 pp, HC, 978-1-879045-85-9 **$24.95**
Vol. 8—*Kabbalat Shabbat* (Welcoming Shabbat in the Synagogue)
7 x 10, 240 pp, HC, 978-1-58023-121-3 **$24.99**
Vol. 9—Welcoming the Night: *Minchah* and *Ma'ariv* (Afternoon and Evening Prayer) 7 x 10, 272 pp, HC, 978-1-58023-262-3 **$24.99**
Vol. 10—Shabbat Morning: *Shacharit* and *Musaf* (Morning and Additional Services) 7 x 10, 240 pp, HC, 978-1-58023-240-1 **$24.99**

Spirituality/Lawrence Kushner

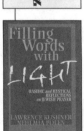

The Book of Letters: A Mystical Hebrew Alphabet
Popular HC Edition, 6 x 9, 80 pp, 2-color text, 978-1-879045-00-2 **$24.95**
Collector's Limited Edition, 9 x 12, 80 pp, gold-foil-embossed pages, w/ limited-edition silkscreened print, 978-1-879045-04-0 **$349.00**

The Book of Miracles: A Young Person's Guide to Jewish Spiritual Awareness
6 x 9, 96 pp, 2-color illus., HC, 978-1-879045-78-1 **$16.95** *For ages 9–13*

The Book of Words: Talking Spiritual Life, Living Spiritual Talk
6 x 9, 160 pp, Quality PB, 978-1-58023-020-9 **$16.95**

Eyes Remade for Wonder: A Lawrence Kushner Reader   *Introduction by Thomas Moore*
6 x 9, 240 pp, Quality PB, 978-1-58023-042-1 **$18.95**

Filling Words with Light: Hasidic and Mystical Reflections on Jewish Prayer
By Rabbi Lawrence Kushner and Rabbi Nehemia Polen
5½ x 8½, 176 pp, Quality PB, 978-1-58023-238-8 **$16.99**; HC, 978-1-58023-216-6 **$21.99**

God Was in This Place & I, i Did Not Know: Finding Self, Spirituality and Ultimate Meaning   6 x 9, 192 pp, Quality PB, 978-1-879045-33-0 **$16.95**

Honey from the Rock: An Introduction to Jewish Mysticism
6 x 9, 176 pp, Quality PB, 978-1-58023-073-5 **$16.95**

Invisible Lines of Connection: Sacred Stories of the Ordinary
5½ x 8½, 160 pp, Quality PB, 978-1-879045-98-9 **$15.95**

Jewish Spirituality: A Brief Introduction for Christians
5½ x 8½, 112 pp, Quality PB, 978-1-58023-150-3 **$12.95**

The River of Light: Jewish Mystical Awareness
6 x 9, 192 pp, Quality PB, 978-1-58023-096-4 **$16.95**

The Way Into Jewish Mystical Tradition
6 x 9, 224 pp, Quality PB, 978-1-58023-200-5 **$18.99**; HC, 978-1-58023-029-2 **$21.95**

Theology/Philosophy/The Way Into... Series

The Way Into... series offers an accessible and highly usable "guided tour" of the Jewish faith, people, history and beliefs—in total, an introduction to Judaism that will enable you to understand and interact with the sacred texts of the Jewish tradition. Each volume is written by a leading contemporary scholar and teacher, and explores one key aspect of Judaism. The Way Into... series enables all readers to achieve a real sense of Jewish cultural literacy through guided study.

The Way Into Encountering God in Judaism
By Rabbi Neil Gillman, PhD
For everyone who wants to understand how Jews have encountered God throughout history and today.
6 x 9, 240 pp, Quality PB, 978-1-58023-199-2 **$18.99**; HC, 978-1-58023-025-4 **$21.95**
Also Available: **The Jewish Approach to God:** A Brief Introduction for Christians
By Rabbi Neil Gillman, PhD
5½ x 8½, 192 pp, Quality PB, 978-1-58023-190-9 **$16.95**

The Way Into Jewish Mystical Tradition
By Rabbi Lawrence Kushner
Allows readers to interact directly with the sacred mystical texts of the Jewish tradition. An accessible introduction to the concepts of Jewish mysticism, their religious and spiritual significance, and how they relate to life today.
6 x 9, 224 pp, Quality PB, 978-1-58023-200-5 **$18.99**; HC, 978-1-58023-029-2 **$21.95**

The Way Into Jewish Prayer
By Rabbi Lawrence A. Hoffman, PhD
Opens the door to 3,000 years of Jewish prayer, making anyone feel at home in the Jewish way of communicating with God.
6 x 9, 208 pp, Quality PB, 978-1-58023-201-2 **$18.99**

Also Available: **The Way Into Jewish Prayer Teacher's Guide**
By Rabbi Jennifer Ossakow Goldsmith
8½ x 11, 42 pp, PB, 978-1-58023-345-3 **$8.99**
Download a free copy at www.jewishlights.com.

The Way Into Judaism and the Environment
By Jeremy Benstein, PhD
Explores the ways in which Judaism contributes to contemporary social-environmental issues, the extent to which Judaism is part of the problem and how it can be part of the solution.
6 x 9, 288 pp, Quality PB, 978-1-58023-368-2 **$18.99**; HC, 978-1-58023-268-5 **$24.99**

The Way Into *Tikkun Olam* (Repairing the World)
By Rabbi Elliot N. Dorff, PhD
An accessible introduction to the Jewish concept of the individual's responsibility to care for others and repair the world.
6 x 9, 304 pp, Quality PB, 978-1-58023-328-6 **$18.99**; 320 pp, HC, 978-1-58023-269-2 **$24.99**

The Way Into Torah
By Rabbi Norman J. Cohen, PhD
Helps guide you in the exploration of the origins and development of Torah, explains why it should be studied and how to do it.
6 x 9, 176 pp, Quality PB, 978-1-58023-198-5 **$16.99**

The Way Into the Varieties of Jewishness
By Sylvia Barack Fishman, PhD
Explores the religious and historical understanding of what it has meant to be Jewish from ancient times to the present controversy over "Who is a Jew?"
6 x 9, 288 pp, Quality PB, 978-1-58023-367-5 **$18.99**; HC, 978-1-58023-030-8 **$24.99**

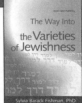

Theology/Philosophy

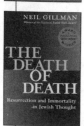

Jewish Theology in Our Time: A New Generation Explores the Foundations and Future of Jewish Belief *Edited by Rabbi Elliot J. Cosgrove, PhD*
A powerful and challenging examination of what Jews can believe—by a new generation's most dynamic and innovative thinkers.
6 x 9, 272 pp, HC, 978-1-58023-413-9 **$24.99**

Maimonides, Spinoza and Us: Toward an Intellectually Vibrant Judaism
By Rabbi Marc D. Angel, PhD A challenging look at two great Jewish philosophers and what their thinking means to our understanding of God, truth, revelation and reason. 6 x 9, 224 pp, HC, 978-1-58023-411-5 **$24.99**

The Death of Death: Resurrection and Immortality in Jewish Thought
By Rabbi Neil Gillman, PhD 6 x 9, 336 pp, Quality PB, 978-1-58023-081-0 **$18.95**

Doing Jewish Theology: God, Torah & Israel in Modern Judaism *By Rabbi Neil Gillman, PhD*
6 x 9, 304 pp, Quality PB, 978-1-58023-439-9 **$18.99**; HC, 978-1-58023-322-4 **$24.99**

Ethics of the Sages: Pirke Avot—Annotated & Explained
Translation & Annotation by Rabbi Rami Shapiro 5½ x 8¼, 192 pp, Quality PB, 978-1-59473-207-2 **$16.99***

Hasidic Tales: Annotated & Explained *Translation & Annotation by Rabbi Rami Shapiro*
5½ x 8¼, 240 pp, Quality PB, 978-1-893361-86-7 **$16.95***

A Heart of Many Rooms: Celebrating the Many Voices within Judaism
By Dr. David Hartman 6 x 9, 352 pp, Quality PB, 978-1-58023-156-5 **$19.95**

The Hebrew Prophets: Selections Annotated & Explained
Translation & Annotation by Rabbi Rami Shapiro; Foreword by Rabbi Zalman M. Schachter-Shalomi
5½ x 8¼, 224 pp, Quality PB, 978-1-59473-037-5 **$16.99***

A Jewish Understanding of the New Testament *By Rabbi Samuel Sandmel;*
Preface by Rabbi David Sandmel 5½ x 8¼, 368 pp, Quality PB, 978-1-59473-048-1 **$19.99***

Jews and Judaism in the 21st Century: Human Responsibility, the Presence of God and the Future of the Covenant *Edited by Rabbi Edward Feinstein; Foreword by Paula E. Hyman*
6 x 9, 192 pp, Quality PB, 978-1-58023-374-3 **$19.99**; HC, 978-1-58023-315-6 **$24.99**

A Living Covenant: The Innovative Spirit in Traditional Judaism
By Dr. David Hartman 6 x 9, 368 pp, Quality PB, 978-1-58023-011-7 **$25.00**

Love and Terror in the God Encounter: The Theological Legacy of Rabbi Joseph B. Soloveitchik *By Dr. David Hartman* 6 x 9, 240 pp, Quality PB, 978-1-58023-176-3 **$19.95**

The Personhood of God: Biblical Theology, Human Faith and the Divine Image
By Dr. Yochanan Muffs; Foreword by Dr. David Hartman
6 x 9, 240 pp, Quality PB, 978-1-58023-338-5 **$18.99**; HC, 978-1-58023-265-4 **$24.99**

A Touch of the Sacred: A Theologian's Informal Guide to Jewish Belief
By Dr. Eugene B. Borowitz and Frances W. Schwartz
6 x 9, 256 pp, Quality PB, 978-1-58023-416-0 **$16.99**; HC, 978-1-58023-337-8 **$21.99**

Traces of God: Seeing God in Torah, History and Everyday Life *By Rabbi Neil Gillman, PhD*
6 x 9, 240 pp, Quality PB, 978-1-58023-369-9 **$16.99**

We Jews and Jesus: Exploring Theological Differences for Mutual Understanding *By Rabbi Samuel Sandmel; Preface by Rabbi David Sandmel* 6 x 9, 192 pp, Quality PB, 978-1-59473-208-9 **$16.99***

Your Word Is Fire: The Hasidic Masters on Contemplative Prayer
Edited and translated by Rabbi Arthur Green, PhD, and Barry W. Holtz
6 x 9, 160 pp, Quality PB, 978-1-879045-25-5 **$15.95**

I Am Jewish

Personal Reflections Inspired by the Last Words of Daniel Pearl
Almost 150 Jews—both famous and not—from all walks of life, from all around the world, write about many aspects of their Judaism.
Edited by Judea and Ruth Pearl 6 x 9, 304 pp, Deluxe PB w/ flaps, 978-1-58023-259-3 **$18.99**
Download a free copy of the *I Am Jewish Teacher's Guide* at www.jewishlights.com.

Hannah Senesh: Her Life and Diary, The First Complete Edition
By Hannah Senesh; Foreword by Marge Piercy; Preface by Eitan Senesh; Afterword by Roberta Grossman
6 x 9, 368 pp, b/w photos, Quality PB, 978-1-58023-342-2 **$19.99**

*A book from SkyLight Paths, Jewish Lights' sister imprint

Social Justice

There Shall Be No Needy
Pursuing Social Justice through Jewish Law and Tradition
By Rabbi Jill Jacobs; Foreword by Rabbi Elliot N. Dorff, PhD; Preface by Simon Greer
Confronts the most pressing issues of twenty-first-century America from a deeply
Jewish perspective.
6 x 9, 288 pp, Quality PB, 978-1-58023-425-2 **$16.99**; HC, 978-1-58023-394-1 **$21.99**
  Also Available: **There Shall Be No Needy Teacher's Guide**
  8½ x 11, 56 pp, PB, 978-1-58023-429-0 **$8.99**

Conscience: The Duty to Obey and the Duty to Disobey
By Rabbi Harold M. Schulweis
This clarion call to rethink our moral and political behavior examines the idea of
conscience and the role conscience plays in our relationships to government, law,
ethics, religion, human nature, God—and to each other.
6 x 9, 160 pp, Quality PB, 978-1-58023-419-1 **$16.99**; HC, 978-1-58023-375-0 **$19.99**

Judaism and Justice: The Jewish Passion to Repair the World
By Rabbi Sidney Schwarz; Foreword by Ruth Messinger
Explores the relationship between Judaism, social justice and the Jewish identity
of American Jews.
6 x 9, 352 pp, Quality PB, 978-1-58023-353-8 **$19.99**; HC, 978-1-58023-312-5 **$24.99**

Spiritual Activism: A Jewish Guide to Leadership and Repairing the World
By Rabbi Avraham Weiss; Foreword by Alan M. Dershowitz
6 x 9, 224 pp, Quality PB, 978-1-58023-418-4 **$16.99**; HC, 978-1-58023-355-2 **$24.99**

Righteous Indignation: A Jewish Call for Justice   *Edited by Rabbi Or N. Rose,*
Jo Ellen Green Kaiser and Margie Klein; Foreword by Rabbi David Ellenson, PhD
Leading progressive Jewish activists explore meaningful intellectual and spiritual
foundations for their social justice work.
6 x 9, 384 pp, Quality PB, 978-1-58023-414-6 **$19.99**; HC, 978-1-58023-336-1 **$24.99**

Spirituality/Women's Interest

New Jewish Feminism: Probing the Past, Forging the Future
Edited by Rabbi Elyse Goldstein; Foreword by Anita Diamant
Looks at the growth and accomplishments of Jewish feminism and what they
mean for Jewish women today and tomorrow.
6 x 9, 480 pp, HC, 978-1-58023-359-0 **$24.99**

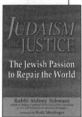

The Divine Feminine in Biblical Wisdom Literature
Selections Annotated & Explained
Translation & Annotation by Rabbi Rami Shapiro
5½ x 8½, 240 pp, Quality PB, 978-1-59473-109-9 **$16.99**
(A book from SkyLight Paths, Jewish Lights' sister imprint)

The Quotable Jewish Woman: Wisdom, Inspiration & Humor from the Mind & Heart
Edited by Elaine Bernstein Partnow   6 x 9, 496 pp, Quality PB, 978-1-58023-236-4 **$19.99**

The Women's Haftarah Commentary: New Insights from Women
Rabbis on the 54 Weekly Haftarah Portions, the 5 Megillot & Special Shabbatot
Edited by Rabbi Elyse Goldstein   Illuminates the historical significance of female
portrayals in the Haftarah and the Five Megillot.
6 x 9, 560 pp, Quality PB, 978-1-58023-371-2 **$19.99**

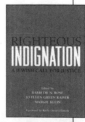

The Women's Torah Commentary: New Insights from Women
Rabbis on the 54 Weekly Torah Portions
Edited by Rabbi Elyse Goldstein
Over fifty women rabbis offer inspiring insights on the Torah, in a week-by-week format.
6 x 9, 496 pp, Quality PB, 978-1-58023-370-5 **$19.99**; HC, 978-1-58023-076-6 **$34.95**

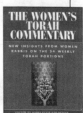

See Passover for *The Women's Passover Companion: Women's Reflections on
the Festival of Freedom* and *The Women's Seder Sourcebook: Rituals &
Readings for Use at the Passover Seder.*

About Jewish Lights

People of all faiths and backgrounds yearn for books that attract, engage, educate, and spiritually inspire.

Our principal goal is to stimulate thought and help all people learn about who the Jewish People are, where they come from, and what the future can be made to hold. While people of our diverse Jewish heritage are the primary audience, our books speak to people in the Christian world as well and will broaden their understanding of Judaism and the roots of their own faith.

We bring to you authors who are at the forefront of spiritual thought and experience. While each has something different to say, they all say it in a voice that you can hear.

Our books are designed to welcome you and then to engage, stimulate, and inspire. We judge our success not only by whether or not our books are beautiful and commercially successful, but by whether or not they make a difference in your life.

For your information and convenience, at the back of this book we have provided a list of other Jewish Lights books you might find interesting and useful. They cover all the categories of your life:

Bar/Bat Mitzvah	Life Cycle
Bible Study / Midrash	Meditation
Children's Books	Men's Interest
Congregation Resources	Parenting
Current Events / History	Prayer / Ritual / Sacred Practice
Ecology / Environment	Social Justice
Fiction: Mystery, Science Fiction	Spirituality
Grief / Healing	Theology / Philosophy
Holidays / Holy Days	Travel
Inspiration	Twelve Steps
Kabbalah / Mysticism / Enneagram	Women's Interest

Stuart M. Matlins

Stuart M. Matlins, Publisher

Or phone, fax, mail or e-mail to: **JEWISH LIGHTS** Publishing
Sunset Farm Offices, Route 4 • P.O. Box 237 • Woodstock, Vermont 05091
Tel: (802) 457-4000 • Fax: (802) 457-4004 • www.jewishlights.com
Credit card orders: (800) 962-4544 (8:30AM–5:30PM ET Monday–Friday)
Generous discounts on quantity orders. SATISFACTION GUARANTEED. Prices subject to change.